BUSINESS SKILLS FOR ACCOUNTANTS

ework

AAT Level 4 Diploma in Business Skills

British Library Cataloguing-in-Publication Data

A catalogue record for this book is available from the British Library.

Published by
Kaplan Publishing UK
Unit 2, The Business Centre
Molly Millars Lane
Wokingham
Berkshire
RG41 2QZ

ISBN 978 1 78415 205 5

Printed and bound in Great Britain.

We are grateful to the Association of Accounting Technicians for permission to reproduce past assessment materials and example tasks based on the new syllabus. The solutions to past assessments and similar activities in the style of the new syllabus have been prepared by Kaplan Publishing.

CONTENTS

Introduction	v
Unit Guides	vi
Assessments	xvi
Study Skills	xvii

STUDY TEXT

1	The role of the accountant in business	1
2	Developing commercial awareness – business organisations	11
3	Developing commercial awareness – external relationships	53
4	Working in teams	89
5	Planning and delivering business communication activities	131
6	Presentations and presentation software	165
7	Organising and facilitating meetings and workshops	207
8	Managing project finances	247
9	Spreadsheet software and the use of information technology	297
10	Performance evaluation	309
11	Skills-based scenario – a project in practice	343
Practice assessment		363
Practice assessment answers		383
Index		I.1

INTRODUCTION

HOW TO USE THESE MATERIALS

These Kaplan Publishing learning materials have been carefully designed to make your learning experience as easy as possible and to give you the best chance of success in your AAT assessments.

They contain a number of features to help you in the study process.

The sections on the Unit Guide, the Assessment and Study Skills should be read before you commence your studies.

They are designed to familiarise you with the nature and content of the assessment and to give you tips on how best to approach your studies.

ICONS

The study chapters include the following icons throughout.

They are designed to assist you in your studies by identifying key definitions and the points at which you can test yourself on the knowledge gained.

Definition

These sections explain important areas of knowledge which must be understood and reproduced in an assessment

Example

The illustrative examples can be used to help develop an understanding of topics before attempting the activity exercises

Activity

These are exercises which give the opportunity to assess your understanding of all the assessment areas.

UNIT GUIDES

This section contains the Learning outcomes and Assessment criteria for the AAT Level 4 Business Skills units listed separately.

Developing commercial awareness (DVCA)

1. Understand own employer's business

1.1 Explain own employer's objectives and strategy and its position in the market.

1.2 Explain own employer's organisational structure and that of its senior leadership team.

1.3 Analyse the services and/or products and how it makes money.

1.4 Explain how own employer adds value to its clients through the services and/or products it provides.

2. Understand how relationships are managed between own employer and clients

2.1 Evaluate own employer's and client's role and responsibilities on a project.

2.2 Explain the contractual obligations that apply between own employer and client.

2.3 Evaluate the impact on individuals and own employer of not fulfilling agreements made with colleagues, clients and stakeholders.

3. Understand a client's business

3.1 Analyse a client's organisational structure and that of its senior management team.

3.2 Explain what services and/or products a client provides and how it makes money.

3.3 Analyse the objectives and strategy of a clients' business and its position in the market.

4. Understand the implications of operating ethically

4.1 Explain what operating ethically means in a business context.

4.2 Explain the implications for a business and its stakeholders of operating ethically.

Working in teams (WKTM)

1. Understand the importance of teams to individual team members and to the team itself

1.1 Explain the advantages and disadvantages of team working.

1.2 Identify the factors that can contribute to a team's success.

1.3 Identify the different roles and responsibilities within a team.

1.4 Explain the stages of team development.

1.5 Explain the personal skills and behaviours required of individuals in a team for effective team working.

1.6 Describe the working relationships in teams.

2. Understand leadership attributes and skills

2.1 Explain the difference between leadership and management.

2.2 Evaluate the impact of different leadership styles on performance of individuals and a team.

2.3 Explain skills and behaviour of team leaders required for successful leadership.

3. Be able to contribute effectively to team work

3.1 Use appropriate skills and behaviour when working as part of a team.

3.2 Assess own contribution to achieving team goals.

4. Understand how to manage potential conflicts within a team

4.1 Explain how to identify and manage potential conflicts within a team.

Planning and delivering business communications activities (PDBC)

1. Understand how to plan business communication activities

1.1 Identify the purpose, the intended audience and desired outcomes of a communication activity.

1.2 Assess the effectiveness of business communications in achieving their purpose and desired outcomes.

1.3 Explain the purpose of and when to keep a file copy of what information has been communicated.

1.4 Explain the importance of reviewing written communications for errors and mistakes.

2. Be able to produce written business communications

2.1 Prepare written communication using language as appropriate for the purpose, audience and desired outcomes including accurate grammar, spelling and punctuation, and plain English.

2.2 Present written information in a structure and style as appropriate for the purpose, audience and desired outcomes.

3. Understand how to communicate verbally in a business environment

3.1 Explain how to use adapt own verbal contributions to professional discussions as appropriate to the audience, purpose of discussion, and the situation.

3.2 Explain what body language and tone of voice to adopt for a specific audience and the situation.

4. Be able to communicate information verbally to the business environment

4.1 Present information and ideas verbally so that they are clear, accurate, convincing and/or persuasive.

4.2 Lead professional discussions to achieve pre-defined objectives.

4.3 Adopt appropriate active listening techniques to gain information from others.

4.4 Deliver well-argued responses to questions appropriate to the situation and audience.

Deliver a presentation (DLPR)

1. Understand the purpose of preparing for and evaluating a presentation

1.1 Explain the purpose of using different types of presentation and equipment.

1.2 Explain different ways of delivering presentations and their features.

1.3 Explain the procedures to be followed when preparing a presentation.

1.4 Explain the benefits of preparing for giving a presentation.

1.5 Describe the types of problems that may occur with equipment and how to deal with them.

1.6 Explain the purpose and benefits of contingency planning.

1.7 Explain the purpose and benefits of collecting feedback from the audience on the presentation.

1.8 Explain the purpose and benefits of evaluating presentations and own performance.

2. Understand the techniques used in enhancing a presentation

2.1 Explain and illustrate how presentations may be enhanced by materials and equipment.

2.2 Explain and illustrate how presentations may be enhanced by use of communication and interpersonal skills.

2.3 Describe how to gauge audience reaction to the presentation.

2.4 Explain the purpose and benefits of summarising important features of the presentation.

2.5 Describe the purpose and benefits of giving the audience opportunities to ask questions.

3. Be able to prepare for delivery of a presentation

3.1 Select any equipment needed and plan how to use it to best effect.

3.2 Make contingency plans in case of equipment failure or other problems, if required.

3.3 Practise the presentation and its timing.

3.4 Obtain feedback on planned presentation and make adjustments, if required.

4. Be able to deliver a presentation

4.1 Check equipment and resources.

4.2 Circulate presentation materials.

4.3 Introduce self to audience and state aims of the presentation.

4.4 Address the audience, speaking clearly and confidently, using language to suit the topic and audience.

4.5 Vary tone, pace and volume to emphasise key points.

4.6 Gauge audience reaction during the presentation and adapt if required.

4.7 Summarise throughout the presentation to emphasise key points and help to maintain audience interest.

4.8 Use body language in a way that reinforces presented information.

4.9 Use equipment, where appropriate, to enhance the presentation, and deal with any problems that may occur.

4.10 Provide the audience with opportunities to ask questions.

4.11 Listen carefully to questions and respond in a way that meets the audience's needs.

5. Be able to evaluate a presentation

5.1 Collect feedback on the presentation.

5.2 Reflect on own performance and identify learning points.

Presentation software

1. Input and combine text and other information within presentation slides

1.1 Explain what types of information are required for the presentation.

1.2 Enter text and other information using layouts appropriate to type of information.

1.3 Insert charts and tables and link to source data.

1.4 Insert images, video or sound to enhance the presentation.

1.5 Identify any constraints which may affect the presentation.

1.6 Organise and combine information for presentations in line with any constraints.

1.7 Store and retrieve presentation files effectively, in line with local guidelines and conventions where available.

2. Use presentation software tools to structure, edit and format presentations

2.1 Explain when and how to use and change slide structure and themes for slides.

2.2 Create, amend and use appropriate templates and themes for slides.

2.3 Explain how interactive and presentation effects can be used to aid meaning or impact.

2.4 Select and use appropriate techniques to edit and format presentations to meet needs.

2.5 Create and use interactive elements to enhance presentations.

2.6 Select and use animation and transition techniques appropriately to enhance presentations.

3. Prepare interactive slideshow for presentation

3.1 Explain how to present slides to communicate effectively for different contexts.

3.2 Prepare interactive slideshow and associated products for presentation.

3.3 Check presentation meets needs, using IT tools and making corrections as necessary.

3.4 Evaluate presentations, identify any quality problems and discuss how to respond to them.

3.5 Respond appropriately to quality problems to ensure that presentations meet needs and are fit for purpose.

3.6 Evaluate the presentation and own performance and identify changes that will improve future presentations.

Organising and facilitating meetings and workshops (OFMW)

1. Be able to take responsibility for meetings and workshop arrangements

1.1 Set up meetings and workshops using calendar/scheduling software.

1.2 Manage the communications regarding meeting and workshop arrangements with intended audience, venue, technology and catering providers, as necessary.

1.3 Assess the needs of the context and audience for meetings and workshops to determine requirements, including venue, audio/visual technology and catering.

2. Understand how to facilitate meetings and workshops

2.1 Assess how to structure meetings and workshops appropriate to the context, objectives and audience of meetings and workshops.

2.2 Assess different methods of communicating information in meetings and workshops.

2.3 Assess what questions are relevant to the meeting situation and audience.

2.4 Assess when it is appropriate to give others opportunity to verbally contribute ideas and opinions.

3. Be able to facilitate meetings and workshops

3.1 Establish ground rules, purposes and objectives for meetings and workshops.

3.2 Lead a meeting and workshop to achieve objectives.

3.3 Communicate information clearly at appropriate points during meetings and workshops.

3.4 Summarise discussions and decisions during meetings and workshops to the appropriate level of details.

3.5 Record meeting actions and decisions.

3.6 Review progress against actions as appropriate.

Managing project finances (MPFS)

1. Be able to develop a budget for a project

1.1 Estimate the costs of different project options, in parallel with other planning processes (including scope, schedule and resource management).

1.2 Recommend a budget (including cost estimate, contingency and management reserve).

1.3 Review actual expenditure against planned expenditure using cost control mechanisms.

1.4 Manage base costs for the project using cost control mechanisms.

1.5 Forecast when funds will need to be released for project activities using cost control mechanisms.

1.6 Anticipate where expenditure may exceed to tolerances, and take the necessary steps to address the issue.

1.7 Analyse and report financial performance at the required intervals.

2. Be able to complete financial transactions and evaluate project costs

2.1 Confirm that all financial liabilities relating to the project are accounted for on project completion.

2.2 Analyse the financial performance of the project at completion.

2.3 Report the financial performance of the project to stakeholders at completion.

3. Be able to comply with standards of financial management

3.1 Identify relevant standards applying to financial procedures within the project (including legal, organisational and professional standards).

3.2 Operate the financial procedures in compliance with the relevant standards (including the legal, organisational and professional standards).

Spreadsheet software (SPSO)

1. Use a spreadsheet to enter, edit and organise numerical and other data

1.1 Use a spreadsheet to enter, edit and organise numerical and other data.

1.2 Enter and edit numerical and other data accurately.

1.3 Combine and link data from different sources.

1.4 Store and retrieve spreadsheet files effectively, in line with local guidelines and conventions where available.

2. Select and use appropriate formulas and data analysis tools and techniques to meet requirements

2.1 Explain what methods can be used to summarise, analyse and interpret spreadsheet data and when to use them.

2.2 Select and use a wide range of appropriate functions and formulas to meet calculation requirements.

2.3 Select and use Select and use a range of tools and techniques to analyse and interpret data to meet requirements.

2.4 Select and use forecasting tools and techniques.

3. Use tools and techniques to present, and format and publish spreadsheet information

3.1 Explain how to present and format spreadsheet information effectively to meet needs.

3.2 Select and use appropriate tools and techniques to format spreadsheet cells, rows columns and worksheets effectively.

3.3 Select and use appropriate tools and techniques to generate, develop and format charts and graphs.

3.4 Select and use appropriate page layout to present, print and publish spreadsheet information.

3.5 Explain how to find and sort out any errors in formulas.

3.6 Check spreadsheet information meets needs, using IT tools and making corrections as necessary.

3.7 Use auditing tools to identify and respond appropriately to any problems with spreadsheets.

Evaluate and improve own performance in a business environment (EPBE)

1. Understand how to evaluate and improve own performance

1.1 Analyse the purpose and benefits of continuously improving work.

1.2 Evaluate the purpose and benefits of encouraging and accepting feedback from others.

1.3 Analyse ways on evaluating own work.

1.4 Evaluate the purpose and benefits of trying out possible improvements of own work.

1.5 Analyse how learning and development can improve own work, benefit organisations and further own career.

1.6 Evaluate possible career progression routes and the opportunities they offer.

1.7 Analyse possible development opportunities and the benefits the offer.

1.8 Evaluate the advantages and disadvantages of a learning plan.

2. Be able to evaluate and improve own performance using feedback from others

2.1 Encourage and accept feedback from other people.

2.2 Make recommendations to improve work performance.

2.3 Complete work tasks, consistently using recommended new ways of working.

2.4 Evaluate work completed for improvements and effectiveness.

2.5 Evaluate changes made for improvements and effectiveness.

3. Be able to use evaluation and feedback to develop and use a learning plan

3.1 Evaluate own performance, using feedback from others, and identify where further learning and development will improve own work.

3.2 Make recommendations and develop a learning plan to improve own work performance, that meets own needs.

3.3 Implement a learning plan for improvement to own work.

3.4 Review and evaluate progress against learning plan and make updates for improving own work and further learning.

THE ASSESSMENTS

The format of the assessment

The method of assessment for each unit is the gathering of Work Place Evidence (WPE) or Recognition of Prior Learning (RPL) in the form of a portfolio submitted online.

All assessment criteria must be evidenced.

Examples of the type of evidence which may be submitted for RPL assessment include:

- workplace documents
- witness testimonies
- personal statements
- professional discussion
- assessor observation activities
- certificates issued following an informal or formal course of learning. For certified achievement a detailed specification of the learning/qualification gained will be needed in order to make up the mapping process possible.

Some candidates may be able to generate workplace assessment evidence from activities undertaken in their workplace.

Students who wish to present workplace evidence for assessment should be tasked to

- collect workplace documents that evidence the assessment criteria for the unit
- explain their role in the production of the evidence. This explanation can be through a personal statement or statements on each piece and will provide the context for the assessor.

Workplace evidence must always consist of workplace documents, questions and answers, and witness testimony. This evidence should then be mapped to the appropriate criteria.

STUDY SKILLS

Preparing to study

Devise a study plan

Determine which times of the week you will study.

Split these times into sessions of at least one hour for study of new material. Any shorter periods could be used for revision or practice.

Put the times you plan to study onto a study plan for the weeks from now until the assessment and set yourself targets for each period of study – in your sessions make sure you cover the whole course, activities and the associated questions with answers at the back of the Study Text.

If you are studying more than one unit at a time, try to vary your subjects as this can help to keep you interested and see subjects as part of wider knowledge.

When working through your course, compare your progress with your plan and, if necessary, re-plan your work (perhaps including extra sessions) or, if you are ahead, do some extra revision/practice questions.

Effective studying

Active reading

You are not expected to learn the text by rote, rather, you must understand what you are reading and be able to use it to pass the assessment and develop good practice.

A good technique is to use SQ3Rs – Survey, Question, Read, Recall, Review:

1 **Survey the chapter**

Look at the headings and read the introduction, knowledge, skills and content, so as to get an overview of what the chapter deals with.

2 **Question**

Whilst undertaking the survey ask yourself the questions you hope the chapter will answer for you.

3 **Read**

Read through the chapter thoroughly working through the activities and, at the end, making sure that you can meet the learning objectives shown within the summary.

4 **Recall**

At the end of each section and at the end of the chapter, try to recall the main ideas of the section/chapter without referring to the text. This is best done after short break of a couple of minutes after the reading stage.

5 **Review**

Check that your recall notes are correct.

You may also find it helpful to re-read the chapter to try and see the topic(s) it deals with as a whole.

Note taking

Taking notes is a useful way of learning, but do not simply copy out the text.

The notes must:

- be in your own words
- be concise
- cover the key points
- be well organised
- be modified as you study further chapters in this text or in related ones.

Trying to summarise a chapter without referring to the text can be a useful way of determining which areas you know and which you don't.

Three ways of taking notes

1 **Summarise the key points of a chapter**

2 **Make linear notes**

A list of headings, subdivided with sub-headings listing the key points.

If you use linear notes, you can use different colours to highlight key points and keep topic areas together.

Use plenty of space to make your notes easy to use.

3 **Try a diagrammatic form**

The most common of which is a mind map.

To make a mind map, put the main heading in the centre of the paper and put a circle around it.

Draw lines radiating from this to the main sub-headings which again have circles around them.

Continue the process from the sub-headings to sub-sub-headings.

Highlighting and underlining

You may find it useful to underline or highlight key points in your study text – but do be selective.

You may also wish to make notes in the margins.

Further reading

In addition to this text, you should also read the 'Student section' of the 'Accounting Technician' magazine every month to keep abreast of any guidance from the examiners.

The role of the accountant in business

1

Introduction

This chapter serves as an introduction to the rest of the Text by clarifying the importance of accounting professionals in a business environment.

It shows the role of the accounting function in relation to other business units and introduces the core professional competencies to be addressed in forthcoming chapters.

Finally, the chapter focuses on the bedrock from which these skills can be developed – personal organisation.

ASSESSMENT CRITERIA

As an introduction, this chapter establishes a good foundation for all further assessment criteria.

CONTENTS

1 Business skills for accountants
2 The accounting function
3 Departments in a business
4 The importance of accounting and finance
5 Core competencies
6 Time management and personal effectiveness

1 Business skills for accountants

1.1 Introduction

To be a successful accountant requires a wide range of accounting skills, which have been covered in depth during your previous studies. This Text addresses the wider professional skills that an accountant needs to progress in their career and establish a good understanding of the company for which they work.

Due to technological change and evolving expectations, these other business skills are increasingly important to the modern accountant.

2 The accounting function

2.1 What is accounting?

Definition

Accounting is the systematic recording, reporting and analysis of financial transactions within a business.

In larger organisations, the range of tasks that the accounting function needs to perform can be very wide. This often means that the finance department can be split into a number of different functions, each with their own diverse set of responsibilities.

In general terms, these can be divided into three functions:

- the financial accounting function
- the management accounting function
- the treasury function

2.2 Financial accounting

Definition

Financial accounting is concerned with the production of financial statements and the recording and reporting of business transactions.

This therefore includes the books of prime entry, the main financial statements (statement of profit or loss, statement of financial position, statement of cash flows) and the general reporting on the company's performance in line with accounting standards and legal requirements.

2.3 Management accounting

Definition

Management accounting is concerned with the process of measuring, analysing, interpreting and communicating information to management, often using the records produced by the financial accounting processes.

This therefore includes costing, budgets and variance reports. Therefore most of the reports provided by this function will be analytical and for internal use. Unlike the information provided by the financial accounting division above, non-financial elements are also considered.

2.4 The treasury

The treasury handles all matters relating to corporate finance, including the generation of external and internal funds for business, the management of currencies and cash flows, financing and tax planning. This section will therefore monitor the organisation's working capital and investments and borrowings, including raising equity and managing debt.

Activity 1

Which of the following is not typically prepared by the management accounting function of a business?

A. Budgets

B. Investment appraisals

C. Business tax calculations

D. Variance reports

Activity 2

Which of the following is normally the treasury function's responsibility?

A. Break-even analysis

B. Costing of products

C. Production of financial statements

D. Foreign exchange management

3 Departments in a business

3.1 The relationship between accounting and other departments

There are few decisions made or policies enforced within an organisation which do not require the input of the finance or accounting department.

3.2 The functions of major departments

Most businesses operate with the same common departments, for which the roles and key concerns are listed below:

Department	Role	Key concerns
Finance	Bookkeeping Accounts Payable Accounts Receivable Financial reporting Financial controls Budgeting Raising of capital	Accuracy of record keeping Monthly management reports Annual financial reporting
Research and Development	Improving existing products Developing new products	Anticipating customer needs Generating new ideas Testing Cost
Purchasing	Acquiring goods, raw materials and services necessary for the business	Price and payment terms Quality Stock levels and delivery schedules
Production	Converting raw materials into finished goods	Quality Costs Efficiency Stock levels and production schedules
Sales and Marketing	Identifying customer needs Market research Product design Pricing Promotion Distribution	Customer needs Quality Promotional strategy Pricing strategy Distribution channels
Customer service and service provision	Providing services and solutions to clients	Quality Scheduling and costs
Human Resources	Staff supervision and development Administrative support Disciplinary measures	Quality and efficiency Workforce issues
Administration (Back Office)	Administrative support Processing transactions Premises and supplies	Efficiency Information processing

Specialist roles outside of, or incorporated into, one of the departments above include:

- Compliance
- Estates Management
- Facilities Management
- Health and Safety
- Investor Relations
- Intellectual Property
- Learning and Development
- Legal advice
- Logistics and Supply Chain Management
- Risk Management
- Systems and IT

Chapter 2 will look in detail at how most companies are structured and managed and the organisational hierarchies within these departments.

Many of these specialised functions may be outsourced or relocated to another, cheaper country to both save costs and ensure expertise. The latter process is known as **offshoring.**

3.3 The relationship between accounting and other departments

From the above information, let us consider how accounting and finance could have an impact on all staff and also separate departments.

Example

Examples of the daily impact of the accounting function on a business:

All staff – payroll, payslips, management of petty cash

Sales –processing, invoicing and credit control of sales orders

Marketing –purchasing promotional materials and cost-benefit analysis

Production – the requisition, ordering and payment of component parts and the management of stock inventory

Human resources – funding for staff recruitment and training, management of resources for disciplinary procedures

The accounting department are also responsible for organisational control, such as the prevention of fraud, the efficient running of the company and its key projects and the safeguarding of company assets.

4 The importance of finance and accounting

4.1 The traditional role of finance

Historically, the role of the finance function in a business was cost control, variance analysis and reporting on past performance.

4.2 The current role of finance

This role has developed over the years into a more proactive, value adding role. Therefore, it could be said that instead of merely reporting on performance, the modern accountant may be required to enhance it.

Later in this Text, we will focus on how accountants play a role in projects and how they are required to inform business strategy. They are also seen as regulators, risk-assessors and reliable advisors.

In the modern world, the finance function can be responsible for cutting costs, processing and analysing vast amounts of data and meeting the increasing regulatory requirements of the markets in which they operate. All of these roles are particularly crucial in the recent times of fast technological evolution and worldwide economic crises.

4.3 Threats to the accounting function

Although the above descriptions of a developing and more varied role for accountants in business implies exciting times for accounting and finance professionals, a cautionary note must be raised.

In their attempts to cut costs, more companies are taking a different approach to their administrative operations. As described above, increasingly the finance function (and others) is being outsourced to external providers or consolidated as part of a shared service centre offering. Although this does not necessarily mean that the accountancy profession will suffer as a whole, the role that accountants currently play, especially in terms of management information and control, could be drastically altered. This said, although moving finance operations away from a company's own administration can lead to a reduced accountancy department in some contexts, in others it can enable greater specialisation of the remaining staff.

5 Core competencies

5.1 Introduction to core competencies

Therefore it is essential that the accountant possesses a number of other core competencies in addition to their financial capabilities.

Broadly speaking, these benchmarks can be characterised as core skills. Many of these skills will be addressed in this Text, for example:

- Communication skills (chapters 3, 5, 6 and 7)
- Presentation skills (chapter 6)
- Administrative, legal and professional skills (chapter 3)
- Team work (chapters 2 and 4)
- Problem-solving (all chapters)
- Conflict resolution (chapter 4)
- IT skills (chapters 6 and 9)

Before addressing all of the above, we will focus briefly on another key attribute required to achieve personal effectiveness in the workplace – time management. Without a sense of organisation and prioritisation, it will be difficult for any professional to exhibit the skills above. Therefore time management can be seen as the bedrock of personal effectiveness.

6 Time management and personal effectiveness

6.1 What is time management?

Definitions

Time management is the process of planning and controlling the amount of time that is spent on specific activities, usually with the aim of increasing overall efficiency or productivity.

Time management has several key purposes. These include:

- plan the best use of time

- complete more in the time available
- eliminate wastage
- devote more time to the really important issues

This allow professionals to:

- refuse excessive workloads
- monitor the progress of key projects
- allocate your time to more important tasks first
- plan each day efficiently, so you get as much done as possible

Time is a scarce resource – failure to manage it properly will lead to:

- low productivity
- wasted time spent on non-essential tasks
- missed deadlines
- poor quality work being produced – perhaps due to work being rushed to meet deadlines

6.2 Time-stealers

Time-stealers are activities that are disproportionately time-consuming, often conflicting with time which had been allocated to other, more important tasks. They can take the form of both business and personal distractions or result from a failure to either refuse unnecessary work or delegate appropriately.

As priorities vary for different people, there is no definitive list of time-stealers, although common examples would include ineffective, overly long meetings, the constant checking of e-mails and social distractions in the office. Social media is one example of the detrimental impact technology can have in terms of time management.

Not all time-stealers are inappropriate – for example, dealing with a distressed colleague may be a worthwhile, if unexpected use of time. Time-stealers are therefore personal and individual, depending on the circumstances.

Activity 3

List three time-stealers you encounter regularly and how you could address them.

6.3 Time management techniques

Spend time planning and organising

Using time to think and plan is essential for good time management. Not only should you plan what tasks you wish to accomplish each day or week, you should also spend time reviewing your schedules to check for problems or changes to your workload that require rescheduling.

It is important to note the old saying – 'failing to plan is planning to fail!'

Effective suggestions to help manage your time include:

Producing an activity log

This could include a breakdown of the time spent in a typical week, divided between different activities such as work, home, study, leisure and travel. Consider what proportion of your time is important to you, important to you others and what can be delegated to others or avoided completely.

Costing your time

Every occasion when you 'save' an hour, or put it to better use, you become more cost-effective. If everything is achieved on a list, offer a reward as a recognition.

Making lists

Plan the coming week in advance, then make a list every day before you start work. Refuse to do anything that is not on the list for each day.

Prioritisation

Look at the list and assess tasks based on their importance (if the consequences of failure are significant or it comes from a powerful stakeholder, such as a manager) and urgency (whether the deadline for the accomplishment of the task is near). If the item is not prioritised, be assertive and ignore it.

Activity 4

Sian earns £25,000 per annum basic pay. On top of this the direct and indirect costs of her employment are £10,000. She works 37.5 hours per week for 44 weeks of the year.

What is the cost of Sian's time per hour?

A £9.09

B £21.21

C £568.18

D £1,650.00

6.4 Consequences of ineffectiveness at work

If individual workers are not effective at work, for example by producing poor quality work or not communicating effectively with others, this can lead to the organisation losing its reputation, experiencing diminished productivity and/or motivation and suffering from poor quality information.

It is therefore in the organisation's best interests to encourage staff to develop and continually improve, a theme revisited in Chapter 10.

Answers to chapter activities

Activity 1

The correct answer is **C**. Business tax calculations are usually the responsibility of the treasury department.

Activity 2

The correct answer is **D.**

A and B are usually part of the management accounting function, whereas C is financial accounting.

Activity 3

The three time-stealers could include:

- Interruptions from colleagues
- E-mails
- Constant telephone calls
- Ineffective meetings
- Over-commitment to minor tasks

Activity 4

The correct answer is B £21.21.

As £35,000 is divided by 1,650 hours.

Developing commercial awareness – business organisations

2

Introduction

For an accountant to enhance their wider business skills and knowledge, they must firstly develop a sense of commercial awareness.

Commercial awareness can be defined as an understanding of the wider environment in which an organisation operates. It incorporates knowledge of the market trends, customers, competitors and suppliers relevant to that specific business.

This chapter enables the student to consider the nature of different business organisations and assess how those with which they are familiar are structured, managed and positioned in the market. The chapter also suggests how to analyse both internal and external developments relevant to the business' success.

An awareness of the key priorities and culture of the company for which they work will be built upon in Chapter 3, where this will be compared to other companies and shown in action through client relationships.

ASSESSMENT CRITERIA

1 To understand the nature of a business

2 To explain the organisational structure and corporate culture of a business

CONTENTS

1 Business Organisations
2 Objectives
3 Organisational Structure
4 Organisational Culture
5 Business Analysis
6 Sources of Company Information

1 Business Organisations

1.1 Introduction

To develop commercial awareness requires an understanding of the priorities of the business, its competitors and the marketplace, as well as the employee's role and responsibilities within that environment.

The first step to developing business awareness is to understand and compare the nature and structure of different types of organisation.

1.2 What is a business organisation?

It is firstly important to define what a business organisation is and to explain why they are formed.

Definition

Organisations are social arrangements for the controlled performance of collective goals. ***Buchanan & Huczynski***

Within this definition, there are three crucial aspects:

(a) **Collective goals** – the aims and objectives which the organisation strives to achieve. Most commercial ventures seek to make profits as a primary goal, but this is not always the case in the public sector.

(b) **Social arrangements** – organisations are structured to allow people to work together towards the above goals. Individuals working alone cannot be classed as organisations.

(c) **Controlled performance** – systems and procedures are developed to achieve the group goals above (e.g. allocating staff responsibilities and assessing performance).

Organisations enable people to:

- share skills and knowledge
- specialise
- pool resources

1.3 Types of business organisation

Depending on the structure and goals of organisations, they can be classified into several different categories.

Commercial Organisations

Commercial organisations largely see their main objective as maximising financial return (profit-seeking).

Commercial companies can be divided into:

- Sole traders
- Partnerships
- Limited Liability Companies

Not-for-Profit Organisations

Not-for-profit organisations (NFPs or NPOs) do not see profitability as their main objective. Their main goal is to satisfy their members' requirements, although due to their varied nature, these will often be radically different.

Private Sector

The private sector consists of organisations which are owned and run by private individual and groups rather than the government.

Within the private sector, companies operate on many different levels, ranging from SMEs (small and medium sized enterprises) such as solicitors, estate agents and newsagents to multinational companies with a presence all over the world.

Whereas SMEs are traditionally run by the people who own them, bigger companies (household names such as Boots, BP, Marks and Spencer and Tesco) are public companies, listed on the London stock exchange so that people can buy shares.

There are three main reasons why a company would choose to 'go public':

- to enable the founders to take money out of the company
- to enable venture capitalists to get a return on their investment
- to expand the business

Public Sector

The public sector is the part of the economy concerned with providing services to the population and is controlled by government organisations at a local, national or international level. Public services typically include:

- Police
- Military
- Public transport
- Education
- Healthcare

Depending on the scale of provision, public services may be limited to specific regions or parts of the community (e.g. means-tested healthcare).

Non-governmental organisations (NGOs) are those where although profit is not necessarily their primary goal, they are not directly linked to national government. They tend to promote social, political or environmental causes (e.g. Red Cross and Greenpeace).

Activity 1

Which of the following organisations is most likely to be classified as part of the public sector?

A. A charity

B. A social club

C. A school

D. A public limited company

1.4 Key differences between organisations

Ownership, Funding and Liability

Public sector organisations are controlled by and tend to secure funds from central or local government. Private companies are likely to be owned and funded by individual owners, shareholders and other investors, such as venture capitalists. Unlike the public sector, they rely heavily on profits for further investment. Charities and non-governmental organisations tend to rely on both corporate and personal donations.

The owners of sole traders and partnerships are liable for losses that the business makes; owners of limited companies have a limited liability to the value of their shareholding.

Objectives

To develop a sound awareness of any organisation, it is crucial to fully comprehend the aims and objectives it seeks to achieve. Some of these aims will be fairly orthodox across all industries and sectors:

- efficiency
- cost-effectiveness
- customer satisfaction
- business/service development

Within the private sector, the primary objective of most companies is usually the generation of revenue in order to maximise profit.

In the public sector and for not-for-profit organisations, objectives can vary depending on the service being provided.

Example

NFPs and their objectives:

Government departments and agencies seek to implement policy.

Schools' main objective is to educate their pupils.

Hospitals have the primary goal of treating patients.

A charity's goal is to provide financial or practical help for those in need.

Local councils may prioritise caring for their communities.

Size

The concept of a company's size is ambiguous but can be judged by:

- total number of employees
- volume of output
- sales revenue
- profits earned
- assets employed
- net worth in real terms
- geographical spread
- relative success compared to competitors

Technology

Some organisations, for example mobile telephone manufacturers, have a high technology usage compared to others, for example a window cleaning company.

Activity

The nature of an organisation and the market in which it operates will determine which activities will be required for it to meet its objectives.

Each sector will therefore have different requirements and specialisations.

Example

There are a large number of different sectors, which include:

- **Agriculture** – production, processing and packaging of food and farm produce
- **Extractive industries** – oil, gas, coal, mineral extraction and processing
- **Construction** – buildings, roads, airports, ports
- **Financial services** – banks, investors, insurance
- **Healthcare and pharmaceuticals** – medical institutions, treatments
- **Manufacturing** – including heavy industry/mass production
- **Public administration** – government services at local and national levels
- **Professional services** – provision of intangible goods and services such as accountancy, law and surveying
- **Retailers** – sale of goods produced by manufacturers to consumers in shops and online
- **Sport, Arts and the Media** – including film, TV and publishing
- **Technology** – innovation and product development
- **Training and Education** – schools, colleges and training companies
- **Transportation** – solutions to move goods and people across locations

Social aspects

Historically organisations focused on their economic responsibilities to operate an efficient and profitable organisation. The current trend is to emphasise social, ecological and ethical responsibilities.

These include:

- relations with customers and suppliers
- attitudes to employees
- attitudes to both the local and world communities
- attitudes to the environment
- the type and quality of product and/or service

Activity 2

Which of the following statements are correct?

A. Private limited companies can sell shares to the public.

B. Shareholders in limited companies typically have limited liability.

C. Most sole traders and partnerships have the aim of maximising wealth.

D. Public sector organisations are controlled by the central government.

E. Charities form part of the public sector.

1.5 Common factors in organisations

Despite the differences among various organisations, there are many common factors, including:

- people
- objectives
- structure
- management

It is the interaction of people in order to achieve objectives which forms the basis of an organisation. Some form of structure is needed by which people's interactions and efforts are channelled and co-ordinated and some process of management by which the activities of the organisation, and the efforts of its members, are directed and controlled.

Activity 3

Briefly describe the nature of the organisation for which you work. Use the above classifications to define the company's business activities, services/products and market position.

(AAT Assessment criteria 1.1 and 1.3)

2 Objectives

2.1 The importance of objectives

Definition

Objectives are defined as the important ends towards which the organisational and individual activities are directed.

Without clear objectives, the activities of an organisation and its employees can lack purpose, direction and co-ordination. As well as acting as targets to motivate and manage staff members, objectives can also be used as standards by which the performance of the organisation as a whole can be measured.

The aim of an organisation is sometimes outlined in its mission statement, which sits at the top of the hierarchy of organisational objectives:

Mission	All embracing
Goals	General
Objectives	Specific
Strategy	Detailed targets
Tactics	Implemented targets
Operational plans	Action targets

- The mission statement describes the basic purpose of an organisation and states in one place what it is trying to achieve. The statement can be quite lengthy or short and punchy. Typically, a mission statement will answer three questions:
  - Why do we exist?
  - What are we providing?
  - For whom do we exist?

- Goals are derived from the mission. They are the long-term, open-ended outcomes the organisation seeks and are sufficient for the satisfaction of the mission.
- Objectives are time-assigned, specific targets derived from the goals.
- Strategies relate to broad areas of an enterprise's operations and can be used as a framework for more detailed tactical planning.
- Tactics are the actions carried out to put strategic decisions into action and can therefore be seen as the detailed implementation of a strategy. In addition, some tactical decisions will be made in response to changing circumstances.
- Actions, programmes and rules are the operational practices that will translate the intention of the tactics into action by individuals and are therefore detailed, short term and subject to immediate control.

If your organisation has a mission statement, you will find it in the latest Company Report and Accounts or similar documentation. Many companies also include mission statements in promotional literature.

Example

Mission statements:

British Airways – seeks to be 'the world's favourite airline'

Starbucks – 'to inspire and nurture the human spirit – one person, one cup and one neighbourhood at a time'

BBC – 'to enrich people's lives with programmes and services that inform, educate and entertain'.

In addition to a Mission statement, some organisations also state a vision for the future. For example, the BBC aim 'to be the most creative organisation in the world'.

An organisation will establish goals, objectives and strategies and then determine the policies and procedures necessary to achieve its stated aims. Once the objectives are set, management will structure the tasks that need to be performed and decide which department and which individuals will complete which task and when.

2.2 Corporate objectives

Corporate objectives are concerned with the business as a whole. They outline the expectations of the firm and the strategic planning process provides the means for achieving the objectives. Objectives should relate to the key (or critical) factors for business success, which are typically:

- profitability (return on investment)
- market share
- growth
- cash flow
- customer satisfaction
- the quality of the firm's products
- industrial relations
- added value

Objectives should be explicit, quantifiable and capable of being achieved. The acronym **SMART** in relation to characteristics of good objectives is useful.

- **S**pecific – all objectives should be specific and deal with a manageable feature of the organisation or individual such as profit, return on capital or output (e.g. 'improve performance' is too vague; 'improve profit after tax' is better).
- **M**easurable – they should have a quantifiable yardstick of attainment (e.g. 'improve image' is difficult to verify compared to 'increase profit after tax by 5%').
- **A**chievable – to avoid discouraging people with unattainable objectives (e.g. 'improve profit after tax by 1000%' probably will be impossible to achieve).
- **R**elevant (or realistic) e.g. 'resurface car park' will not have the same impact as 'avoid liquidation'.
- **T**ime bounded – means that there should be a deadline to complete the objective (e.g. 'eliminate hospital waiting lists' – when? By the end of the year or the decade).

Example

Corporate objectives for two departmental managers:

Sales/Marketing manager

- Increase the turnover by X% in six months.
- Increase our share of the market for Widgets from 15% to 20% in the next 18 months.
- Successfully introduce our new baby Widget and obtain sales of £10,000 per week after three months.
- Recruit and train effectively six new sales people.

Production manager

- Operate plant at maximum practical operating output.
- Reduce overall costs of manufacturing by 5% over a six-month period using the new equipment.
- Improve the performance of junior managers and supervisors by the use of in-plant training courses.
- Contain wage levels to the lowest possible increase but in any case no larger than X% in line with expected domestic inflation.

2.3 The profit objective

As well as making a profit, other objectives of a business organisation are generally to survive and to develop and grow. However, profit maximisation must be seen as the main objective of a company as it tries to satisfy the desire of shareholders for high dividends. Profitability, as a financial objective, can be expressed as a return on capital employed (ROCE) or a return on investment (ROI), a return on shareholders' capital or earnings per share. Development and growth is not itself a prime objective but a means of satisfying the shareholders' demand for an adequate return. It also requires profit to provide for future investments.

The notion of generating profits is, however, not simply to increase the wealth of the individuals. Other reasons why making profit is essential include:

- reinvesting in technology
- developing new products and markets
- rewarding backers and customers

The current commercial environment is constantly changing due to new market demands and the scale of innovation and change. In order to compete in the modern world, it is necessary not only to develop new ideas and more efficient ways of operating, but also to be aware of how external factors can influence your future development.

Profit maximisation may be the primary goal but management must also consider the quality of the product/service, the operational costs and the environmental influences. If the expenditure on quality, after-sales service, R&D, sales promotion, management development, satisfaction of staff and their employment conditions is cut, this may increase profitability in the short term but it is likely to jeopardise future growth and development and may even put the survival of the organisation at risk.

2.4 Non-financial objectives

Although it is possible that a business enterprise's declared primary objective may not to be to make a profit, many other major objectives (e.g. customer satisfaction, market share and social responsibility) actually also lead to greater profits and as such are secondary objectives at best. In particular, the opportunities offered by expanding a product portfolio or extending geographical coverage and the publicity resulting from fulfilling environmental goals can increase business and therefore profits.

2.5 Levels of strategy

Organisations will have a whole range of objectives. Some are short-term in nature while others are longer term. Some may be the objectives of a small department whilst others may cover the whole organisation.

Example

Mainwaring & Sons Ltd is a menswear clothing retailer. Their long-term objectives are to 'sell high quality tailored suits' and 'to provide a satisfying work environment for employees'.

To support this, Mainwaring & Sons have created the following action plans:

- 'to increase online sales by 10% within one year'
- 'to increase our market share for local wedding suit hire to 25% within two years'
- 'to launch two new stores within three years'

Unlike the open-ended and qualitative objectives initially stated, these are capable of being interpreted in quantitative terms and given a limited time scale. They include profitability, market share, sales volume growth, research and development and production.

Within an organisation, each level of management will have different roles and responsibilities. This is especially the case when developing a strategy for the organisation's future.

Managers at different levels in the organisational hierarchy are concerned with different kinds of objectives.

The Anthony Triangle can be used to illustrate the types of strategic planning at each level of the organisation's hierarchy:

- **Strategic Planning** is undertaken by the board of directors and senior managers. It involves determining the overall objectives and mission and making long-term decisions for the entire organisation.
- **Tactical Planning** is undertaken by middle management. They set objectives for specific divisions or departments and plan how to use resources.
- **Operational Planning** is undertaken by junior managers and supervisors. This planning is short-term, detailed and practical, often focusing solely on their own department or unit.

Example

The above planning levels could be applied to a supermarket as follows:

- Strategic planning would involve making plans for the whole business. This could involve which locations are suitable for new stores or store closures, national marketing messages and whether to seek outside investment.
- Tactical planning would be the creation of strategies for particular stores, such as special offers, local advertising and stock levels.
- Operational planning would be the practical, day-to-day strategies such as shift patterns, display positions and staff recruitment.

In order to be successful, all levels must support each other.

For example, if a strategic decision is to improve customer service, this could be supported by a tactical decision to hire and train new customer service staff and an operational strategy to select the most suitable candidates for particular roles.

Activity 4

Mainwaring & Sons is a menswear clothing retailer with several stores. It has three strategies in place:

1 To hire a total of fifty extra checkout operators within the next five weeks to reduce customer queue times

2 To begin the sale of children's clothing in all stores within the next two years

3 To relocate one of its stores in Town A to a new, more suitable site, located by the store manager

Using the Anthony triangle model, what would each of these strategies be classified as?

A. Strategic

B. Tactical

C. Operational

Activity 5

Explain your company's primary objectives with reference to any relevant mission statements or relevant documentation.

Include examples of both strategic and operational objectives.

(AAT Assessment criteria 1.1)

3 Organisational Structure

3.1 Introduction

In order for a company to meet its objectives and be run efficiently and effectively, a defined organisational structure is crucial.

Definition

Organisational structure is concerned with the way in which work is divided up and allocated. It outlines the roles and responsibilities of individuals and groups within an organisation.

As soon as an organisation has grown too big for administration by a single individual, key activities and functions must be grouped, roles and responsibilities must be allocated and lines of authority and responsibility must be established.

An important feature of any organisation is the optimum number of people who report to any single individual. Attempts by managers to resolve this problem have produced various forms of organisation. The type of structure chosen depends on the degree of specialisation within the organisation, the number of levels of authority deemed desirable and the amount of decentralisation permitted.

3.2 Delegation

Definition

Delegation is the act by which a person transfers part of their authority to a subordinate person. This creates a chain of command where authority flows downwards from the top management to each level.

The term **hierarchy** refers to the number of levels and the distribution of authority, responsibility and accountability within the organisation. Delegated authority passes down through the ranks so that at each level those receiving delegated authority are answerable to their superiors.

This chain gives employees the means to resolve or refer queries to the appropriate person. It is illustrated below with arrows showing delegation:

Shareholders	– Owners of the business who are too numerous or too widely dispersed so delegate the running of the organisation
Board of Directors	– The board decide on the policy but delegate how to carry it out
Managing Director	– Implements policy but, because it is too much for one person, MD delegates the running
Functional managers e.g. sales, purchasing	– Carry out company policy in their department but cannot oversee every job and must delegate
Junior managers of superiors	– Carry out policy relating to their section but delegate the various tasks
Operatives	– Perform the tasks specified

The basis of delegation is illustrated below showing how the subordinate is responsible to the manager for doing the job, the manager is responsible for seeing that the job gets done and the manager is accountable to the superior for the actions of subordinates.

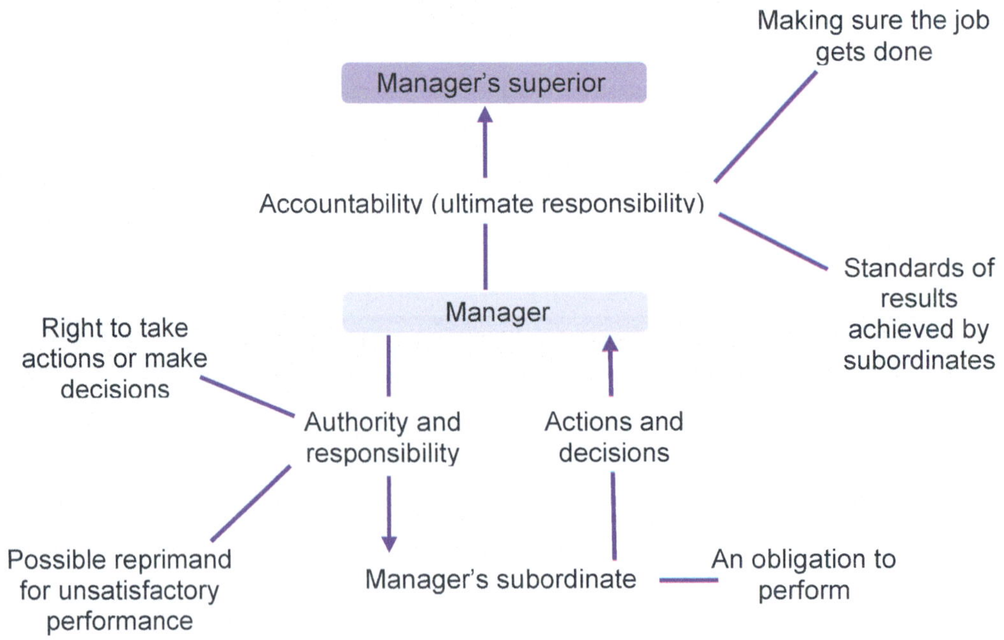

3.3 Organisational levels and spans of control

An essential feature of the hierarchy is that, within the organisation, authority passes downwards, and accountability upwards.

Definition

A scalar chain is the line of authority which can be traced up and down the chain from the most senior member of staff to the most junior. The vertical length of the chain is therefore the number of levels of authority and responsibility within an organisation.

Definition

A manager's span of control is number of people for whom he or she is directly responsible.

The vertical structure of an organisation can be either tall or flat, as below:

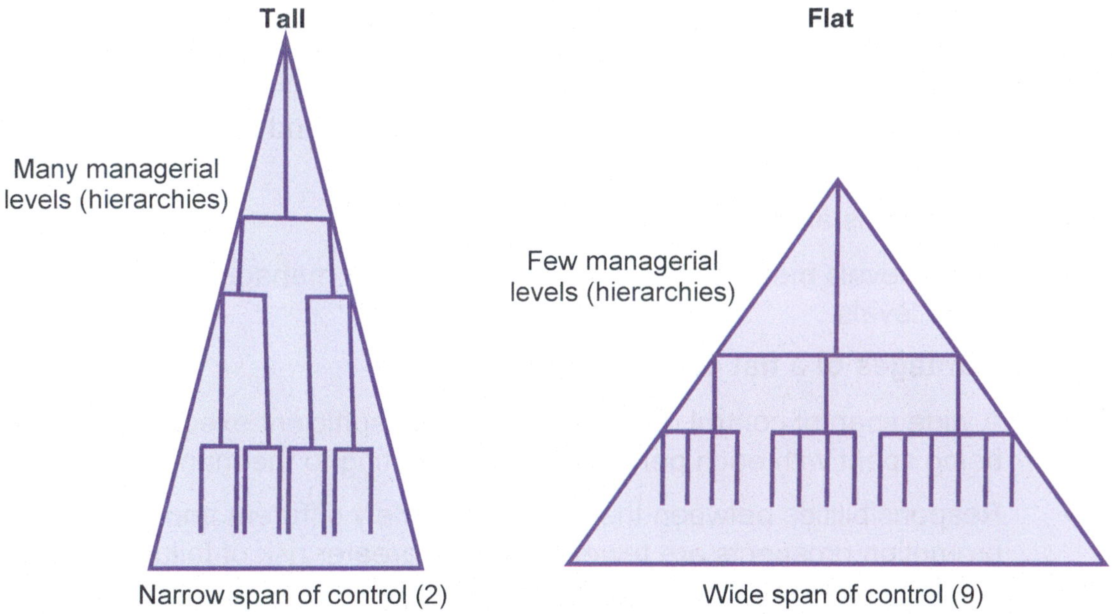

A 'tall' organisation has many levels of management (a long scalar chain) and a narrow span of control. An example of this would be the National Health Service.

A 'flat' organisation has few levels of management (a short scalar chain) and a wide span of control. For example, if the job is relatively simple, and most employees in the department are doing the same tasks then large numbers can be controlled by one manager or supervisor quite easily.

There is no universally correct size for the span of control. It will depend on the nature of the work, the ability and training of staff at all levels, the effectiveness of communications and the personality of the manager.

Activity 6

Wilson Ltd is a financial services company. The work undertaken is simple and focused, meaning that each manager looks after a large number of employees. Due to this, there are relatively few levels of management within the company.

Which of the following is correct with regards to Wilson Ltd's structure?

A. Wide span of control, short scalar chain

B. Narrow span of control, short scalar chain

C. Wide span of control, long scalar chain

D. Narrow span of control, long scalar chain

Advantages of a flat organisation

- A wide span of control encourages delegation and therefore motivation through job enrichment.
- There are usually lower management overhead costs.
- Communications tend to be better as horizontal and lateral communication is encouraged.
- Promotions are real and meaningful.
- Fewer levels mean closer contact between top management and lower levels.

Disadvantages of a flat organisation

- A wide span of control could lead to lack of sufficient executive time being spent with each person directly reporting to the manager.
- Responsibilities between the levels are widely different and so promotion prospects are fewer and carry greater risk of failure than in a tall organisation where there may be an overlap of responsibilities between manager and subordinate.

Advantages of a tall organisation

- A steady flow of promotion opportunities occurs and progression from one level to another is relatively smooth since there is only a minor increase in authority and responsibility.
- Spans of control can be kept small hence increasing the opportunities for personal contact between manager and each subordinate. This can be important in such areas as research and marketing where the role of the boss is often to act as a sounding board in discussing subordinates' initiatives.

Disadvantages of a tall organisation

- More expensive in terms of management overheads.
- Real increases in power and responsibility between one level and another are minor and this creates overlapping of responsibility and artificial, meaningless differences of status (e.g. size of carpets, number of chairs in the room).
- Messages, plans, etc. pass through more levels and so multiply communication difficulties.
- Planning and co-ordination become more difficult as more levels of management and more people become involved.
- The number of levels between senior management and shop floor creates a remoteness which is detrimental to staff motivation and performance.
- There is little scope for delegation, job enrichment or team building – status barriers and overlapping of responsibilities mitigate against such initiatives.

Activity 7

Which of the following would be a typical feature of a flat organisation?

A. Easy career progression for employees

B. Close supervision of employees by managers

C. Faster decision-making

D. High levels of bureaucracy

3.4 Organisation charts

The organisation chart describes the structure of the organisation in diagrammatic form. It is the skeleton upon which every other activity depends. More importantly, it is the framework that explains the communication pattern, process and the linking mechanisms between the roles. It illustrates to everyone who communicates with whom, how the control system works, who is in control, who has authority and above all, who is responsible. It explains how the organisation is co-ordinated and how individual departments relate. Formal structures are often based on specific tasks and it is how these tasks are allocated and the authority that they carry that is explained by the organisational structure.

Authority relationships can be traced by following the lines of an organisational chart downwards. Responsibility relationships can be traced by following those same lines upwards.

3.5 The different types of organisational structure

The structure of an organisation is concerned with the grouping of the activities so that it can meet its objectives in the best possible way. It achieves this by assigning certain activities to various parts of the organisation and by providing for the necessary authority and co-ordination.

It must ensure that there is no duplication of effort, since apart from the additional costs involved, this might result in the organisation not being competitive within the marketplace that is, not being able to sell its goods or services as cheaply as someone else.

Work can be divided, and activities linked together, in a variety of different ways. The main types of organisational structure are as follows:

- entrepreneurial structure
- functional structure
- product or service structure
- geographical or territorial structure
- matrix structure
- boundaryless structure

As a business develops, the organisational structure may change.

Small businesses in the early stages of their development often adopt an **entrepreneurial structure**. In this model, the owner-manager typically has specialist knowledge and makes decisions with little input from others. There is very little in the way of job descriptions and everybody helps out with all ongoing tasks. Although the absence of formal roles and procedures may be suitable for small organisations and this structure can lead to quick, responsive decisions, the company may struggle to cope with diversification or growth due to its reliance on one person.

For organisations which have outgrown the entrepreneurial structure, but have relatively few products or locations, a **functional (or departmental) structure** is more common. This is most people's idea of the 'classical' approach to organisational structure. This structure incorporates specialised departments to manage the different functions of the business, under the overall leadership of the directors.

This is illustrated in the organisation chart below.

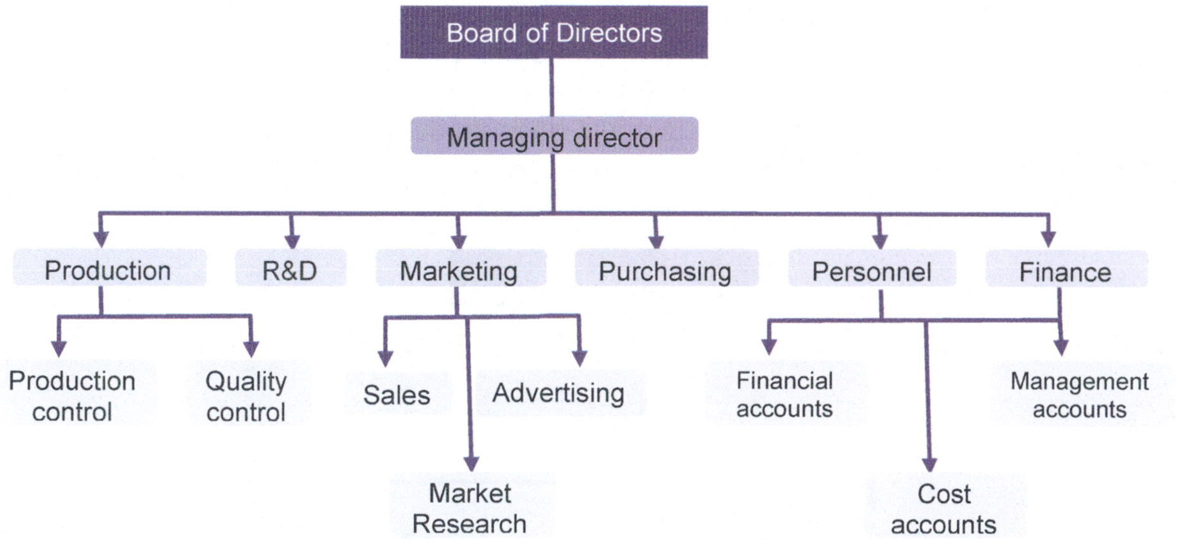

The Board will decide overall company policy. The Managing Director has responsibility for the running of the company and thus is accountable to members of the Board for the implementation of policy. The Board itself is responsible to the shareholders for the success of the company.

Each department head is responsible for the smooth running of their department and has authority to make day-to-day decisions as problems arise, whilst remaining accountable to the Managing Director. Within each department, some authority is delegated to senior staff, e.g. supervisors in the accounting department, team leaders in the production department or buyers in the purchasing department. Such employees are accountable to their department heads.

Although this approach can enable greater specialisation and career opportunities within the individual departments, decision-making can be slower and subject to conflicts between functions.

For larger companies, a **divisional structure** allows several divisions to run autonomously as **strategic business units (SBUs)**. These divisions will typically run with their own, separate departmental structure and therefore have their own sales, purchasing, HR and advertising departments.

Divisional structures can be organised based on a number of factors:

- Product portfolio
- Customer type
- Geographical region

For example, Procter and Gamble divides its organisational structure on the basis of product. Each of the P&G divisions – food products, toilet goods, paper products, packaged soap and detergents, coffee and industrial food – is headed by a vice-president.

This structure establishes each product or group of products as an integrated unit within the framework of the company. The main functions of production, sales, personnel and finance are apportioned to the relative products. So each product group could have its own specialist in accounting, personnel, etc. Such a structure allows greater delegation by top management and clear profit accountability by division heads.

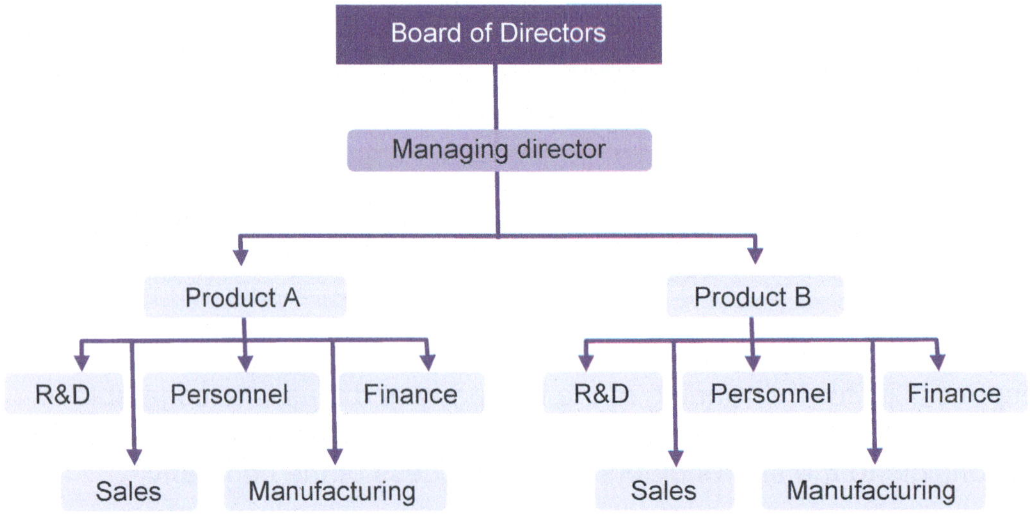

Geographical or territorial structure is a favoured method amongst companies that operate across wide geographical areas and where it is important that activities in any area should be grouped and assigned to a manager. It is a more suitable method where customer needs or product characteristics are regionally based and when the product itself is not so complex or capital insensitive as to make the establishment of regional operations too costly or impractical.

This would typically happen when demands of customers varied greatly between geographical areas and could best be satisfied by local bases. Consider the differing needs of an estate agency chain, which must be geographically based, and that of an insurance agency, which can be centralised.

In many modern organisations where conventional communication structures are less formal, communication tends to be horizontal, between individuals and departments, rather than the upwards or downward flow. A project team may be set up as a separate unit on a temporary basis to accomplish a specific task and when this is completed, the team is disbanded or members of the unit are reassigned to a new task. **A matrix organisation** is a combination of functional departments, which provide a stable base for specialised activities and a permanent location for members of staff, and units that integrate various activities or departments on a project team, product, programme or geographical basis. It establishes a grid with a two-way flow of authority and responsibility.

Its great advantage is that it is cross-functional – maintaining functions and the commitment and specialisation of individual departments. At the same time it allows adaptation to change, encourages commitment to the organisation as a whole, improves communication and perhaps most importantly of all, reduces the need for slow, laborious communication up and down the traditional hierarchical structure.

This is illustrated below:

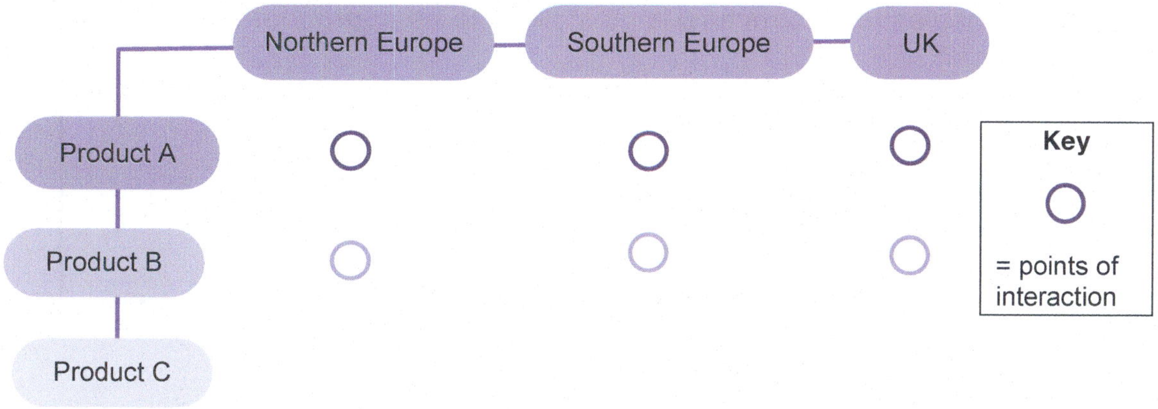

In the above the team working on Product C would be responsible not only to the head of that product, but also to the heads of each geographical region.

Boundaryless structures adopt a more flexible approach than the above, traditional models. Unrestricted by rigid chains of command or formal departments, they instead focus on flexibility.

Example

Types of boundaryless organisation:

Hollow organisations – split their functions into core and non-core activities. Anything classified as core remains in-house and non-core operations are outsourced.

Virtual organisations – outsource many functions to other organisations and therefore co-ordinate processes using a small central staff.

Modular organisations – primarily manufacturing companies, they outsource elements of the production process to others. In an extreme case, these organisations simply assemble others' products to create a final product.

Activity 8

Godfrey plc is a large company operating in only one country. It manufactures a variety of electric products, each of which is highly complex and specialised. Its sales have grown significantly over a number of years, with each of the products producing a roughly equal amount of Godfrey's overall revenue.

Which organisational structure is most likely to be appropriate for Godfrey plc?

A. Divisional – geographic

B. Divisional – product

C. Functional/departmental

D. Entrepreneurial

3.6 Centralisation or decentralisation?

A method of analysing structures is by reference to the level at which decisions are made.

Definition

In a **centralised structure**, the upper levels of management retain the authority to make decisions and functions are typically managed from the company's headquarters.

In a **decentralised structure**, the authority to make decisions is delegated down to divisional units and those responsible for the day-to-day operations of the business. people at lower levels. In fact, it has been defined as 'the delegation of the freedom to make decisions'.

The advantages and disadvantages of a decentralised structure are:

Advantages	Disadvantages
Senior management free to concentrate to strategy	Loss of control by senior management
Better local decisions due to local expertise	Lack of goal congruence and co-ordination in decisions
Better motivation due to increased training	Inexperienced managers making decisions
Easier career progression	Additional training costs

Quicker responses due to smaller chain of command	Duplication of roles within organisation
More flexibility on decisions	Extra costs in obtaining information

Decentralised structures however rely heavily on the ability of employees at a local level to be able to make sound decisions.

Activity 9

Explain your organisation's organisational structure and the extent of its operations at a local, national and international level. Using an organisation chart, determine how the management of the company is structured.

(AAT Assessment criteria 1.2)

4 Organisational culture

4.1 Defining a corporate culture

There are many definitions of corporate culture. Put simply though it is sum total of all of the beliefs, attitudes, norms and customs that prevail within an organisation. For this reason, every company will have its own distinctive cultures and behaviour acceptable in one may be discouraged in another.

The culture within a company can change overnight with a change of ownership or leadership or if the organisation is threatened by external factors such as the constraints of a period of economic uncertainty.

Crucially, the corporate culture not only has an impact on how employees relate to and work with each other, but also on how they portray the company to outsiders, including potential customers.

The key factors which determine the culture of an organisation are:

- the size of the organisation (turnover, number of sites, employees)
- age (how old is the business and how experienced is its key staff?)
- history (who has worked there in the past and how did they react to certain situations?)

- diversity (how varied is the company's product/service offering and what is the geographical or cultural spread of its stakeholders?)
- ownership (who are the shareholders and what is their involvement?)
- technology (how advanced are the systems in place)
- creativity (does the organisation support those willing to take risks or use their own initiative?)
- formality (are communications and office attire and layout strict/hierarchical or more relaxed?)
- interaction (are different groups encouraged to work together?)
- focus (is there a clear direction and is everyone aware of company objectives?)

Definition

The **informal organisation** is the network of relationships which exist within an organisation, which evolve over time. These informal structures are largely due to organic relationships between staff members from different divisions.
Such informal structures should be seen as both a consequence of and a crucial aspect of the corporate culture. Although they are unwritten, they can greatly enhance or hold back a business and they key decision-makers within the formal structure should consider how best to adapt formal organisation to complement informal groups and activities.

Activity 10

Sum up your organisation's organisational/corporate culture in no more than two sentences. Do the same for one of your company's competitors and note the differences.

(AAT Assessment criteria 1.2)

5 Business Analysis

5.1 SWOT Analysis

Before any long-term planning or a decision can be made, four factors have to be taken into consideration:

The organisation's **strengths** and **weaknesses**, and the **opportunities** and **threats** presented to the organisation by its environment (SWOT analysis)

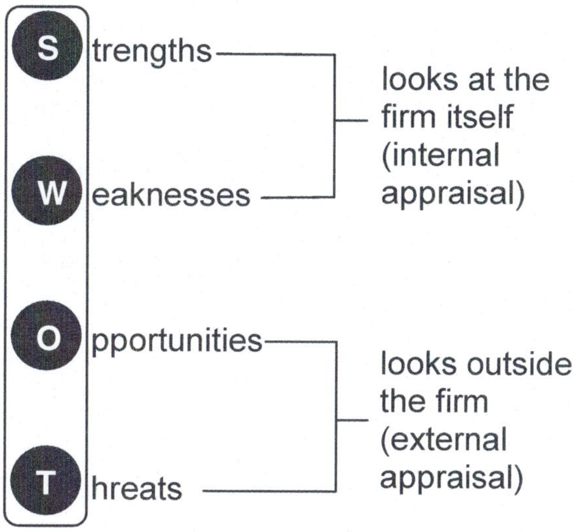

SWOT analysis is the simplest and most well-known model for a business to analyse its position and form a strategy for the future.

The objective is to ascertain the company's strengths and weaknesses, and to forecast what the results may be if the company continues as it is, in the light of information at present available to it.

It identifies the company's

- **S**trengths (things that are going well)
- **W**eaknesses (things that are not being done or are being done badly)
- **O**pportunities (events or changes in the external environment which may lead to gaining new customers, markets)
- **T**hreats (from competitors or changes in the external environment, such as government actions, the economic climate or technological developments)

The review should be organised and co-ordinated throughout the company and carried out in a way that motivates management to face up to the true issues and think constructively and not defensively.

The analysis should include the following.

- A comprehensive review of the company's results.
- An investigation to ascertain the strengths of the company (the areas in which it has exclusive skills or does well as compared with competitive standards) and areas where significant improvements

are needed.

- Comparisons with competitors, and other industries where useful.

The main areas considered in an internal appraisal would include the following:

- **products** e.g. age, life span, life cycle stage, quality comparisons
- **marketing** e.g. market share, presence in target segments, identifiable and non-identifiable benefits, success of promotions, advertising
- **distribution** e.g. delivery promise performance, depot location
- **production** e.g. age/obsolescence, valuation, capacity
- **research and development** e.g. number of commercially viable products, costs/benefits, relevance of projects
- **human resources** e.g. manpower plan, management in depth, training levels, morale
- **finance** e.g. cash availability, risk exposure, short and long-term funding, contribution levels.

An outline of a SWOT analysis process is shown on below.

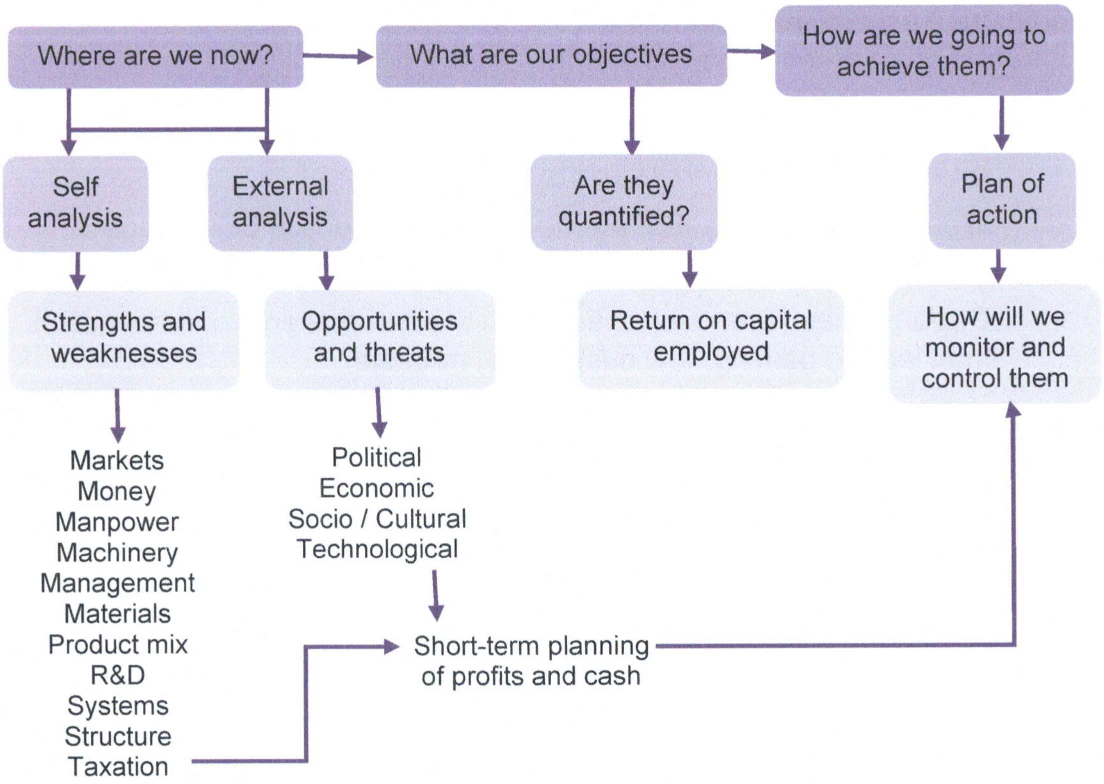

The strengths and weaknesses refer to the internal aspects of the organisation compared both to the expectations of the market place and to the competition.

The external analysis aims to highlight opportunities and potential constraints for the organisation. In the light of both the internal and external analyses, previously established objectives may be seen as either unachievable or too easy, so the objectives may have to be modified.

The internal and external appraisals will be brought together and perhaps shown in some form of chart so that potential strategies can be identified. For example, the results of a SWOT analysis could be as follows:

Strengths Committed employees Good community links New equipment Established products	**Weaknesses** Reactive approach Outdated IT systems No new R & D projects No international presence
Opportunities Socio-cultural New technologies R & D funding International partnerships	**Threats** Competitive market – initiation of price wars New legislation Negative consumer trends

Activity 11

Tick the correct box to identify which of the issues below is a strength, weakness, opportunity or threat.

	S	W	O	T
A growing overdraft				
A well trained workforce				
A new competitor entering the market				
A new piece of software is developed that may be useful to us				

Activity 12

A greater percentage of teenagers in the UK are going to university than ever before.

Give examples of three firms who will be affected by this and state whether they would view the development as an opportunity or a threat in each case.

5.2 External factors – PEST Analysis

As mentioned above when introducing SWOT analysis, no company or market exists in a vacuum without impact from the outside world. In order to fully understand an organisation and to evaluate its performance and create a strategy, we also need to consider the business environment in which it operates.

The aim of external analysis is to identify and understand the opportunities and threats facing the organisation, both present and potential. A threat is a trend or event that will have no strategic response as well as a significant downward departure from current sales and profit patterns e.g. consumers' concern for healthy eating and foods that affect cholesterol represents a threat to the dairy industry. An opportunity is a trend or event that could lead to a significant upward change in sales and profit patterns, given a suitable strategic response.

There are four components of external analysis – customer analysis, competitive analysis, industry analysis and environmental analysis.

- **Customer analysis** – identifies the organisation's customer segments and each segment's motivations and unmet needs.
- **Competitive analysis** – covers the identification of current and potential competitors. Some competitors will compete more intensely than others and, although they should be examined in more detail, all competitors are usually relevant to the strategy development.
- **Industry analysis** – to measure the attractiveness of the market and understand its dynamics so that threats and opportunities can be detected and strategies formed. The analysis will include an examination of the market size, profitability, growth, cost structure, channels, trends and key (or critical) success factors.
- **Environmental analysis** – to identify and understand emerging opportunities and threats created by forces beyond the normal scope of the organisation and its market.

Such an analysis of external factors can be referred to as PEST (or PESTLE) analysis. This would include the following factors:

- **P**olitical factors
- **E**conomic factors
- **S**ocial factors
- **T**echnological factors
- **L**egal factors (if not included with the Political category)
- **E**nvironmental factors (if not included with the Political or Social factors)

Overview

Political/legal Taxation policy Foreign trade regulations Environmental protection Anti-monopoly legislation Government stability	**Economic** Interest rates Inflation Unemployment Disposable income Business cycles GNP trends Energy availability and cost
Socio-Cultural Lifestyle changes Education levels Attitudes to leisure Consumerism	**Technological** New discoveries New developments Speed of technology transfer Rates of obsolescence Government spending on R&D

Political Factors

Decisions made by national and local governments affect business on a daily basis. The business must be aware of and react to government policies and legislation relating to trading, pricing, dividends, tax, employment, monopolies, environmental protection laws, foreign trade regulations and health and safety regulations in particular. Although many regulatory constraints can be seen as threats, there are opportunities resulting from governmental scheme - for example, companies could make use of grants and tax concessions available within an industry.

Economic Factors

General economic conditions and trends are critical to the success of an organisation. They include interest rates and the availability of credit, inflation, exchange rates, business cycles, the level of unemployment and disposable income. Inflationary effects on wages, supplier and competitor pricing affect both the costs of producing products or offering services.

Common economic indicators measure national income and output (GNP), savings, investment, prices, wages, productivity, employment, government activities and international transactions.

International economic issues may also be important to the organisation. The organisation needs to know what the economic prospects and inflation forecasts are for the countries that it operates in and how they will affect strategy.

Social Factors

Changes in demographic variables – such as age, sex, family size, income, occupation, education, nationality and social class – can have a major impact on businesses. For example in Western Europe people are living longer and in many countries the birth rate is falling, leading to an ageing population. This has obvious implications for the types of products and services that organisations may plan to offer.

People's tastes and values are important considerations and are reflected in their lifestyles and consumer patterns. For example, attitudes towards work have changed, and with the increased use of technology, working from home has also become more common and can enable a business to operate in a different way.

Technological Factors

The level of technology in a particular industry determines to some extent what products and services will be produced, what equipment will be used and how operations will be managed. Companies often spend vast amounts of money on technology, in the hope that they will gain some form of competitive advantage, leading to higher profits.

This is an area in which change takes place very rapidly and the organisation needs to be constantly aware of what is going on. Technological change can influence the following:

- changes in production techniques
- the type of products that are made and sold
- how services are provided
- how we identify markets.

Technological factors may include changes in retailing methods (such as direct selling via the Internet), changes in production methods (greater use of automation) and greater integration between buyers and suppliers via computer link-ups. The managers would need to know to what extent the existing technologies are maturing and what technological developments or trends are affecting or could affect the industry. The effect of technological development and change includes the following:

- markets and customers analysed more effectively (using sophisticated databases)
- new products and services being developed
- changes in work methods leading to a reduction in production and other costs
- better quality products and services at no increased cost
- products and services available and delivered quicker or more effectively than previously
- employees freed from repetitive work and able to demonstrate more creativity
- short product life cycles – an organisation needs to be innovative

Legal Factors

Businesses cannot operate effectively without a good working knowledge of the laws and regulations that govern them. They need to be fully aware of the implications of employment and consumer law, as will be addressed in Chapter 3. Companies are also required to comply with a generally accepted financial reporting framework, which is the International Financial Reporting Standards (IFRS), which are issues by the International Accounting Standards Board (IASB).

Example

A haulage firm might consider the following factors using PEST analysis:

- **Political**
  Government steps to reduce pollution from lorries
  Congestion charges in cities
  Plans to build new roads
  Fuel tax
- **Economic**
  Overall state of the national economy
  Fuel prices
  Interest rate fluctuations
- **Social**
  Public concerns over road safety could lead to restrictions
- **Technological**
  Developments in satellite navigation software
  Anti-theft devices
  Tracking systems to monitor driver performance
  Tyre technology

5.3 Competitive Analysis: Porter's Five Forces

The degree of competition between organisations already operating within the market is likely to be based on:

- whether there is a dominant organisation
- whether the market is growing or declining
- whether the product or service can be differentiated between competitors
- whether the economy is in recession or booming (generally as an economy goes into recession competitive rivalry will intensify).

Porter's Five Forces looks in detail at the competitive environment by analysing five key forces, which determine the overall profit potential of the industry for the company.

The five forces to be assessed are:

- **Competitive rivalry** (number and strength of competitors, the rate of growth, how aggressive pricing/marketing strategies are, how easy it is to switch)
- **Power of customers** (will have greater power where they have alternative sources of supply and are well informed of their choices)
- **Power of suppliers** (will have greater power where there are fewer companies offering products, where products are clearly differentiated and where switching costs are high)
- **New entrants to the market** (will intensify competition, but may also face considerable barriers to entry)
- **Substitutes** (the better the price-performance alternative offered, the greater the threat)

The 'degree' of competition will be reduced by the effectiveness of any barriers to entry. Typical barriers to entry are as follows:

(a) **Financial or capital requirement of entry.** The amount of capital required may not be the major barrier to entry but rather the availability and cost of raising finance.

(b) **The patterns of distribution or access to distribution channels.** The soft drinks industry in the UK for example, was traditionally dominated by two companies because brewers owned the soft drinks companies and the distribution outlets (i.e. the public houses).This pattern of distribution, however, has been forced to change with government legislation now restricting the number of public houses that can be owned by brewers.

(c) **Government legislation** and changes in such legislation obviously have a major effect on barriers to entry. Deregulation and privatisation has meant that extensive barriers to entry have now been lowered in an attempt to make markets contestable.

There are other barriers to entry such as advertising, patents and trade secrets, but it is not possible to state which are the most important. What is important is the recognition that barriers to entry have a major impact on the threat of potential entry.

Example

Porter's five forces applied to the an established fast food restaurant chain, such as McDonalds:

- **Competitive Rivalry: very high**

  Many major competitors with vast marketing budgets eg Burger King, KFC

- **Power of Customers: low**

  Customers could switch easily for no cost and could easily go to a different restaurant, but as individuals they have very low buying power or ability to negotiate

- **Power of Suppliers: low**

  McDonalds buys from small suppliers all over the world

- **Threat of New Entrants: low**

  Significant barriers to entry including the capital investment required, the strengths of existing brands in the market and economies of scale

- **Threat of Substitutes: medium**

  Numerous other fast food options are available eg. Pizzas, Fried Chicken, coffee shop food

Therefore the key issue here is competitive rivalry.

Activity 13

Pike.com is an online DVD and CD retailer. It has a large number of competitors within the market. It has recently cut its prices and is now selling at a price which is significantly lower than its rivals. Pike.com believes that it will be difficult for any other company to match its pricing structure.

Which of Porter's five forces would this strategy NOT help to deal with?

A. Power of suppliers

B. Power of customers

C. New entrants

D. Competitive rivalry

Activity 14

Perform a SWOT Analysis and PESTLE Analysis on your own company.

Use Porter's Five Forces theory to assess your market's current competitive position.

(AAT Assessment criteria 1.1)

Activity 15

Kellehers is a national chain of Irish-themed bars considering extending their operations overseas. Match up the following factors with the heading they would be analysed under in a PESTLE analysis:

A The age at which people are allowed to drink alcohol

B Government tax on alcohol sales

C The level of disposable income people have

D People's religious beliefs and attitudes towards alcohol

Choose one of the following words from the Picklist to describe each of the above.

Picklist

Political	Social	Environmental
Economic	Technological	Legal

6 Sources of Company Information

In order to relate this to your own company or one with which you are familiar, the following sources will be of particular use:

- Company promotional brochures supplied to prospective clients
- The staff handbook
- The company website
- The company's annual report
- Other employees' views and experiences
- Competitor websites and promotional materials, as a means of comparison

Activity 16

Using the sources of information listed, identify the key services and products that your company offers to market and consider how the company makes money.

(AAT Assessment criteria 1.3)

Answers to chapter activities

Activity 1

C A school

This is the only one likely to be controlled and funded by the central government. Although private schools do exist, the majority are subject to public policy and finance.

Of the remaining three, all are typically private enterprises with no involvement from the government.

Activity 2

A **Incorrect.** Only public limited companies can sell shares to the public

B **Correct.** Shareholders in limited companies have limited liability

C **Correct.** Most sole traders and partnerships aim to maximise wealth

D **Correct.** Public sector organisations are controlled by central government

E **Incorrect.** Charities form part of the private sector

Activity 3

This answer will depend on the company, but should include reference to the industry sector they operate in, the ownership and size of the company, its primary objective and market position. For example:

- I work for a pet food company in the food manufacturing and retail sector. The company is a private enterprise and limited company. Customers are spread across the UK and there are thirty staff. Turnover is £3 million. Technology is developing. It is primarily concerned with making profits, although customer care is a high priority. It has over twenty main competitors, most operating on a larger scale, but is increasing its market share every year and trying to remain specialised.
- I work for a local government office specialising in housing policy. The organisation is part of the public sector, specialising in public administration services. The main objective is to provide the public with affordable housing and therefore improve the state of the local

community. The department is not profit generating and is accountable to the public.

Activity 4

1 **C Operational** –a practical, short-term policy

2 **A Strategic** –a long-term plan, affecting the whole business

3 **B Tactical** – affects a particular store and is made by a middle manager

Activity 5

This answer will depend on the individual's company, but the mission statement and primary objectives should be available in most company literature, including handbooks and reports. In addition to the mission statement, students should also state the main goals resulting from this.

A mission statement will typically make reference to the company's aims in terms of the market and its competitors, as well as to make promises to customers and staff. For example:

We aim to be the largest provider of pet food in the UK, providing our customers with the best quality products and our staff with the working environment to inspire them to success.

(As usual, the real objective here is to make profit!)

Activity 6

A Wide span of control, short scalar chain

There are few levels of management, meaning the scalar chain is short. The fact that each manager has a large number of subordinates indicates a wide span of control.

Activity 7

C Faster decision-making

Flat organisations have shorter scalar chains so there will be relatively few managerial positions. As a result, opportunities for progression would be limited but decisions will be quicker. Due to the wide span of control, monitoring individual staff would be more difficult.

Activity 8

B Divisional – product range

Due to the complex nature of the products, a division to look after each would seem the most logical option.

Activity 9

This answer will depend on the company, but the answer should include an organisational chart with the following annotations or explanations:

- How is authority and responsibility delegated?
- Does the company have a Tall or Wide structure and why?
- Does the organisation follow an entrepreneurial/ functional/ divisional - product/ divisional – geographical/ matrix/ boundaryless structure and why?
- Are functions and decisions centralised or decentralised?

Activity 10

This answer will depend on the individual's company, but the answer should include reference to key factors determining an organisation's corporate culture. For example:

- The history of the company
- The ownership
- The demographics of the workforce
- The use of technology
- The role in the community
- Key policies and priorities

The student should also highlight at least two crucial differences in their company's culture compared to the competitor as a good means of summarising their activities. For example, one could be a relatively new company and one quite old in comparison; one could be at the cutting edge of technology and the other slow to pick up on its advantages.

Activity 11

	S	W	O	T
A growing overdraft		√		
A well trained workforce	√			
A new competitor entering the market				√
A new piece of software is developed			√	

Activity 12

Examples could include:

1. Firms who rent out properties in university towns and cities would see it as an opportunity.
2. Providers of stationary and study materials would see it as an opportunity.
3. Student loan and service providers (e.g. student insurance, student travel specialists) would see it as an opportunity.
4. Any firms who look to recruit high quality workers straight from school could see it as a threat to their recruitment.
5. Graduates are likely to expect higher wages which is also a threat.

Activity 13

The strategy would NOT help to deal with

A Power of suppliers

Cutting prices would reduce customer bargaining power, as they will be unable to find a cheaper alternative. The lower prices would also deter those looking to enter the market and almost certainly attract customers from its rivals, reducing the impact of competitive rivalry.

Activity 14

This answer will depend on the individual's company, but the answer should include:

- Examples of Strengths, Weaknesses, Opportunities and Threats to the company
- Examples from the external environment of Political, Economic, Social, Technological, Legal and Environmental factors which could impact the business
- Analysis of competitive rivalry, the power of suppliers and customers and barriers to entry specific to the business.

Activity 15

A The age at which people are allowed to drink alcohol = **Legal**

B Government tax on alcohol sales = **Political**

C The level of disposable income people have = **Economic**

D People's religious beliefs and attitudes towards alcohol = **Social**

Activity 16

This answer will depend on the individual's company, but the answer should include descriptions of the products and services offered and how crucial their sales are to the success of the business.

3 Developing commercial awareness – external relationships

Introduction

In Chapter 2, we developed an understanding of the nature of organisations and how they are strategically managed. It is now crucial to look beyond the internal workings of a company and see how the business can have an impact on a variety of external parties, including customers and competitors.

As explained in Chapter 2, most enterprises are created to generate revenue and maximise profits. Therefore a further examination of how one of these groups, the customer, is required. This chapter will look at the nature of different stakeholders and assess how companies achieve their primary objective by delivering effective client relationships.

ASSESSMENT CRITERIA

2 Understand how relationships are managed between an organisation and its clients

3 Understand a client's business

4 Explain the contractual and ethical obligations that apply between an organisation and its stakeholders

CONTENTS

1 Stakeholders
2 Customer Acquisition
3 Customer Relationships
4 Legal Obligations
5 Ethical Considerations

1 Stakeholders

1.1 Stakeholders

Definition

A stakeholder is an individual or group who has an interest in what the organisation does, or who affects, or can be affected by, the organisation's actions.

A business' strategic decision-making must therefore consider the needs of important stakeholders and assess the ramifications of their actions on them.

1.2 Primary Stakeholders

Internal stakeholders are those within the organisation itself and include:

- **Employees** – generally concerned with job security, pay and conditions and job satisfaction
- **Managers and directors** – generally concerned with pay and status, job security and individual performance measures. If an organisation follows a strategy that threatens a manager's department, they are likely to be hostile

Connected stakeholders are those who either invest in or have regular dealings with the company and include:

- **Shareholders / Investors** – generally concerned with a steady flow of income, capital growth and business development. If an organisation wishes to follow strategies requiring a large capital injection, the shareholders will be unhappy if this has an adverse effect on their income stream.
- **Customers** – generally concerned with receiving goods and services of a reasonable quality and at a reasonable price. If an organisation wishes to change its offering, customers may switch provider.
- **Suppliers / Contractors** – generally concerned with being paid promptly for goods and services or receiving regular repayments of capital they have provided (e.g. banks). If an organisation wishes to follow a strategy that improves working capital management by paying suppliers late, existing suppliers may decide to sever links with them, leading to the increased cost of finding new suppliers.

- **Advisors** – generally concerned with ensuring that the organisation is appreciative of their expertise.

Both of the above groups are known as **primary stakeholders.**

1.3 Secondary Stakeholders

External or secondary stakeholders do not have a direct or contractual link to the organisation but can be influenced by its activities. They include:

- **The government** – generally concerned that the organisation is meeting legal requirements and does not harm their environment. For example, if an organisation wishes to follow a strategy focusing on out-of-town retail centres, this will be affected by government policy towards increased road building and urban redevelopment.
- **The community** – generally concerned that the organisation is operating in a way that is socially and environmentally acceptable. For the example of out-of-town shopping, society's attitude towards this method of retail and consumer trends would need consideration.
- **Trade unions** – generally concerned with taking an active part in the decision-making process. This includes consultation on key employment issues such as the closing of a manufacturing plant.
- **Pressure groups** - generally concerned that the organisation is meeting relevant legal requirements and that it does not harm the outside environment.

Assessing the expectations of stakeholders enables an organisation to gauge whether its objectives will provide the means to satisfy their needs.

Activity 1

Which of the following would be classified as an internal stakeholder?

A. Customers

B. Suppliers

C. Shareholders

D. Directors

Activity 2

A supermarket buys its goods on credit and sells them for cash, therefore ensuring it has strong cash flows at all times. What are the needs of the supplier to such a supermarket with regards to their business relationship?

1.4 Mendelow's Matrix

If an organisation is having difficulty deciding who the dominant stakeholder is, they can use Mendelow's power-interest matrix:

Level of power \ Level of interest	Low	High
Low	Minimal effort	Keep informed
High	Keep satisfied	Key players

By plotting each stakeholder according to the level of power and the level of interest they have in a particular decision, companies can determine who the key players are and therefore consider them more widely in the formulation and evaluation of strategic policy.

Example

Windsor Electricals is a leading manufacturer and supplier of electrical appliances, primarily to commercial customers.

The directors at Windsor Electricals are assessing their strategy for the forthcoming year. They are currently seen to be wasting time, energy and money on certain stakeholders.

They use Mendelow's matrix to decide strategies for the following:

- Mooney Homes is a property and land management company and owner of housing developments all over the country. Windsor Electricals have an exclusive contract with Mooney Homes and work extremely closely with them on large projects. The team at Mooney Homes require constant information and are always happy to stress how important their business is. In truth, they are one of Windsor Electricals' top five customers.
- Mrs L is the largest shareholder in Windsor Electricals. She owns over 35% of the shares, which is significantly more than the other shareholders. She knows the team at Windsor Electricals well so is more than happy to let them run the company as they see fit, without any intervention.
- Morse and Marshall provide a variety of components crucial in electrical appliance manufacturing. They are a small company and tend to rely on repeat business without applying much effort. They are happy to supply to Windsor Electricals when required, but do

not seek any sort of intensification of their partnership or further information.

- Geoffrey lives in the house opposite Windsor Electricals. He has done so for most of his life and knows many of the staff well. He is also a customer, largely purchasing equipment for the small restaurant he owns in the neighbouring village. These orders are rare, but Geoffrey asks a lot of questions and spends vast amounts of time deciding what he needs. He also often contacts senior staff to ask logistical questions about the road they are both located on.

Using Mendelow's Matrix, the stakeholders could be mapped as follows:

POWER	Mrs L (High power, low interest) **KEEP SATISFIED**	Mooney Homes (High interest, high power) **KEY PLAYER**
	Morse and Marshall (Low power, low interest) **MINIMAL INTEREST**	Geoffrey (High interest, lower power) **KEEP INFORMED**
	INTEREST	

Therefore, Mooney Homes are Key Players, Mrs L falls into the Keep Satisfied quadrant, Morse and Marshall would require Minimal Effort and Geoffrey would be considered to need to be Kept Informed.

Activity 3

With reference to your own company, provide an example of each of the following:

i. An internal stakeholder

ii. A connected stakeholder

iii. An external stakeholder

For each of the above,

a) Describe how the needs and expectations of the three stakeholders differ with reference to your company's objectives.

b) Assess their importance using Mendelow's matrix.

(AAT Assessment criteria 1.4, 2.3)

2 Customer Acquisition

2.1 The importance of customers

As we have seen, the customer is a crucial stakeholder for any business organisation and no business can survive without customers (often referred to as 'clients' for professional service firms such as accountancy practices, solicitors or surveyors) purchasing its goods or services. From a local accountancy practice up to a transnational IT equipment supplier, the customer's financial endorsement is key to success. Put simply, customer acquisition and retention is how businesses make money.

Therefore the focus on business development and converting opportunities into purchasing customers is understandable within businesses of all sizes.

There are two principle types of customers organisations sell to:

- business-to-consumer (B2C)
- business-to-business (B2B)

B2C (also known as retail sales) involves largely selling to the general public and promoting the company's offering to mass markets.

However, some companies will receive the majority of their business from other enterprises. Where a company targets other commercial organisations for the majority of its income, they tend to be more focused, specific and sophisticated in terms of brand messages. Mass marketing is usually not appropriate as the audience is obvious and specialised.

2.2 The role of marketing

Despite popular misconceptions, marketing is much more than simply advertising. To get a customer to buy your products or services, it is crucial to differentiate your offering and explain your USP (unique selling points or unique selling proposition). This is achieved through a marketing strategy which not only defines and anticipates customer needs but also appeals directly to them.

Companies who show a **marketing orientation** as opposed to a **product orientation** are those who consider customer needs as more important than technological advancements.

Activity 4

Marketing is mainly concerned with which of the following?

A. Increasing sales revenue

B. Streamlining production

C. Anticipating and meeting customer needs

D. Maximising profit

2.3 Brand messages

Definition

Brand management is about how companies communicate and project their goods and services to the market.

Having decided on which groups to target and which products/services seem the most attractive, it must then be decided how to differentiate the company's brand from its competitors.

The most common and obvious distinctions used in advertising are:

- Price
- Quality

Some companies promote affordable products to appeal to the cash-conscious consumer (often 'own-brand' or 'no-frills' alternatives), whereas others use higher pricing to imply a higher standard of product.

Global brands have defined themselves based on other factors:

- High level customer service
- Innovation (e.g. Apple)
- Luxury (e.g. Louis Vuitton)
- Environmentally friendly approach (e.g. Body Shop)
- Ethical policies
- Charity and community

Activity 5

Summarise your company's brand message in one sentence.

(AAT Assessment criteria 1.3 and 1.4)

Marketing is covered in greater depth as part of business communication activities in Chapter 5.

3 Customer Relationships

3.1 Customer Relationship Management

Customer (or Client) Relationship Management (CRM) is a crucial part of the B2B sales process, realising that success is not simply a case of winning business, but also the often more complex task of keeping it.

This involves the continual monitoring of customer activities and opinions and forging strong relationships to enable business development. Companies therefore track and organise their contacts for both current and prospective clients, often using software to manage this. As the number of potential customers is smaller than with B2C marketing, more time and customisation can be used to focus on a group of key targets.

3.2 Understanding a client's business

As discussed in Chapter 1, there are many ways to classify business organisations, their organisational structures and corporate culture. It is crucial to understand how a client operates and what its priorities are in order to initially gain, retain and empathise with their business.

Unlike your own business, where information may be freely available, to ascertain the nature of a client's business, further research may be required.

Using similar methods to those identified in Chapter 2, relevant press and promotional literature, company reports and the website of the client should establish a good overview. Depending on your relationship with the client, formal or informal questionnaires may also prove revealing.

As you research, here are some of the areas you may wish to consider:

- How would you classify the company in terms of its market sector, size and technological development?
- What is the company's stated mission statement?
- How would you sum up the company's true objectives in one sentence?
- What are the company's stated or implied core corporate values?
- Do the staff all share these?

- What products and services are offered?
- How would you classify the target market for each?
- What do customers say about the company?
- Who are the competitors and how do they compare?
- What is the primary focus of the company's marketing?
- What is particularly strong about the brand and how has it been portrayed in press and advertising?
- Is there a rigid structure to the organisation or is it more flexible?
- What is the company's turnover?
- How many offices and staff does it have? Does it operate globally?
- Has the company won any awards?

3.3 What makes business organisations different?

When researching companies, whether suppliers or customers, it is important to compare them to the other organisations. To do so, a comparative framework is useful.

Example

Let us compare a large transnational IT manufacturing company with a local accountancy practice using five different criteria:

- **Objectives:** The manufacturing company is likely to have a large number of objectives and resulting goals across varied divisions and possibly geographical locations, whereas the accountancy firm would probably have more specific and less complex goals. Although both may share the maximisation of profit as their principal mission, the manufacturing company are likely to set goals on productivity, research and development and geographical expansion whereas the accountancy firm would probably look to increase market share, awareness and community interaction.
- **Offering:** The manufacturing company offers a product, whereas the accountancy practice offers a largely intangible service. As an IT company, the transnational business would be likely to focus more on product and technology, whereas the accountancy firm would promote its expertise and customer care.
- **Organisational Structure:** The manufacturing company is likely to have a more rigid, corporate structure due to its size. It would probably adopt a divisional structure, whereas the accountancy

firm would be more likely to follow an entrepreneurial or functional structure. The manufacturing company will most probably be answerable to a larger number of stakeholders, with more creditors and shareholders than a smaller entity.

- **Operational Costs:** The manufacturing company is likely to have greater costs of sale and much of its cash tied up in stock, whereas the accountancy firm's cash would be typically tied up in work in progress and therefore easier to convert. Overheads would be greater for the manufacturing company due to its size, however in terms of per employee expenditure on wages and facilities, the accountancy firm would probably have greater relative costs.
- **Operational Systems:** The manufacturing company is likely to have automated rather than people-oriented operating systems. It will rely more heavily on external suppliers than the accountancy firm. As there are likely to be departments responsible for each area of operation, a more complex system is required. For the accountancy firm, the systems in place can be relatively fluid as a few members of staff are likely to be required to fulfil multiple roles.

Another way to compare organisational structure and corporate culture would be McKinsey's 7-S Framework. This states there are seven factors that make organisations different:

- Structure
- Systems
- Style
- Skills
- Staff
- Shared Values
- Strategy

By comparing different clients with each other and your own company using the above seven factors, you are able to develop a better overall view of their unique qualities and varied cultures.

Activity 6

Consider two companies your organisation has regular dealings with (whether suppliers or customers). Compare the companies using each of the factors from McKinsey's 7-S Framework.

(AAT Assessment criteria 3.1, 3.3)

3.4 Customer Acquisition

If an organisation's brand message and marketing have been successful, they will inevitably gain new customers.

As explained earlier in this chapter, the primary motivation for the customer choosing to use the company's products or services will vary. If you consider some of the key clients your organisation works with, they will have different reasons for having made their decision.

This said, there are some key tools and messages to generate new business.

- Price promotion and discounts
- Quality of products and services
- Reliable and prompt delivery of products and services
- Best available 'value for money'
- Reputation with the public and within the market
- Environmentally and socially friendly policies
- After-sales service including warranties and guarantees
- 'Added value' such as loyalty schemes and early payment discounts

Activity 7

Explain how your company attracts and retains customers through its marketing of the products or services it provides.

Consider the following:

- How does your company add value to its clients?
- What does the company offer which is unique?
- How important is pricing and promotion?

(AAT Assessment criteria 1.4)

3.5 Customer Retention and Business Development

For many enterprises, the key to long-term success is repeat business. By fostering a positive relationship with customers through CRM and delivering on their promised offering, businesses are able to either acquire further sales revenue or recommendations from their customers.

Customer care is critical to this process. Building lasting relationships with different clients will require an adaptable approach, but the following are crucial to maintaining a client's happiness:

- **Constant and prompt communication** – keeping customers adequately informed of developments within the company or their specific requirements
- **Efficiency and timeliness** – responding quickly both in terms of customer service queries and providing goods or services
- **Responsiveness** – listening to the client's needs and concerns
- **Reliability and honesty** – engendering trust by providing accurate information and have their needs in mind
- **Mutual interest** – it is important that both parties feel that the relationship is rewarding, whether on a corporate/financial or personal level

In addition to this, some businesses offer their clients incentives or rewards for remaining loyal.

- **Loyalty or frequent purchaser schemes** – providing rewards for repeat or increased business
- **Referral bonuses** – should the client recommend your business to others
- **Beneficial account terms** – delivery and payment terms to meet the customer's requirements
- **Key client account management** – dedicated specialist staff looking after the daily management of a small number of crucial customers
- **Partnerships and networking opportunities** – allowing the client to develop their own business

3.6 Project relationships

At times, the relationship between companies will focus on one particular project or tender. Depending on the nature of this project, your company may become part of a supply chain to deliver a key objective to another client and in turn, may be reliant on other companies supplying materials and services to enable your company to meet the requirements. Where this happens, the strength of relationships with both customers and suppliers is tested.

To successfully gain large contracts from customers often requires a formal or informal tendering process, where your company and their competitors will offer competing terms to secure the business. This will involve a thorough cost-benefit analysis and the involvement of many parts of the business. It is often seen that proposals and tenders are the responsibility of the sales and marketing teams, but in truth they rely on constructive input from many departments, especially the finance function. For more details on this, refer back to Chapter 1 and see Chapter 8 which deals specifically with project management.

There are many considerations for a customer when choosing a supplier as part of a project, some of which are as follows:

- What does the company charge?
- Does it offer discounts or incentives?
- Can it deliver the required quality of product or service?
- Can it customise its offering?
- How does it ship its products and what costs are involved?
- Will deliveries be prompt and accurate?
- Is technical support available?
- Do they have adequate technology?
- How will invoices be administered?
- Is the company financially secure?
- Are they widely seen to be ethical and reliable?

Bear the above factors in mind both when analysing your company's relationship with your suppliers and how your company is viewed when supplying to others.

The relationship between customers and suppliers was traditionally an antagonistic one. Purchasers would aggressively seek the lowest price available and happily switch supplier to get a better deal. In response to this, supplier contracts would be laden with heavy penalty causes due to this mutual mistrust. Information was withheld between the two businesses, meaning that the knowledge and skills of the supplier could not be exploited effectively as they were not fully aware of the situation. Due to this antagonist relationship, trading relationships were not as cost-effective and companies regularly dealing with each other rarely benefited from mutual market intelligence and shared good practice.

The modern trend is for a closer working partnership between companies, especially when working on projects. Collaboration can lead to both parties increasing their market share and prospering from each other's success. The nature of these partnerships can be both ad hoc or formal and sustained, depending on the industry and the requirements of end users at a given time (see PEST analysis). Co-operation enables organisations to:

- understand how to provide better value and customer service to their clients based on actual intelligence rather than assumptions and guesswork
- get the products and services they need – suppliers and customers are now actively involved when new products or systems are being designed, often leading to better and more appropriate products being offered to market
- agree to long-term contracts to provide stability and mutual trust
- reward each other for their support and by doing so create a better working relationship
- improve customer care so that specific needs are met
- have greater co-ordination and synergy of their own working practices
- create better industry intelligence and respond to regulatory requirements
- work together on new or difficult business areas, such as CSR policies (discussed later in this chapter)

Definition

Corporate social responsibility (CSR) refers to the idea that a company should be sensitive to the needs and wants of its stakeholders, rather than just the shareholders.

It is closely linked to sustainable development and matters such as employee rights, environmental protection, customer and supplier relations and community involvement.

One way the relationship between customer and supplier can be formalised and procedures decided is the creation of a Service Level Agreement, which clearly defines expectations.

This would include:

- a detailed explanation of exactly what services and products are being supplied
- the targets/benchmarks to be used and the consequences of failing to meet them
- expected communication deadlines for technical or service queries
- expected response times to recover the operations in the event of an unexpected issue

- the procedure for dealing with complaints
- the information and reporting procedures to be adopted
- the frequency and purpose of meetings
- financial responsibilities
- the procedures for cancelling the contract.

Activity 8

Following a series of meetings, Mooney Homes has decided to enter into a more formal relationship with Windsor Electricals.

As part of this arrangement, they require a service level agreement from Windsor Electricals to guarantee the account benefits and product and service levels they require.

Establish at least five clauses for such an agreement.

(AAT Assessment criteria 2.1, 2.2, 3.2)

4 Legal obligations

4.1 Contractual obligations

So far we have seen how relationships between companies flourish for mutually beneficial outcomes and seen how partnerships are now the norm for everyday business operations. If this is to be a long-term arrangement, however formal, legal arrangements may be required.

A contract is a legally enforceable agreement. Contracts form the basis of most commercial transactions and are of vital importance in business life. They can be either in writing or implied by the conduct of the parties involved in the agreement. As a general rule, the more at stake and the more complex the agreement, the more advisable it is for written form.

On a daily basis, legal contracts can be seen across business operations, including all dealings in land and goods, credit, insurance, carriage of goods, the formation and ownership of business organisations and the employment of their staff.

All everyday transactions from buying a newspaper to purchasing a house involve contracts.

To amount to a valid contract, the following essential elements must be present between the parties involved:

- Agreement – usually in the form of an offer by one participant which is accepted by the other.
- Consideration – in English law, a contract must be a two-sided bargain, with each side promising to provide some consideration in return for what the other is to provide.
- Intention to create legal relations – both parties must have intended for the agreement to be legally binding.
- Reality of the consent – those involved should have freely entered into the agreement.
- Capacity to contract – each party must have the legal power to bind itself contractually.
- Legality – the agreement must be reached with the laws of the land in mind.

A contract will include a series of terms, as agreed by both parties. These can be either express terms (those specifically mentioned and agreed to by the parties either in writing or orally) or implied terms (although not clearly stated in the contract, these terms are implied by assumed intentions, statutes or customs and are imposed as the court feels that both parties would have agreed on the matter had it been considered).

Implied terms will generally be overridden by express terms. However, some statutory terms cannot be overridden by express agreement and this is the case with the Sale of Goods Act 1979.

4.2 Contractual obligations between customers and suppliers

The Sale of Goods Act 1979 (amended in 1994) provides a number of examples of terms implied by statute. These terms impose obligations upon a seller and can be implied into every contract of sale:

- That the seller has (or will have) the right to sell the goods (S12)
- That the goods shall correspond with any description applied to them (S13)
- Where the sale is made in the course of business, that the goods shall be both of satisfactory (formerly 'merchantable') quality and reasonably fit for the required purpose if the seller has been made aware of this (S14)
- That the bulk will correspond with any sample (S15)

Example

In the case of **Rogers v Parish (1987),** the claimant purchased a new Range Rover for £16,000. It had defects in the engine gearbox and bodywork. After several attempts at repair, the car still did not function as desired and the claimant sued.

It was judged that the car was indeed of an unsatisfactory quality and as it was a new Range Rover, this had given rise to expectations above those relating to a more modest car.

The implied terms relating to the provision of services is contained in the Supply of Goods and Services Act 1982. The Act provides a statutory term that 'the supplier will carry out the service with reasonable care and skill'.

Under the Act, an accountant owes the following implied duties:

- to obey a client's instructions (except for anything deemed illegal)
- to demonstrate the level of skill that has been professed
- to take reasonable care
- to keep proper records
- to act in an honest manner
- to show good faith
- to maintain confidentiality

A breach of contract occurs where one of the parties to the agreement fails to comply satisfactorily with their obligations under it.

As a result of the contract being breached, damages or other remedies may be sought. In sale of goods contracts, where the seller is in breach of contract the buyer can either reject the goods or claim damages for their value; where the buyer is in breach of contract the seller can remedy the situation by suing for the prices of the goods or claiming damages for non-acceptance.

In addition to this, the Sale of Goods Act 1979 gives an unpaid seller certain rights over the actual goods:

- If the goods are in the seller's possession, they may hold onto them until payment is received.
- Where the buyer is insolvent, the seller has the right to stop delivery whilst the goods are being transported so they can be recovered.

- If the contract allows, or if the buyer is notified, the seller may rescind the contract and resell the goods if payment is not received in a reasonable time.

Many of the Consumer Protection laws in the United Kingdom result from directives from the European Union. For example, Consumer Protection Act 1987 and Unfair Terms in Consumer Contracts Regulations 1999. The former addressed consumer safety relating to defective products whereas the latter protected the consumer from unreasonable terms or exemption clauses.

Consumer Protection complaints are investigated by the Office of Fair Trading (the UK's official consumer and competition watchdog), who can take the matter to litigation should their investigations prove that a serious breach has occurred.

Activity 9

Gladys buys a new washing machine she saw advertised on Gr8Buys TV, a satellite shopping channel.

When the washing machine arrives, Gladys realises that it is an older model to the one she saw on the television and does not have the key features which attracted to purchase it. She also finds that the machine does not clean her clothes satisfactorily and is incredibly loud, to the point where a neighbour complained to her.

Could Gladys claim Gr8Buys TV has breached the Sale of Goods Act and if so, what is the likely outcome?

Activity 10

Which of the following is a requirement of typical consumer protection legislation?

A. All goods and services must be reasonably priced

B. Goods should be of good quality

C. The seller must have legal title to the good being sold

D. Buyers do not have to make payment until after receipt of the goods

4.3 Other considerations and codes

A **code of conduct** is the set of rules outlining the responsibilities of, or proper practices for an individual or organisation. Often stating the standards and rules by which the business should be run and detailing the procedures and systems to be followed, this code can both protect the business and inform employees of company-wide expectations.

Although the code does not need to be overly detailed, it is a crucial training document and plays a role in defining the organisational culture of the organisation to its stakeholders and employees, however typically it is specific to the company and therefore not intended for internal use.

When working with clients therefore, it is vital to acknowledge that some aspects of the two companies' codes may prove contradictory. For example, dress codes and working hours may be contrary and therefore lead to negotiation.

A **code of practice** is a set of principles and values adopted by a professional group with shared interests to regulate the behaviour of its members. It will often take the form of an ethical code and provide guidance on how to address difficult issues. In a membership context, failure to comply with a code of practice can result in expulsion from the professional organisation.

Although the code of practices for all professions should be considered when working with other departments and external clients, this can also cause conflict, as will be further discussed later in this chapter.

4.4 Employee Contracts

Another relationship which is contractual is that between the employer and employee. It is important here to state the importance of the difference between employees (those who work under a contract of service) and contractors (those who are self-employed and therefore work under a contract for services).

Being a company employee rather than a contractor has a number of consequences. For example, employees receive statutory protection, receive their pay under the PAYE system, can access certain state benefits and are subject to the implied terms in a contract of employment.

To determine an employee's status, the following factors could be considered:

- the degree of control by the 'employer'
- the ownership of tools and equipment
- whether the worker is subject to regular working hours
- whether there is a single or consistent method of payment

- whether there is mutuality of obligations
- the degree of financial risk the worker undertakes
- the ability to provide a substitute

All employees of a company should therefore have a **Contract of Employment.** This consist of a series of terms relating to both the employee and employers.

- Express terms agreed by the two parties (written or oral)
- Terms implied by the courts
- Terms implied by statutes

Express Terms

The Employment Rights Act 1996 requires an employer to provide an employee with a written statement of certain particulars of their employment within two months of the commencement of employment. The statement must include details of:

- Pay rates and frequency
- Job title
- Hours of work
- Place of work
- Length of notice
- Details of disciplinary and grievance procedures
- Date of commencement

If both parties agree to the statement, it is called a contract.

The courts have also implied various terms into the employment contract as a result of past rulings.

Employee's duties include:

- the duty to obey lawful and reasonable orders
- the duty of mutual co-operation
- the duty to exercise reasonable care and skill
- the duty to good faith – to give honest and faithful service
- the duty to render personal service

Employer's duties include:

- the duty to pay reasonable remuneration
- the duty to indemnify the employee
- the duty to provide a safe system of work

- the duty to give reasonable notice of termination of employment
- the duty of mutual co-operation

Terms implied by statute

These largely protect the rights of workers and include:

- Employment Rights Act 1996 includes the right not to be unfairly dismissed, the right to a redundancy payment if applicable and the right to a minimum period of notice.
- Working Time Regulations 1998 limits the average working hours to an average of 48 hours per week and confirms an entitlement to four weeks' paid leave a year.
- Equality Act 2010 protects people from discrimination within the workplace (also covered in Sex Discrimination Act 1975, race Relations Act 1976, Disability Discrimination Act 1995, Sex Discrimination Regulations 2008).
- Equal Pay Act 1970 deals not only with pay but with other terms also. This implies an equality clause into all contracts of employment if workers of differing sexes do the same job or a different job of equal value.
- National Minimum Wage Act 1988 imposes minimum levels of pay.
- Employment Act 2002 relates to the rights of working parents, including flexible working and paternity leave.

4.5 Implications of poor practice

As detailed above, contracts with customers and employees are legally binding. Therefore, any breach can result in legal action being taken (as detailed above for the Sale of Goods Act) and therefore the payment of damages. There also other consequences in terms of the reputation of the company and the level of trust it receives from its customers and employees.

For repeated breaches or more serious instances, a company would use the mechanisms set out in its corporate governance strategy to ensure its practices were improved.

Definition

Corporate Governance is the set of processes and policies by which a company is directed, administered and controlled. It includes the appropriate role of the Board of Directors and the auditors of a company.

Activity 11

Describe a company's legal obligations to its employees and customers, using relevant legislation. Assess the implications should a company not honour these obligations.

(AAT Assessment criteria 2.2, 2.3)

5 Ethical considerations

5.1 Corporate social responsibility

In addition to the legal responsibilities companies have towards their stakeholders (whether internal or external), they are also accountable to their employees and other interested parties in other ways.

In other words, a company needs to recognise that all stakeholders are important, not just its shareholders. As a result of this, their needs have to be assessed not only in terms of financial transactions, but also what they find socially desirable. A criticism of CSR (see definition page 66) is that 'business is business' and that its concern is making money rather than making friends, but there are considerable commercial gains to be made from such strategies.

A socially responsible company may consider the following policies:

- environmentally-friendly factors (e.g. pollution, renewable and non-renewable energies)
- the health impact of products and procedures for users
- the fair treatment of employees
- moral issues such as animal testing
- the safety of products and production processes
- ethical behaviour of employees
- community and charity work

Example

Marks and Spencer promotes itself as a company that takes CSR seriously. It aims to listen and respond to the needs of its shareholders and build up good relationships with employees, suppliers and society at large, using three basic principles:

Products – they promote ethical and environmentally friendly methods in the production, selling and usage of their products

People – they offer a variety of benefits for their own staff and encourage the same of their partners

Places – the company recognises its obligations to the communities in which it trades.

Activity 12

Corporate responsibility means:

A. That the company, not the individual is ultimately responsible for the values of the accounting professionals it employs

B. That a company has the responsibility to do what is in the best interests of its clients, employees and shareholders

C. That a company has to ensure that it has a charitable and environmentally friendly marketing approach

D. That a company reviews and considers the impact of its policies and practices to ensure that it plays a positive and contributory role in relation to its stakeholders, the community and the environment

5.2 CSR and ethics

Although the two terms are often used interchangeably, CSR and ethics have distinct meanings. CSR refers to a firm's obligation to maximise its positive impact on its stakeholders. Therefore, although professional ethics form an essential part of this and ethical considerations instruct the formation of CSR strategy, there may be other factors involved.

5.3 The importance of professional ethics

> **Definition**
>
> **Professional ethics** can be described as the prevailing standards of correct behaviour. Ethics reflect principles and ideals of behaviour that ought to be adhered to. The Code of Practice by which most professions operate is typically an ethical guide to decision-making in that industry.

There are two different approaches to formulating a code of ethics:

- **Rules-based ethics** – explicitly sets out what individuals can and cannot do and states sanctions should they not comply, therefore instilling a sense of fear.
- **A Framework approach** – provides the principles to help individuals arrive at the correct decision and determine the right course of action, therefore providing greater flexibility to respond to complex or new ethical issues.

5.4 The Code of Ethics for Professional Accountants

Published by The International Federation of Accountants (IFAC), the Code of Ethics for Professional Accountants adopts a framework approach, including a set of ethical principles which are deemed to be at the heart of professional behaviour.

The five key principles are:

- **Integrity** – to be straightforward, honest and consistent in all profession business relationships.
- **Objectivity** – to not allow bias, conflict of interest or undue influence of others to override professional or business judgements and base decisions on professional guidelines rather than personal views.
- **Professional Competence and Due Care** – to maintain professional knowledge and skill at the level required to ensure that a client or employer receives competent professional services based on current developments in practice, legislation and techniques and act diligently and in accordance with applicable technical and professional standards.
- **Confidentiality** – to respect the confidentiality of information acquired as a result of professional and business relationships and not disclose any such information to third parties without proper and specific authority, unless there is a legal or professional duty to disclose, not use the information for personal advantage

- **Professional Behaviour** – to comply with relevant laws and regulations and avoid any action that discredits the profession.

Activity 13

Fraser is the accountant for Butterworth and Sons. He has received a complaint from a client because he has been unable to provide a report on time. He told the client that this was due to a technical issue with the company's e-mail system.

Fraser approaches the account manager responsible for the client at Butterworth and Sons and explains the situation, telling his colleague that the report was late because he is still unable to work the company's CRM computer package despite considerable training. He asked the account manager to tell the client that the system was not working. Office practice is for this type of report to be checked by a colleague before sending it on to the client, but Fraser asks the account manager to send it immediately without checking it.

Although the account manager is keen to help, as Fraser is a friend of his, he is concerned. Fraser had both told him more than he needed to know about the situation and asked him not to tell anyone. He said he would take him for a drink to thank him for covering up.

Required:

List all of the actions which breach one of the fundamental principles and state which one is compromised in each case.

Activity 14

Perry is an AAT member currently working as an accountant for a manufacturing company. Recent events at work have been troubling Perry and he discussed them with a former colleague to seek her advice. Perry had been asked by one of the directors to become involved in an arrangement which would lead to financial gain for the director at the expense of the company. The director had made it clear to Perry that he would receive a payrise if he complied, but would lose his job if he refused.

Required:

i. State which ethical principle Perry has breached by speaking about this.

ii. Explain what course of action is most appropriate for Perry to take.

Activity 15

Research whether your company has a CSR policy or code of conduct.

5.5 The benefits of ethical behaviour

At times, ethical policies can hamper the organisation's primary objective, to make a profit. For example, sourcing materials from ethical sources (e.g. Fairtrade food produce) can prove more expensive than other suppliers and having to refuse business from clients deemed unethical can forfeit potential revenue. To introduce a CSR strategy from scratch can also be time-consuming.

Having said this, notable commercial benefits can result from a CSR policy based on good ethical behaviour.

- It can provide differentiation, establishing a strong brand message and therefore attracting new customers
- It can result in a better, happier workforce, as such programmes tend to lead to more recruiting and retaining better and more conscientious staff
- It can save long-term costs, especially in the case of environmental issues where long-term damage can be reduced and money saved by avoiding pollution taxes and reducing energy bills
- It can lead to new market opportunities due to the alignment with social needs and expectations
- It can reduce business risks as some of the greatest commercial disasters and controversies have resulted from a lack of transparency and fairness

Example

Cosby plc owns a small chain of supermarkets with an emphasis on organic, local produce. The Directors of Cosby plc are concerned that, despite having better quality produce than its rivals, it is not competing as well as it would like against the national supermarket chains.

The Marketing Director has proposed that Cosby plc should set up a new CSR policy and code of practice that could be used as part of the marketing effort.

He is convinced that many customers will be influenced by such a code and has suggested the following aspects could be incorporated:

1. All products should be purchased from local farms and suppliers where appropriate.

2. All packing materials should be obtained from renewable sources where feasible.

3. All suppliers to be paid on time.

4. All suppliers to be paid fair prices as determined by the Purchasing Manager.

This is a good example of a Code of Practice being used for commercial purposes, as well as the promotion of sustainable business policies.

5.6 Threats to ethical behaviour

Some examples of threats to ethical behaviour in a client relationship would be:

Integrity

- Prior to the completion of a major project for the client, your manager asks you to report on financial progress and provide a forecast for key stakeholders. He asks you to omit some of the relevant information from your report and therefore deliberately mislead others.

Objectivity

- Your company treats all of your client's staff to excessive hospitality and therefore attempts to influence their independence of mind for future buying decisions.
- The client asks you to help with the recruitment of a new junior member in their accounts team. One of your close personal friends has applied for the role, therefore calling into question whether or not you can remain unbiased.

Professional competence and due care

- At the conclusion of the project with the client, you are asked to perform tax computations covering areas you have not looked at for many years. Due to your lack of expertise, you are unable to perform this role competently.

Confidentiality

- Your client has just won another major tender for work elsewhere in the country. You not only tell others within the industry of the developments but also purchase shares in the company for your personal gain.

- Your client is knowingly selling faulty products to consumers and informs you of this. Here is an example where it **would** be necessary to disclose the information to the authorities.

Professional behaviour

- Your client finds your colleagues lacking in professional courtesy and do not trust their judgement.

There are six key values businesses promote in order to safeguard against ethical threats. They can be remembered using the acronym HOTTER:

- **Honesty** – employees should be encouraged to be honest at all times – even when this may be seen as detrimental to the organisation itself. For example, a salesperson should never overstate the benefits or features of the product they are selling.
- **Openness** – this means that the organisation should be willing to freely provide information, as needed, to stakeholders. This should make it easier for shareholders, for example, to decide whether to invest in the business or not.
- **Transparency** – this is similar to openness in many ways and indicates that a company makes it easy for key stakeholders to review its activities. This can be helped by regular audits and the production of detailed reports on business activities.
- **Trust** – organisations need to be trustworthy in their dealings with others and attempt to work in the best interests of as many stakeholders as possible. This could involve, for instance, not overcharging customers.
- **Empowerment** – this involves giving employees and other stakeholders more ability to make their own decisions. This will improve their self-image and their motivation.
- **Respect** – all employees and stakeholders should be treated with dignity by the organisation regardless of their age, gender, ethnicity, religion or sexuality.

5.7 Consequences of unethical behaviour

The personal and commercial consequences of unethical behaviour can be disastrous.

For the individual, the negative impact on their reputation may result in them losing their job, future earning potential, career status, professional memberships and position in the community.

For a business organisation, the loss of public confidence can lead to customers taking their business to more trusted competitors and ultimately therefore the dissolution of the company.

In a wider context, when such unethical behaviour is identified, trust can be undermined in other organisations linked to the company at fault. Clients and suppliers, as well as competitors of a very similar nature, can see their reputations tarnished by association with the scandal.

Accountants are often seen as the key defenders of ethical behaviour in the workplace, but this requires considerable skill and sensitivity when ethical dilemmas present themselves.

Activity 16

What three Rs, together with timeliness and courtesy, constitute the personal qualities one would expect of a professional accountant?

A. Regulation, Registration, Remuneration

B. Respect, Reliability, Realism

C. Reliability, Responsibility, Regulation

D. Respect, Responsibility, Reliability

Activity 17

Consider the five fundamental principles of ethics and identify:

a) Examples of good practice by your company or a client for each

b) Examples of threats to each from your experience of your company or a client

c) The impact on a business and individuals should the code of conduct be breached.

(AAT Assessment criteria 4.1, 4.2)

Activity 18

Windsor Electricals do not currently have a corporate social responsibility policy. Although individual staff members are bound by the professional ethics of their profession, there is also no central code of conduct.

The senior management of Windsor Electricals have identified that some of their competitors are establishing such policies and these seem to be well received by the communities in which they operate, and more importantly perhaps, with their customers.

Required:

a) What are the advantages for Windsor Electricals of this sort of policy?

b) Provide six suggestions for policies which could be included.

c) Explain who should be informed of the new policy.

(AAT Assessment criteria 4.1, 4.2)

Answers to chapter activities

Activity 1

The correct answer is

D. Directors.

would be classified as an internal stakeholder. The other options are connected stakeholders.

Activity 2

The needs of the supplier would include:

- A long-term business relationship so the supplier can plan for the future
- Regular, significant orders
- Agreed quality standards that both parties can work with
- Fair prices
- Prompt payment on the agreed dates

Activity 3

The answer to this question will be based on the individual's work experience and the specific stakeholders they encounter. However, general points to be raised include:

The internal stakeholder should be an employee or manager within the company. The connected stakeholder should be a customer, supplier or shareholder. The external stakeholder should be from society as a whole, including governmental and political agencies.

Their needs could include career satisfaction, pay and security for the internal stakeholders; prices, quality and profits for the connected stakeholders; and compliance with norms and policies for the external stakeholders.

Each should be plotted on Mendelow's matrix accordingly. Those with little power and little interest would be deemed worthy of Minimal Effort; those with a low level of interest but a lot of power would be Keep

Satisfied; those with a high level of interest but little power would be Keep Informed; those with significant power and interest would be Key Players.

Activity 4

The correct answer is

C. Anticipating and meeting customer needs.

Activity 5

The answer will depend on the organisation the individual works for and their marketing strategy. The brand message should aim to clearly differentiate the company from others and have a clear USP or selling message. It should be brief and ideally summed up in one snappy sentence.

Activity 6

The answer will depend on the two companies involved, but the student should make reference to all of the seven qualities identified by McKinsey or a similar frame of reference. They should include consideration of the objectives, organisational structure, financial model, market position, selling messages, staff, specialisations and operational systems of both companies. Some reference should also be made to their own experience of the company.

Most likely this answer will require further research from the sources identified earlier in the chapter, such as press releases, company reports and promotional literature.

Activity 7

This question refers to both branding and marketing strategy and as such is revisited in Chapter 5. For the purposes of this assessment criteria, the student needs to focus on the customers' needs and the 'added value' elements listed. Therefore they should consider extra benefits available to customers who choose to use their products and services and the key factors which make them different to others in the market.

Although pricing and promotion is a major consideration, there will hopefully be other factors beyond this, such as customer care and ethical policies, which the company promotes as part of its selling proposition.

Activity 8

Examples of service level agreement clauses would be:

1. All customer queries will be responded to within 24 hours by e-mail or telephone
2. All deliveries will be made within 5 days of ordering the products unless otherwise advised
3. All technical issues can be addressed via a 24 hour hotline
4. If a minimum of £1 million of products are ordered in from 1st January to 31st December, a 5% rebate will be honoured
5. If a delivery is late by more than two days, the customer will be due a 50% refund

Note that where possible the clauses should be quantitative and follow the guidelines for SMART objectives.

Activity 9

Gladys has two reasons to claim that Gr8Buys TV has breached the Sale of Goods Act:

She bought the washing machine based on the description given on television. As she received a different model with less features, the description given is inaccurate.

In addition, the washing machine does not appear to be of satisfactory quality, as it fails to clean clothes and makes an unhealthy noise.

Gladys should be able to return the machine for a replacement or refund.

Activity 10

The correct answer is **C The seller must have legal title to the good being sold.**

Goods have to be fit for purpose but there are no requirements regarding reasonable pricing or them being of good quality. There is no legal need for customers to pay in advance.

Activity 11

The company's legal obligations take the form of the contracts they have with their clients and employees. The terms of these contracts can be both express and implied.

Key examples for the employee include the Contract of Employment and associated legislation to address equality in the workplace.

Relationships with clients will be affected by the separate contracts agreed by supplier and consumer, as well as legislation such as the Sale of Goods Act and the Supply of Goods and Services Act.

To breach these contracts would be to break the law and in addition to any resulting damages, there would also be a loss of both revenue and financial income for both individuals and the company.

Activity 12

Corporate social responsibility means:

D That a company reviews and considers the impact of its policies and practices to ensure that it plays a positive and contributory role in relation to its stakeholders, the community and the environment.

In terms of the other options given, individuals remain ultimately responsible for their own conduct despite a company's role in supporting them and marketing benefits from ethical values and CSR initiatives are undeniable, but they should not be the main motivating factor behind such policies.

Activity 13

Integrity – The implication that the e-mail system was not working could be termed as telling the client a lie. Likewise, the report not being checked could be seen as acting improperly.

Professional Competence and Due Care – Fraser has both failed to provide the report and work the CRM package, implying a level of incompetence and lack of desire to get up to speed with developments.

Objectivity – The fact that Fraser is good friends with the account manager and has offered to take him for a drink suggests he keen to use his familiarity.

Confidentiality – Fraser appears to share too much information about the client's situation with the account manager.

Professional behaviour - Fraser does not seem keen to follow correct procedures, trying to cover up the customer's complaint.

Activity 14

i. The situation is an example of a breach of Confidentiality.

ii. Perry should talk to the director concerned and explain that the scenario he proposed was unethical. Should this not prove worthwhile, Perry should escalate the matter. His best course of action would be to resign and state his reasons for the resignation. He could then report the situation to external regulators for investigation.

Activity 15

This is a research and evidence-gathering exercise and as such will depend on the individual and the company.

Activity 16

The correct answer is D.

Activity 17

This answer will be dependent on the individual's relevant work experience, but should include examples for all five of the principles with an explanation as to why the practice was either good or bad. Likewise threats should be identified for each and HOTTER could be used to challenge these.

The implications will depend on specifics, but most likely a loss of professional membership and loss of reputation and therefore the ability to make money for both individual and the company will ensue.

Activity 18

The main advantages of a CSR policy are:

- It can increase revenue by attracting new customers
- It can differentiate the company from its competitors
- It can result in a better, happier workforce
- It can save long-term costs
- It can lead to new market opportunities
- It can reduce business risks

New policies could include:

- Using ethical suppliers
- Not trading with undesirable clients
- Offering fair pricing
- Charity and community work
- Staff welfare programmes
- Reducing carbon footprint
- Reducing or modifying packaging

All stakeholders should be informed of the policy. Internal stakeholders need to drive it forward, but the commercial and social benefits will only result if the public and customers are also made aware.

Working in teams

4

Introduction

Having developed awareness of how organisations and commercial partnerships are managed to achieve objectives, this chapter focuses on how individuals can work together within the workplace to help deliver specific goals.

Although individuals have a lot to offer in a business environment, many of the greatest successes come from collaboration, whether with colleagues or clients. Effective teams are not thrown together, but instead are formed to fulfil specific roles and create their own ethos.

This chapter will not only address the roles incumbent in any productive team, but also the way leadership can manage and motivate those involved.

ASSESSMENT CRITERIA

Learning objectives:

1 To understand the importance of teams to individual team members and to the team itself.

2 To understand leadership attributes and skills.

3 To be able to effectively contribute to team work.

4 To understand how to effectively manage potential conflicts within a team

CONTENTS

1 Individuals within a team
2 Groups and teams
3 Team formation and development
4 Team effectiveness
5 Team and individual motivation
6 Team leadership and conflict resolution
7 Your role in the team

1 Individuals within a team

1.1 Characteristics of individual behaviour

Although every individual worker will exhibit different behaviour patterns, the underlying issues affecting their behaviour and performance at work will be largely similar for everyone. Typical issues include:

- **Motivation level**

  The individual's level of desire to perform tasks and the level of effort they devote to their job accordingly. This can be influenced by many factors, including reward levels, recognition from managers, social interactions at work and general working conditions.

- **Perception**

  Messages from managers are subject to individual interpretation, with the employee selecting parts of the message and interpreting it in light of their own experiences, wants and needs.

- **Attitudes**

  These are persistent feelings and behavioural tendencies directed towards specific people, groups, ideas or objects.

- **Personality**

  This is the combination of emotional, attitudinal and behavioural responses of an individual.

Activity 1

A manager has recently emailed two individuals in his team, asking for them to submit reports to him. One worker did so, while the other failed to. The second worker, when asked, stated that she thought that the wording of the email meant that it did not apply to her.

Which characteristic of individual behaviour is the manager having difficulties with?

A. Motivation

B. Perception

C. Attitude

D. Personality

1.2 Role theory

Role Theory suggests that the behaviour of individuals depends on other people's expectations of them and how they are supposed to behave in a given situation.

Definitions

- **A role** is the expected pattern of behaviours associated with someone who occupies a particular position in an organisation.
- **Role behaviour** – certain types of behaviour can be associated with a particular role (e.g. a member of staff who expects promotion may start acting as if they are already in charge).
- **Role set** – this describes the people who respond to an individual in a particular role (e.g. nurses, medical specialists, patients and administrators form part of doctor's role set).
- **Role signs** – these are visible indications of a role (e.g. in the military, different uniforms indicate status and position in the ranks).

These patterns of behaviour may cause the following problems:

- **Role ambiguity** – when an individual or those around them is unsure of what role they are to play (e.g. when a new member joins an established group).
- **Role conflict** – when individuals find a clash between different roles they have adopted (e.g. if an accountant uncovers a fraud perpetrated by a friend, their roles as a professional and a friend may conflict).
- **Role incompatibility** – when individuals experience expectations from outside groups about their role that challenge their own expectations.

Activity 2

Sid has recently started a new job working in a warehouse. He has been asked to wear a yellow high-visibility jacket that identifies him as a junior member of staff and is a different colour to those worn by supervisors.

According to role theory, what is Sid's uniform an example of?

A. Role behaviour

B. Role set

C. Role conflict

D. Role signs

2 Groups and Teams

2.1 Groups

Definition

A group is a collection of individuals.

Groups have the following characteristics:

- **A sense of identity** – the group has defined boundaries and it is clear who is within the group and who is not.
- **Loyalty to the group** – group members accept one another and have certain standard behaviours that the follow. This binds the group together and excludes others.
- **Purpose and leadership** – a group has a purpose and individuals are chosen to join in order to help the group achieve its goals.

There are two main types of group:

- **Informal groups** – these are groups that individuals voluntarily join to meet their social or security needs. Individual members are dependent on each other and influence each other's behaviour, for example, employees who sit together and chat at lunchtime.
- **Formal groups** – these are groups that are created to carry out specific tasks, communicate and solve problems. Membership is normally determined by the organisation – for example, a project team put together to deliver a new payroll system.

Activity 3

Would a number of people queuing to be served at the Post Office be described as:

A. A formal group

B. An informal group

C. Neither of the above

2.2 Group Behaviour

When dealing with other personalities within a group, people can adopt different types of behaviour:

- **Assertive** – this is direct, honest and professional communication. It involves insisting on your rights without violating those of others.
- **Aggressive** – this violates another person's rights and can often lead to conflict.
- **Passive behaviour** – this is giving into another person in the belief that their rights are more important than yours.

Example

Hattie has given her manager a weekly sales report as requested. Upon review, the manager discovers that it is full of errors and it needs to be passed back to Hattie so she can correct the mistakes.

An assertive manager might say: 'I would like you to rework this report because there are several mistakes in it.'

An aggressive manager might say: 'I don't know how you dared to give me a report that has this many mistakes in it.'

A passive manager might say: 'The mistakes in the report were probably my fault for not explaining it to you properly.'

Activity 4

Which of the following members of staff is most likely to defuse conflict when dealing with other people:

A. James, who is assertive

B. William, who is aggressive

C. Howard, who is passive

2.3 Benefits of teams compared to individuals

Organised, well-structured groups can often contribute to a greater extent than individuals in a commercial environment. For this to be the case however, the group needs to be formally organised and act as a team.

Definition

A team is more than a group. A team can be described as any group of people who must significantly relate with each other in order to accomplish shared, specified objectives.

Therefore a team usually:

- shares a common goal
- is committed to achieving that goal
- enjoys working together to achieve it.

A team is therefore a formal group, with its own culture and leader. Where working effectively, the members of a team show collective loyalty and possess a strong sense of **team spirit.**

Benefits of teams include:

- they possess a **mixture of skills and abilities**, often improving the number of creative ideas and appreciation of different points of view. This can also aid problem solving.
- **synergy** – the pooling of ideas and energy may mean greater efficiency than if the workers were acting as individuals. This is sometimes known as the 2 + 2 = 5 principle.
- **increased flexibility**, as the team can easily be configured in different ways, with different people taking over different tasks.
- **better control**, with opportunities for individual performance to be reviewed and controlled by other members.
- **increased motivation**, if worker's social needs are being met.
- **improved communication between workers**.
- **healthy competition** – by splitting employees into groups, the rivalry created may help to boost performance. For instance, a sales department may be split so that the team with the highest sales will be rewarded, motivating all participants to work harder.

However, teams are not always more efficient and there are a number of problems inherent in group work. These include:

- **decision-making can be slow** as discussion is needed.
- **they tend to compromise** when this is not in the business' interests.
- **the group pressure to conform** where members of a close-knit team agree to decisions that they know are wrong because other members of the group support them and they wish to fit in.

- **lack of individual responsibility** which can cause rash or risky decisions as no one will be personally held solely accountable.
- the risk of having **too much social interaction** - meetings may become social events, with little practical work being undertaken.
- **increased competition and conflict** can develop and may be destructive.

Activity 5

Explain the key advantages and disadvantages of team working.

(AAT assessment criteria 1.1)

3 Team Formation and Development

3.1 Roles and responsibilities within a team

Teams must act as one, but by their nature comprise of diverse skillsets, personalities and roles. As highlighted earlier, for any organisation or its constituent parts to operate effectively, organisational structure is required. Therefore it is vital in any team that the chain of command is clear.

Here is an example of an accounting department's organisational chart:

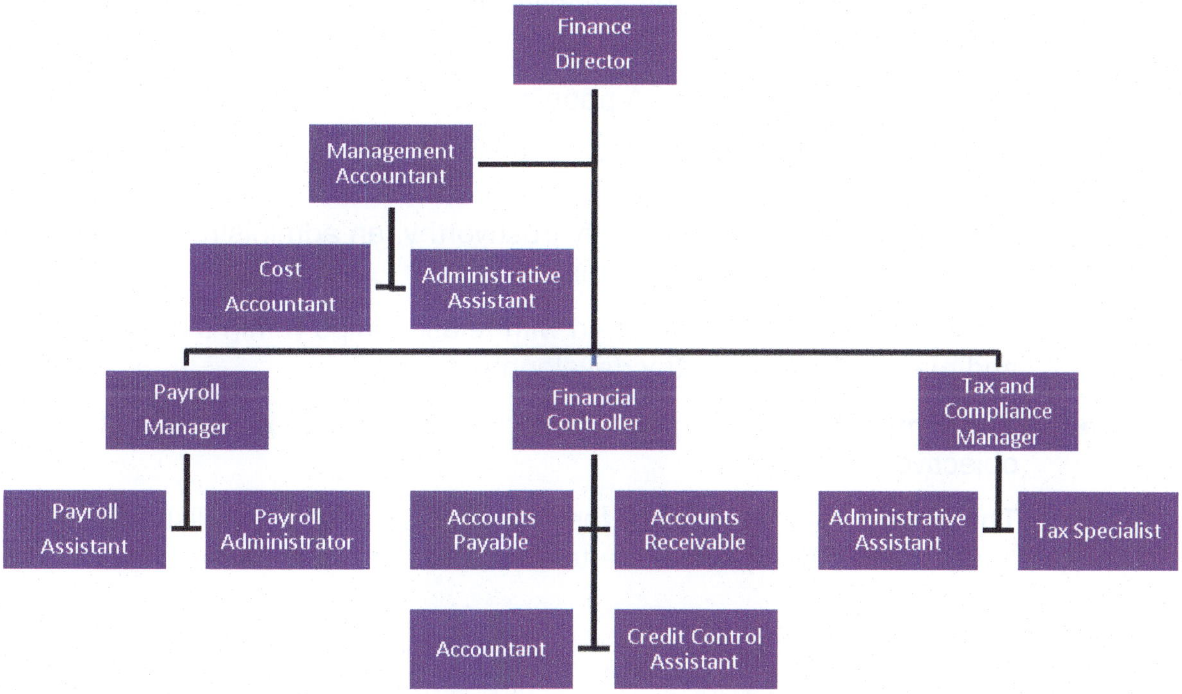

Consider your own department at work and its hierarchy. Within your team, do individuals have clearly defined roles? Is there a blend of personalities within the team? Examine the organisational chart of the department and consider your own role in the team.

The grouping of activities and allocation of tasks applies as much to a team as it does to the business a whole, however due to the smaller nature of most teams you will experience, the personalities involved and the skills they exhibit are particularly important. These dynamics and the need to position individuals in the most fitting roles make the formation of a team formation a complex but crucial activity.

3.2 Belbin's team roles theory

Belbin suggested that, in order for a team to operate effectively, nine different roles need to be fulfilled. This does not always necessitate nine team members, as individuals within the team could perform multiple roles.

The nine roles are:

- **Leader** - A co-ordinator, typically a balanced and disciplined person good at working with others.
- **Shaper** - Promotes activity and action, dominant and highly task-driven, compulsive and extrovert personality.
- **Plant** – Introvert, thoughtful and thought-provoking, an imaginative person who acts as a source of ideas.
- **Monitor-evaluator** - Not creative but highly analytical and likely to spot flaws or criticise ideas, brings the team down to earth but can be tactless.
- **Resource-investigator –** A popular and social member of the team, a networker with good contacts, always looking for alternative solutions.
- **The Company worker** – Highly trustworthy, an administrator and organiser, with an eye for detail.
- **The Team worker** - Concerned with relationships within the team and maintaining its healthy development.
- **The Finisher** - The progress chaser, pushing the team to meet its objectives.
- **The Expert** - As required by the project, they offer specialist advice and provide a perspective the team's core members cannot.

Example

Let us return to the example of Windsor Electricals.

Kenneth is a team manager at Windsor Electricals. He is in charge of a group of ten people performing varied roles across the research and development department. The group has been working together amicably and successfully for a considerable time. Its members value Kenneth's leadership and the backup given by Joan. Joan is frequently on hand to elaborate on Kenneth's instructions and deals on his behalf with group day-to-day queries, especially when he is out of the office attending meetings.

Much of the success of the group has been due to Peter, who is creative at problem solving and comes up with new ideas, and Barbara who has an encyclopaedic knowledge of sources of supply and information. Charles is an expert on charting and records, and Bernard is invaluable at sorting out disagreements and keeping everyone cheerful. The remaining members of the group also have roles, which are acceptable to themselves and to the others.

Within the group Belbin's role classifications can be applied as follows:

Kenneth – Leader

Joan – Shaper

Peter – Plant

Barbara – Resource-investigator

Charles – Company Worker

Bernard – Team worker

3.3 Tuckman's stages of team development

Tuckman argued that teams progress through four main stages of development. All groups do not automatically follow these stages in this sequence and not all groups pass through all the stages – some get stuck in the middle and remain inefficient and ineffective.

The aim for any company is to reach the Performing stage as quickly as possible, especially for short-term projects.

- **Forming** – At this initial stage, the group is no more than a collection of individuals seeking to define the team's purpose, the nature of its members and how it will operate. It is characterised by early mutual awareness.

- **Storming** – A period of conflict. Norms of attitude and behaviour are challenged and members compete for their chosen roles within the group dynamic. If successful, this stage will have forged a stronger team with greater knowledge of each other and their objectives.
- **Norming** – This stage establishes the norms under which the group operates. Members experiment and test team reaction as norms establish themselves. Typically, the norming stage will establish how the group takes decisions, behaviour patterns, level of trust and openness and individual roles, and this is a period of co-operation.
- **Performing** – A period where the team and productivity prospers. The team is now capable of operating to full potential, since the difficulties of adjustment and definition should have been resolved.

A further stage has also been more recently added:

- **Dorming** - If a team remains for a long time in the performing phase, there is a danger it will switch to automatic pilot. 'Groupthink' occurs to the extent that changing circumstances may be ignored. Instead, maintaining the team dynamic becomes one of its prime objectives.

Example

Following on from the Windsor Electricals example, the following has since occurred:

- Joan resigned to relocate.
- Because the workload has been increasing, Kenneth has recruited three new people to the group.
- Kenneth now finds that various members of the group, including the new recruits, complain to him about what they are expected to do and about other people's failings.
- Barbara has been unusually helpful to Kenneth and has tried to welcome the new staff, but Peter has been less supportive and has questioned many of the recent changes and Barbara's influence.
- Charles has struggled to keep up with administrative duties as he has been involved in staff training and covering for Bernard who has recently married and taken a month's leave for his honeymoon.

According to Tuckman's stages, prior to the above, the team could be described as Performing. Following the changes, with new people recruited and new roles for existing team members, they are back to the Forming and Storming stages of development.

It is also worth noting that the team roles seem to have changed.

Barbara is now taking on the role of Shaper, Peter being more Monitor-Evaluator than Innovator and no one performing as Team worker in Bernard's absence. Without the established Shaper and the person key to team morale and stability, it is clear why conflict and confusion is mounting with both new and established staff.

Activity 6

Butterworths is a leading manufacturer of garden equipment. Under the leadership of Terry, a Product Development team has been set up to focus on a new range.

The Managing Director of Butterworths visits the team and asks Terry to identify the roles being performed by the other members of the team. Terry has observed that:

- Frankie develops new ideas to help the team achieve their objectives.
- Angela constantly checks up on team progress and tries to ensure that all tasks are completed on time.
- Jim identifies the flaws and inaccuracies in other team members' work.
- Pedro is a force for action, ensuring others are aware of their tasks and dominating proceedings.
- Jack is keen to support others by maintaining tight control on the administrative side of their work.

Using Belbin's team roles, which of the above staff is:

A The Company Worker

B The Shaper

C The Plant

D The Finisher

E The Monitor-Evaluator

Terry has also been asked to complete monthly reports on how the team are progressing.

In the first report, Terry noted that 'The team have little or no conflict and are largely trying to determine people's strengths. They are currently dividing up their workload in line with the objectives set.'

In the second report, Terry wrote, 'The team now seem to have accomplished all of their major tasks and are now meeting largely for social reasons'.

Using Tuckman's stages of development (Forming/ Storming/ Performing/ Norming/ Dorming), what is the shift from the first to the second report?

(AAT Assessment criteria 1.3, 1.4 and 1.6)

Activity 7

Describe the working relationships within your team in the workplace. Analyse the interaction between the various roles in your department with reference to

a) the organisational structure for the business and department

b) Belbin's theory

(AAT Assessment criteria 1.3 and 1.6)

4 Team Effectiveness

4.1 Effective Teams

Although every case will be different, effective teams typically possess:

- clear and shared objectives
- co-operation and a sense of mutual self-interest (that everyone 'wins' from being in the team) and respect
- an ability to listen to others and compromise where in the team and business' interests
- a range of skills, expertise and personal styles
- frequent, easy communication
- a willingness to share ideas and knowledge
- a sense of organisation and structure, even if informal

Peters and Waterman define the five key aspects of successful teams as:

- the team should be relatively small – inevitably each member will want to represent the interests of their section/department, meaning that larger teams will be slower and harder to manage.
- the team should have a set duration, existing only to achieve a particular task.
- membership should be voluntary – a member who does not want to be part of the group is unlikely to be contributing or participating.
- communication should be informal and unstructured – there should be little documentation and no status barriers.
- the team should be action-oriented - they should create a plan for action and decide what needs doing to accomplish their goals.

The above would be most applicable to project teams.

4.2 Ineffective teams

It is essential for any business that the teams within the organisation operate effectively. There are many possible results of unhappy or unproductive teams.

- The inability to work towards or complete objectives
- A lack of productivity
- Constant conflict or a lack of trust within the team
- Members of the team becoming marginalised and under-utilised
- Poor or infrequent communication between team members
- Continual interference from management
- Increased staff turnover and absenteeism

4.3 Measuring Team Effectiveness

Therefore it is crucial for the business to monitor how effectively teams are performing. Means of measuring team effectiveness include:

- the degree to which the team achieved its stated objectives and the quality of its output.
- team member satisfaction – this could be measured, amongst other things, by using labour turnover or absenteeism rates.
- efficiency – the resources used to achieve team objectives.

Management could measure these through the use of questionnaires for team members, interviews, or direct observation of the team.

Team rewards could then be designed to not only motivate the individuals within the group, but also encourage co-operation and responsibility-sharing between the team as a whole.

Activity 8

Which of the following would be characteristics of an effective team?

A. A positive atmosphere

B. Small number of members

C. Lack of communication

D. Strong pressure for group members to conform

E. Clear objectives

F. Dominant individual members

G. High labour turnover

H. Low absenteeism

I. High productivity

(AAT Assessment criteria 1.2 and 1.5)

4.4 Improving Team Effectiveness

Teams are not always able to achieve their goals without some outside intervention or support from management. As such, managers may attempt to create **'team building'** exercises for workers. These are tasks designed to develop group members and their ability to work together.

Team building exercises tend to be based around developing the team in several areas, including:

- improved communication
- problem-solving
- building trust
- social interaction

These exercises are designed to

- develop skills
- benefit from shared best practice and see new perspectives
- reduce conflict and increase co-operation

- set standards for teamwork

In addition to formal teambuilding exercises, managers can attempt to reinforce the individual identity of the team using other methods. For example, giving the team its own name, its own office/space or its own uniforms will strengthen the sense of belonging of its members.

Activity 9

Considering your own workplace, identify the necessary skills and behaviour required for effective teamwork and describe the possible impact of the team working ineffectively.

(AAT Assessment criteria 3.1)

5 Team and Individual Motivation

5.1 What is motivation?

Definitions

In an organisation, **motivation refers to the willingness of individuals to perform certain tasks or actions.**

It is the incentive or reason for them behaving in a particular way.

In practice, motivation is taken as meaning how hard an employee is willing to work in their job and how dedicated they are. For an individual to appear motivated, they may need to not merely follow the rules, but instead go beyond expectations.

While the two are linked, it is important to distinguish between motivation and satisfaction. Motivation looks at how hard someone is willing to work, while satisfaction looks at whether they are content with their existing job and not looking for another. Although satisfied staff are more likely to be motivated, motivation can also come from negative factors such as an aggressive manager who the team member fears.

5.2 The benefits of motivated staff

Having motivated staff members has a range of benefits – from the perspectives of both the organisation and the individuals or teams themselves.

Benefits for the Organisation

- Harder working employees
- Fewer mistakes and errors
- Less waste of time and resources
- More suggestions and ideas generated

Benefits for the Individual

- Greater job satisfaction
- Improved health, due to less stress
- Improved career prospects
- Finding the job more interesting and enjoyable

Benefits for the Team

- Increased co-operation
- More commitment to team needs
- Better ideas generation and evaluation

5.3 Motivation Theories

Maslow's hierarchy of needs

Maslow's theory may be summarised by saying that everyone wants certain things throughout life, and these can be placed in five ascending categories, namely:

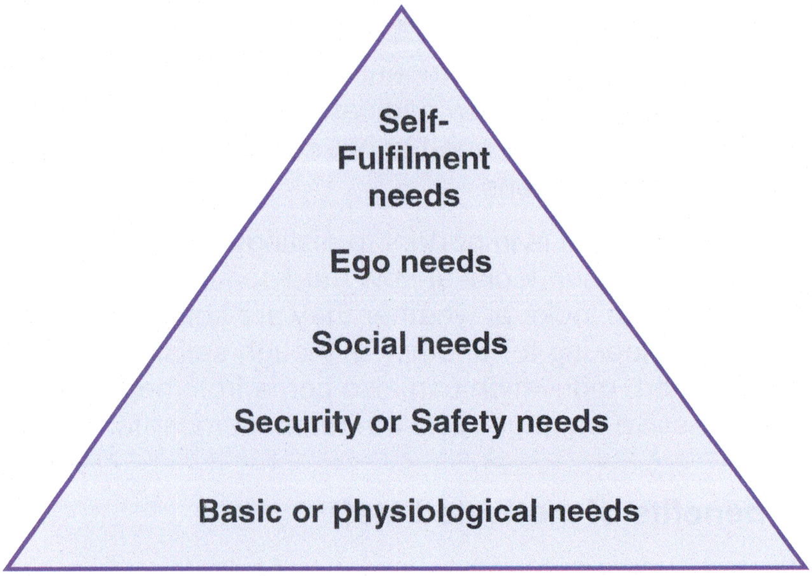

- **Basic or physiological needs** – the things needed to stay alive, such as food, shelter and clothing. Such needs can be satisfied by money.
- **Safety or security needs** – people want protection against unemployment, the consequences of sickness and retirement as well as being safeguarded against unfair treatment. These needs can be satisfied by the rules and benefits of employment, i.e. pension scheme, sick fund, employment legislation.
- **Social needs** – the vast majority of people want to be part of a group and it is only through group activities that this need can be satisfied. Thus the way that work is organised, enabling people to feel part of a group, is fundamental to satisfaction of this need.
- **Ego needs** – these needs may be expressed as wanting the esteem and respect of other people and thinking well of oneself. While status and promotion can offer short-term satisfaction, building up the job itself and giving people a greater say in how their work is organised gives satisfaction of a more permanent nature.
- **Self-fulfilment needs** – this is quite simply the need to achieve something worthwhile in life. It is a need that is satisfied only by continuing success, for example opening and running a new office.

Example

Returning to the example of Windsor Electricals, Kenneth has been promoted to the role of Managing Director and now sits on the board. Consequently, he has a generous pay package and pension arrangements. When discussing his new role with colleagues, he described his new job as 'constantly challenging and always changing'.

It therefore appears that Kenneth has reached the self-fulfilment level of Maslow's hierarchy of needs.

He has certainly achieved security (through the attractive pay and pension scheme), his social needs are met by being part of the board of directors and his ego needs are likely to have been met by being promoted to such an important role.

The fact that Kenneth describes his role as being challenging and constantly changing indicated he has reached self-fulfilment in his role.

Activity 10

Which level of Maslow's hierarchy do the following factors relate to?

A. New job title

B. Large pay rises

C. Sick pay

D. Christmas parties

E. Challenging work

F. Enough cash to live on

Activity 11

Due to a departmental restructuring at Windsor Electricals, Peter is now working part-time hours in a different, less desirable department. He has three young children and recently moved house. His wife works full-time elsewhere but they cannot afford the costs of living on her salary alone. Which of Maslow's hierarchy of needs is likely to be motivating Peter?

A. Basic

B. Safety

C. Social

D. Ego

Criticisms of Maslow's hierarchy include:

- Individuals have different needs and may not necessarily reach them in the same order as each other (for example, a recent university graduate starting a new job may seek to fulfil social needs before looking at security needs such as a pension).
- Individuals may seek to satisfy several needs at the same time.
- Not all needs are, or can be, satisfied through work.

Herzberg's two factor theory

Herzberg's model examined two sets of factors that can be used to help get the best out of workers.

Hygiene factors

These are issues that must be addressed to avoid workers becoming dissatisfied with their jobs. They include:

- policies and procedures for staff treatment
- appropriate level of pay and conditions for the job
- suitable levels of supervision
- team working and interpersonal relationships at work
- pleasant physical working environment

The absence of these will reduce satisfaction levels and lead to employees looking for work elsewhere. However, their presence may not result in positive motivation.

Motivators

These are issues that will motivate workers and stimulate improved performance. According to Herzberg, they included:

- a sense of achievement
- recognition of good work by management
- increasing levels of responsibility
- career progression and status increases
- enjoying the job itself

You will notice that the main motivators are to do with the value and satisfaction gained from the job itself and are largely non-financial in nature. Herzberg argued that the potential boost to employee motivation caused by increases to pay were in fact extremely limited.

Example

Parallels can be drawn between Maslow's hierarchy of needs and Herzberg's two-factor theory.

- Maslow's 'security' need can be linked to Herzberg's hygiene factor of pay, benefits and working conditions.
- Maslow's 'social' need can be linked to Herzberg's hygiene factor of interpersonal relationships at work.
- Maslow's 'ego' need can be linked to Herzberg's motivating factors of recognition of good work and status increases.

Maslow's 'self-fulfilment' need can be linked to Herzberg's motivating factors relating to a sense of achievement, career progression and enjoying the job.

Herzberg suggested three types of job design that could be an effective tool for motivating employees:

- **Job enrichment** is a deliberate, planned process to improve the responsibility, challenge and creativity of a job. It involves giving an employee a greater level of responsibility and autonomy within their job – often involving problem solving or delegation. For instance, an accountant who is currently responsible for producing quarterly management accounts could have their role enriched so that they also have to submit and explain them to senior management.
- **Job enlargement** is an attempt to widen the employee's job by giving them a larger workload. It does not involve higher level work, simply more of the existing work that the employee already undertakes.
- **Job rotation** is the planned rotation of staff between jobs to alleviate monotony and provide a fresh, challenging job. Job rotation would ensure that where there were unattractive tasks to be performed, individuals would spend equal time on each job. While this would reduce boredom for workers, Herzberg argued that it would often simply improve satisfaction, rather than providing motivation.

Activity 12

Modern trends in job design have been aimed at the quality of working life for the worker and labour flexibility. Which of Herzberg's three definitions would these be attributed to?

A. Job rotation

B. Job enrichment

C. Job enlargement

Vroom's expectancy theory

Vroom believed that team members will only be motivated to complete tasks if they are confident that the tasks will help them to reach their goals.

This can be seen as a formula:

Strength of motivation = preference for outcome x expectancy

Expectancy can be defined as the probability of success.

Example

Windsor Electricals have been asked to submit a tender for a contract. Kenneth needs to decide whether this would be worthwhile. In other words, he needs to judge how motivated he would be to partake in the process and how motivated his staff would be to devote their efforts to the tender.

According to Vroom's expectancy theory, Kenneth needs to determine:

- The preference for the outcome – if the contract was worth considerable financial gain or a significant increase in the company's status, the outcome would be more desirable and therefore motivation to try to win the contract would be greater.
- Expectancy – if Windsor plc had successfully been successful with similar tenders or if the contract covered an area where their expertise was developed, they would perceive their chances of being successful as higher.

5.4 Reward Systems

Definitions

- **A reward** is something given to an individual or group in recognition of their services, efforts or achievements.
- The rewards offered by an organisation can be both **intrinsic** (arising from performance of the job itself) or **extrinsic** (separate to the job and dependent on the decisions of others).

Example

The following are typical rewards offered to employees.

Intrinsic Rewards

- Career progression
- Training
- Enjoyment of the job
- Interest in the job
- Level of satisfaction
- Higher level decision-making

Extrinsic Rewards

- Salary
- Sick pay allowances
- Holiday entitlement
- Maternity entitlement
- Bonuses
- Company car

The offering of positive rewards to employees is a key motivational issue for most organisations. However, rewards systems should be carefully designed in order to ensure that they:

- are fair and consistent for all employees, even for those workers with different job sizes or required levels of skill
- are sufficient to attract and retain staff
- maintain and improve levels of employee performance
- reward progression and promotion
- comply with legislation and regulation (i.e. minimum wage laws)
- control salary costs

Employees can be rewarded in a number of ways, including through ongoing development and training (which will boost their future career prospects). This links back to Maslow's hierarchy of needs, as continuous development will help to meet self-fulfilment and ego needs.

However, most employees will be particularly interested in their remuneration. One way that businesses tie the performance of their employees to their pay is through the use of incentive schemes.

There are three main types of incentive scheme:

- **Performance related pay (PRP)**

  Based on meeting specific targets or objectives (eg. speed/volume of production, level of cost reduction, commission for sales growth).

- **Bonus schemes**

  Usually a one-off as opposed to PRP schemes which are usually continuous. Group bonuses can help the team to pull together and work as a cohesive unit, but may lead to conflict if some members of the team are seen to be doing less work than others.

- **Profit sharing**

  Usually available to a wide group of employees where payments are made in the light of the overall profitability of the company. Share issues may be part of the scheme.

Incentives need to encourage effort or action towards the delivery of organisational objectives, so there may be potential conflict when contrasting long and short term objectives (e.g. sales staff offering discounts to customers to win extra orders this year to get a bonus, at the expense of next year's sales).

Activity 13

Which of the following is NOT an issue that needs taking account of when setting the basic salary level for employees?

A. Rewards offered by similar or rival organisations

B. Legislation and regulation

C. Motivation of employees

D. Control of total salary costs

Activity 14

Considering your own workplace, explain the factors which cause you and your colleagues to contribute towards and effectively achieve team goals. Include reference to motivation theories.

(AAT Assessment criteria 3.2)

6 Team Leadership

6.1 Leadership vs Management

Definitions

Leadership is an interpersonal influence directed toward the achievement of a goal or goals. Leadership is therefore a conscious activity and is concerned with setting goals and then inspiring people to achieve them.

Management is the effective use and co-ordination of business resources in order to achieve key objectives with maximum efficiency. Managers have an overall aim of ensuring that tasks are achieved in line with business needs.

Note that **a manager is not necessarily a leader**. A manager will only be a leader if he or she is able to influence people to achieve the goals of the organisation without relying on the use of formal authority.

Typically, leaders are keen to innovate and look to the future, whereas managers rely on control and have an eye on the bottom line.

A supervisor is a person given responsibility for planning and controlling the work of a group of employees. They are responsible for ensuring that specified tasks are performed correctly and efficiently by the group. Supervisors are therefore the lowest level of management and act as an interface between management and the workforce, as they work on the front line of the organisation.

Managers therefore rely more heavily on the authority inherent with their position than leaders, who are able to influence their staff in other ways.

To be effective leaders, those responsible for the team must have the ability to influence their subordinates in order to work productively as a group. Leaders can use different forms of 'power' to gain this influence and ensure that their team are both cohesive and compliant.

French and Raven identified five possible sources of a power:

- **Reward Power** – where the leader can offer intrinsic and/or extrinsic rewards
- **Coercive Power** – where the leader can use penalties or punishments to force behaviour
- **Referent Power** – where the leader had desirable personal characteristics or charisma
- **Expert Power** – where the leader has vast expertise or knowledge
- **Legitimate Power** – where the leader has the authority awarded to them by their status.

Therefore for a manager to also be termed a leader, he or she would need to avoid the use of Legitimate Power to achieve results and more likely rely on Referent Power and Expert Power to inspire their colleagues.

Activity 15

Explain the difference between leadership and management, providing examples.

(AAT Assessment criteria 2.1)

6.2 Effective Management

There have been many theories regarding successful management. Two crucial theories to be aware of are Drucker's five basic functions and Mintzberg's ten skills.

Drucker argued that all effective managers perform five basic functions.

- **Set objectives** – determining the goals the team is working towards and deciding how they can be achieved
- **Organise** –dividing the work it into manageable activities and allocate staff and time accordingly
- **Motivate and communicate** – making a team out of the people that are responsible for various jobs through leadership
- **Establish yardsticks** – making measurements available, focused on the performance of the individual and the whole organisation.
- **Develop people, including themselves.**

Mintzberg identified ten skills that managers need if they are to maximise their effectiveness. The skills are grouped into three main categories - interpersonal, informational and decisional.

Interpersonal

- *Figurehead:* Managers perform a symbolic role, obliged to carry out social, inspirational, legal and ceremonial duties (e.g. receiving visitors and making presentations).
- *Leader:* Managers form crucial relationships with their subordinates, especially in allocating tasks, hiring, training and motivating staff (e.g. seeking to build teamwork and foster employee commitment).
- *Liaison:* The development of a network of contacts outside the chain of command through which information and favours can be traded for mutual benefits (e.g. lunches with suppliers/customers).

Informational

- *Monitor:* Managers collect and analyse information regarding the organisation and its environment as a basis for decision-making (e.g. reading reports and seeking staff feedback).
- *Disseminator:* Managers spread important information widely (e.g. passing privileged information to subordinates).
- *Spokesperson:* Managers transmit information to various external groups by acting in a PR capacity, informing others about the organisation's performance, plans and policies (e.g. a sales presentation to prospective customers).

Decisional

- *Entrepreneur*: Managers are continually seeking opportunities to improve and innovate (e.g. launching a new idea or introducing procedures such as a cost reduction programme).
- *Disturbance-handler:* A manager has to respond to pressures over which the department has no control.
- *Resource-allocator:* Choosing from among competing demands for money, equipment, personnel and management time *(e*.g. approving expenditure on a project).
- *Negotiator*: Managers must take charge when their organisation engages in negotiations with others. In these negotiations, the manager acts as a figurehead, spokesperson and resource allocator (e.g. drawing up contracts with suppliers).

6.3 Styles of leadership

Managers approach the responsibilities identified by Drucker and Mintzberg using different styles of leadership.

Ashridge Management College

The research at Ashridge Management College distinguished four styles:

- **Tells (autocratic)** – the manager makes all the decisions and issues instructions which are to be obeyed without question.
- **Sells (persuasive)** – the manager still makes all the decisions, but believes that team members must be motivated to accept them in order to carry them out properly.
- **Consults (participative)** – the manager confers with the team and takes their views into account, although still retains the final say.
- **Joins (democratic)** – the leader and the team members make the decision together on the basis of consensus.

Ashridge discovered that most people preferred operating under the 'consults' style, although staff valued consistency and disliked it when managers changed between different styles. This said, it is undeniable that different styles may well be needed to solve particular issues.

Activity 16

In his capacity as Managing Director at Windsor Electricals, Kenneth has asked his senior management team for suggestions as to how they can improve the efficiency of their departmental operations. The managers have made several suggestions, but Kenneth does not feel they are practical and has decided to adopt a different approach.

According to the Ashridge Management College, what management style is Kenneth demonstrating?

A. Joins

B. Tells

C. Consults

D. Sells

6.4 Blake and Mouton – The Managerial Grid

The Blake and Mouton managerial grid charts people-oriented versus task-oriented styles of leadership. These two extremes can be described as follows:

- Task-centred leadership – where the main concern of the leader is completing the task and achieving the objectives. The leader sees the group simply as a means to an ends.
- Group-centred leadership – where the main concern of the leader is to ensure that the group are happy and productive as individuals.

The grid therefore scores the manager based on two concerns:

- their concern for people
- their concern for production/output

The combinations of scores for the above two factors lead to certain leadership styles, as shown in the grid below.

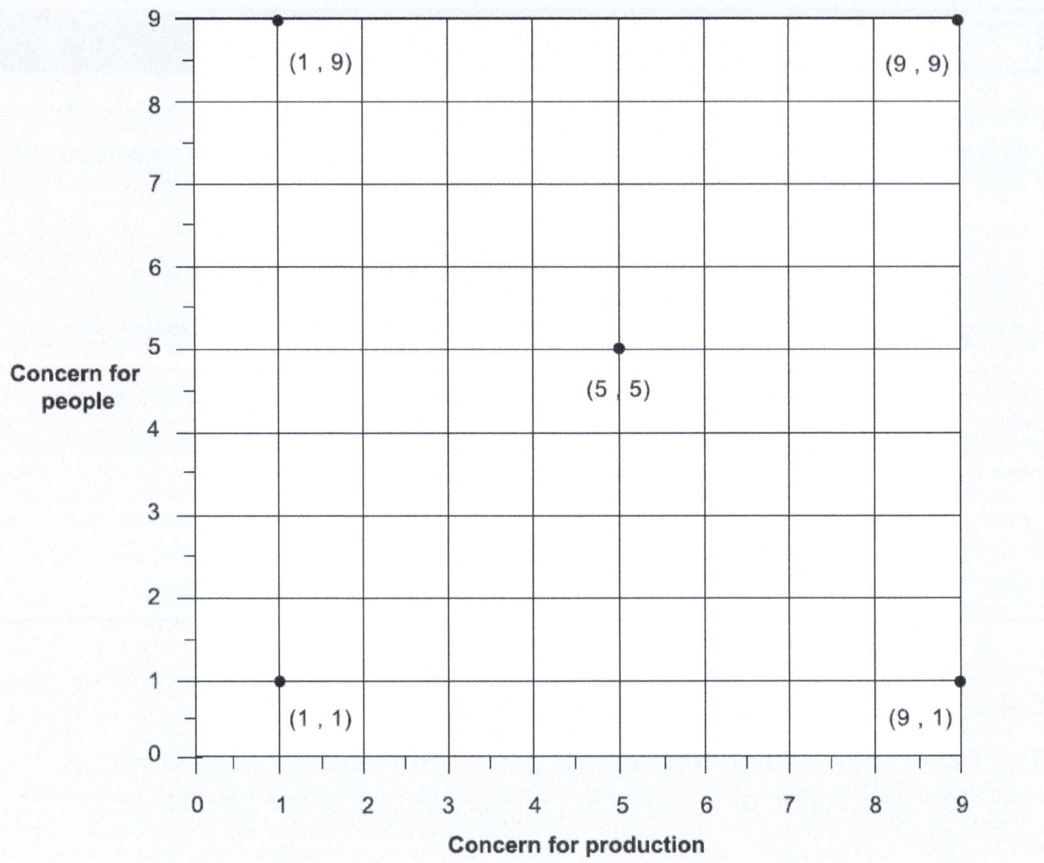

Impoverished style (1.1) – these managers have little interest in the company or their colleagues and therefore appear to have few management skills. They would typically be frustrated, disillusioned individuals shut off from the team.

Middle road (5.5) – this is a happy medium and most managers will score in this area. They have concern for both people and tasks, but are willing to be flexible and not go to extremes.

Task-oriented (9.1) – these managers concentrate wholeheartedly on the performance and production of the team and as a result can treat staff like commodities or machines. They tend not to address personal or development issues and instead focus on processes and output.

Country club (1.9) – these managers emphasise the people in the team, ensuring that they are happy and motivated. They encourage and delegate, but at times, the output can suffer and drawbacks are ignored.

The team style – the goal (9.9) – this sort of manager is rare and it is perhaps too idealistic to suggest that such a high level of concern for both production and people is possible. Within this model, it is assumed that happy workers will be motivated enough to produce accordingly.

6.5 Action-centred leadership and other theories

Adair suggested that any leader has to strive to balance three interrelated goals in order to be effective. These three goals relate to the needs of the group, the individual and the task. If a manager is able to juggle all three types of goal, they are showing exemplary leadership qualities.

Hersey and Blanchard add an extra dimension, suggesting that the level of maturity of the followers enables a leader to switch from task-related behaviour to relationship behaviour.

The way a leader interacts with people is also the subject of many studies. Fielder distinguishes between psychologically close and psychologically distant managers, the former preferring informal and people-oriented management to the latter's task-oriented style.

Bennis classifies leaders as the transactional and the transformational, with the latter being more inspiring and dynamic.

Activity 17

Explain the skills and behaviour of team leaders required for successful leadership of teams. Use examples from your own workplace of how leaders have influenced your own personal effectiveness.

(AAT Assessment criteria 2.2 and 2.3)

6.6 Conflict within a team

For a team to work effectively, both the leadership and members need to be aware of potential sources of conflict that could damage its effectiveness and prove destructive to the relationships formed.

Definition

Conflict is defined as any personal divergence of interests between groups and individuals.

While some conflict can be positive or constructive within the organisation – leading to change and problem-solving – conflict can also create hostility and bad feeling. Such destructive conflict will, in turn, normally damage the interests of the organisation as a whole, causing alienation and demotivating staff.

Example

Daft (1989) suggested the following negative consequences of conflict for a team:

- **Diversion of energy** away from the common objectives and focused on the resolution of the conflict and related issues
- **Altered judgement** within the team, meaning that emotions can impact decision-making
- **Loser effects** such as the loser distorting the reality of losing, seeking scapegoats or threatening the team dynamic
- **Poor co-ordination and a lack of compromise** due to people refusing to communicate effectively with others

There are two main types of conflict:

Vertical: conflict between individuals and groups at different levels of the organisation's hierarchy. For example, this could be the conflict between a junior employee and his or her manager.

There may be many causes, including:

- lack of communication, leading to junior workers feeling alienated or unimportant
- disagreements over remuneration or working conditions
- disagreements over employee workloads, due to poor coordination
- personality clashes.

Horizontal: conflict between individuals and groups at the same level of the organisation's hierarchy. For instance, this could be conflict between individual directors on the Board of Directors.

Again, there may be many reasons for such conflict, including:

- personality clashes
- role ambiguity, where individuals' authority overlaps
- conflicting objectives or priorities
- a lack of available resources.

Example

At Windsor Electricals, Isa is the Director of Human Resources and Bernard is the Finance Director. They find themselves in conflict over the hiring of new members of staff.

Isa is keen to offer competitive rates of pay for employees in order to attract the very best possible staff, thereby maximising business effectiveness and profitability. Bernard has the same goal of maximising company profit, but feels that this is best accomplished by offering lower levels of pay, thereby lowering costs.

This is an example of horizontal conflict. Both of these individuals are at the same level in the business hierarchy, but they disagree about the way that the organisation's goals should be achieved and the allocation of resources. Conflict will also arise if it is unclear which of the directors' approaches should be followed.

This could lead to several problems for the company itself. The relationship between the two directors could be damaged, making it difficult for them to cooperate in the future. In addition, the conflict, if unresolved, could mean that the company finds itself lacking key new members of staff for the immediate future.

Where possible, then, we can see that destructive conflict should be avoided. This can be accomplished through:

- **Good communication** – Conflict can be caused by simple misunderstandings. Making sure that managers and staff freely and regularly communicate with each other about issues that arise is therefore important.
- **Motivated staff** – Those who are happy in their job role and feel fulfilled are less likely to cause problems for others.
- **Rules and procedures** – Having clearly defined rules can help to avoid conflict. If all employees know what they are responsible for within the organisation, they are less likely to conflict with each other.
- **Avoiding a 'blame culture'** – Managers need to lead by example here. If a manager is in regular conflict with other employees, this is likely to be imitated by other, more junior members of staff.
- **Ensuring a fair allocation of resources** – Managers should ensure that staff, cash and other resources are fairly allocated between departments and individuals. This should help to reduce disagreements and conflict.

6.7 Strategies to Resolve Conflict

If conflict cannot be avoided, the individuals within the team need to adopt a strategy to resolve it. How those involved will respond will depend on the relationships within the team, the rules and procedures of the company and the nature and severity of the conflict.

Some conflicts can be handled on an informal basis by the members of the team involved, whereas others will require more formal procedures and the involvement of the management.

For a junior team member experiencing conflict, they must firstly decide whether to deal with the matter themselves or refer it to a more senior manager. Although handling the matter in an informal way can lead to a quicker and more friendly resolution, it can also make the matter worse should the approach of those involved not be aligned.

When judging whether to escalate a conflict to the management of the team or take further steps, the team member should consider:

- the nature of the conflict – how long has it lasted; how aggressive or destructive has it become; how important are the issues it concerns
- the people involved – what is the history of the relationships between those in the conflict; what is the involvement of other team members
- the rules and procedures of the company
- the potential further conflicts which could be caused by either informal or formal approaches to resolution

For relatively minor or personal issues, employees may seek to take action themselves. This could involve discussing the matter informally or avoiding the conflict completely and seeking to restore relationships in other ways. Examples where this approach may be best would include office gossip, not being invited to a social gathering or a disagreement over which supplier to use for one contract. This said, should any of the above persist, a case could be made for referring the issue to management.

Activity 18

Identify three conflicts which either you have experienced in the workplace. For each conflict explain whether you would resolve the conflict yourself (and if so how this would be achieved) or refer the matter to a senior manager.

(AAT Assessment criteria 4.1)

There are numerous possible approaches a manager can take, including:

- **Avoidance** – this involves the manager ignoring the conflict and hoping that it blows over without needing any intervention. This may well work for minor conflicts between employees.
- **Suppression** – the manager can threaten the conflicting parties with punishment if they fail to overcome their problems. This is likely to be a short-term solution and will not be successful for major conflicts.
- **Compromise/negotiation** – the manager can act as a neutral third party and negotiate a compromise agreement between the conflicting parties. This tends to be the most common approach, with both parties getting some (but not all) of what they want.
- **Resolution** – the manager seeks to find the root cause of the conflict and solve it. This will hopefully produce a 'win-win' solution where both parties end up satisfied. It is often time-consuming and complex, though it may provide a lasting solution to the conflict.

Activity 19

Let us return to the example of Butterworths, a leading manufacturer of garden equipment. Following a successful period of product development, they are due to launch their new product range.

They are planning to attend two exhibitions later this month to promote their new products to the general public and trade buyers.

Under the leadership of Terry, Frankie has been made responsible for one exhibition and Pedro has been put in charge of the other.

They both require support from Jack, who handles administrative support and finances, and Fenella, who is a marketing specialist.

As the exhibitions are taking place at similar times, both Frankie and Douglas want access to Jack and Fenella, both seeing their needs as being more important than the others'.

This has caused considerable conflict, with Frankie and Pedro frequently arguing across the office and both putting pressure on Jack and Fenella to prioritise their workload.

Terry has taken the decision to try to deal with the conflict. He has four options:

1. Do nothing and assume the managers will be able to deal with the problem by themselves.
2. Talk with the managers and see if an agreement can be reached to share the Jack and Fenella's time between them.

3. Investigate to see if any other workers within the company have the same, specialist skills. There would then be enough skilled employees for both projects.
4. Order the two managers to sort out the problem quickly, or they will lose their bonus for the year.

Required:

a) For each of the four approaches, state which conflict management strategy Terry would be taking.

b) Explain how you would approach this problem if you were in Terry's position.

(AAT Assessment criteria 4.1)

Activity 20

Think of an example of a conflict within your workplace. Assess why the matter was resolved effectively.

(AAT Assessment criteria 4.1)

7 Your role in the team

This chapter has focused on how successful team work can deliver business objectives and simultaneously foster healthy working relationships. Although we need to be able to operate as individuals, the benefits of productive teams and the ideas they share cannot be denied.

To be an effective team player, you need to define your own role in the team, whether by responsibilities you have or by your personality traits and which of Belbin's nine team members you tend to become. Your role in the team can change depending on the other people involved, but consider which of characteristics you have and what that would add to a team dynamic – think about how you react to people, tasks and the working environment and start to define your role.

For example, are you an ideas person – someone who suggests new ways of doing things and likes to be active and challenge the accepted norms? Or maybe you are in a supportive role, either as a pacifier or to encourage others? Or perhaps you a forceful, animated individual who likes to take responsibility? All have a team role to play.

Cloke and Goldsmith refer to ten special 'skills' required for successful teamwork, all of which are interrelated:

- Self-management – a sense of ownership, personal responsibility and commitment
- Responsibility – collective responsibility for all decisions and actions
- Leadership – organising, co-ordinating, facilitating and mentoring team members
- Strategic planning – identifying challenges and creating solutions
- Feedback and evaluation – learning, self-evaluation and consideration of team processes and relationships
- Communication – collaboration and sharing of ideas
- Shaping successful meetings – team decisions made in consenus
- Resolving conflicts – responding to issues as they arise and ensuring conflict is constructive rather than destructive
- Supportive diversity – overcoming any prejudices to allow free communication and different perspectives
- Enjoyment – team members working in unison and producing results.

Consider all of the above and how the team in which you work exhibit these skills.

Activity 21

You have been asked to present to a group of decision-makers from local companies on the subject of 'Effective Teamwork – Skills and Behaviours Required'.

This presentation will be further covered in Chapter 6, but as this stage, make a list of all of the key points you need to include in the presentation. In particular focus on the roles in the team and how they contribute, with reference to Belbin, Cloke and Goldsmith and other relevant theories. Start also to consider your own role and think of examples of how you personally have had a positive impact on a team.

(AAT Assessment criteria 1.5, 3.2)

Answers to chapter activities

Activity 1

The correct answer is B.

The two individuals have interpreted the email in different ways indicating that they have different perceptions of what the email meant.

Activity 2

According to role theory, Sid's uniform is an example of:

D Role signs

A role sign is a visible indication of an individual's role within the organisation and a different uniform to other people's would indicate this.

Activity 3

The correct answer is C

Those in the Post Office queue would be considered more as a random crowd than a group. They lack a sense of identity, as there are no acknowledged boundaries or leadership. There is unlikely to be any loyalty or collective objective (despite them sharing the individual aim of being served in a timely fashion).

This said, if they are forced to wait for a long time or knowingly join the queue each week, they may eventually create an informal group.

Activity 4

A James, who is assertive is more likely to handle conflict effectively.

William's aggressive behaviour could cause more conflict and areas of disagreement, whereas Howard's passive approach could mean the conflict is either ignored or left unchallenged.

Activity 5

Advantages of teams include they possess a mixture of skills and abilities, they provide greater energy, focus and control, they allow increased flexibility, increased motivation, improved communication between workers and healthy competition.

Disadvantages of teams include slow decision-making, constant compromise, group pressure to conform, lack of individual responsibility, too much social interaction and the destructive element of increased competition and more opportunities for conflict.

Activity 6

A The Company Worker is Jack

B The Shaper is Pedro

C The Plant is Frankie

D The Finisher is Angela

E The Monitor-Evaluator is Jim

Using Tuckman's stages of development, Terry's first report suggests that the group are largely in the **Norming stage**, where people are aware of each other and working to define roles and organise workload. By the second report the team seem to be in the **Dorming stage**. They appear to have outlived their usefulness and productivity has fallen.

Activity 7

This answer will depend on the individual's experience and the way their business and department are structured. Some explanation of department roles, ideally using an organisational chart, should be provided. It should also be considered what sort of team they are part of and how the members generally interact. Different members of the team should be allocated roles according to Belbin's theory and a judgement of the team's maturity and stage of development using Tuckman or a similar form of classification should be used.

Activity 8

The following would be characteristics of an effective team:

A A positive atmosphere

B Small number of members

E Clear objectives

H Low absenteeism

I High productivity

Lack of communication, pressure being applied to individuals to comply with dubious decisions and dominating characters within the group all suggest that the group are not listened to each other or partaking in the decision-making process. High labour turnover suggests problems within the group and constant newcomers being unclear of how it operates.

Activity 9

Although examples should be provided from the individual's experience, common skills and behaviour can be identified. For example, effective teams will include good listeners willing to compromise, a range of skills and attributes (see Belbin), frequent and easy communication, clear objectives and a sense of mutual self-interest.

The impact of this is likely to be positive and include factors such as increased productivity, a dedicated and loyal workforce and the encouragement of novel ideas to improve the business.

Activity 10

Maslow's hierarchy would be applied as follows:

A New job title - **Ego**

B Large pay rises - **Ego**

C Sick pay - **Safety**

D Christmas parties - **Social**

E Challenging work – **Self-fulfilment**

F Enough cash to live on - **Basic**

Activity 11

The correct answer is **A Basic.**

Peter is performing a role he is not happy in to allow him to pay towards the house for him and his family. He is unlikely to be motivated by anything other than basic needs (for the moment).

Activity 12

The correct answer is **A Job rotation**

Labour flexibility would include multi-skilling which would allow employees to move around the organisation and could be linked to job rotation.

Activity 13

The correct answer is **C Motivation of employees**

Most motivational models argue that the basic salary level set is unlikely to act as a motivator.

Activity 14

This answer will depend on the individual's workplace and the personality of their colleagues. Answers should include reference to reward systems and how different people respond to them, as well as at least one motivation theory (Maslow, Herzberg, Vroom). The motivation of contrasting colleagues should be assessed.

Activity 15

A leader is able to influence their team toward the achievement of a goal or goals. Leadership is therefore a conscious activity and is concerned with setting goals and then inspiring people to achieve them. Managers by contrast rely on the use of formal authority and the co-ordination of business resources rather than their personality.

Activity 16

The correct answer is **C Consults** as this is a participative style.

Activity 17

This answer will depend on the individual's experience in the workplace, but should include some of the skills and roles identified by Drucker and Mintzberg. In addition to stating the strengths of the leader, they should be explained with reference to their impact on others.

Activity 18

This answer will depend on individual experience, but relatively minor or personal issues may be best solved with an informal approach and appealing to the person directly rather than escalating the issue and risking further conflict. Office gossip or emotional reactions to team dynamics would fall under this category. The student should show they considered the people involved, the situation and company policy.

Activity 19

a) Terry's options can be defined as:

1. Avoidance / denial as the conflict is ignored
2. Negotiation as a compromise is sought
3. Resolution as this tries to get to the root of the issue
4. Suppression as this would force a resolution

b) It seems that the conflict is currently intensifying and the issue is worsening. As the dispute seems relatively obvious, it will be difficult for Terry to ignore. The issue has escalated enough that it is clearly becoming personal and others are involved, so Terry must act. Suppression seems like an extreme measure given that the staff are clearly experienced and focused on their work. The solution would be temporary and would undoubtedly flare up in the future to the detriment of everyone, including Jack and Fenella.

As both seem keen to work with Jack and Fenella, most likely a compromise over their time could be reached. If roles were more clearly defined, they could both have access to their support staff equally. If that failed, perhaps other staff could be brought in to assist, but this could cause more disputes between Pedro and Frankie if their initial disagreement is not addressed and the power struggle over Jack and Fenella continues regardless.

Some note should also be made here that given the nature of the dispute, Terry needs to act as a calm conciliator.

Activity 20

This answer will be dependent on the individual's relevant experience in the workplace, but they should consider the nature of the conflict itself (Vertical/Horizontal, Daft), the leadership attributes illustrated, the ethics of the team and the specific strategy used to consider why the conflict was resolved successfully. Links may be made to team roles, motivation and other factors should they be relevant to the situation.

Activity 21

The contents of the presentation should include analysis of everything covered in this chapter, including characteristics of effective teams and their formation. Examples should come from individual experience of teams in the workplace.

Planning and delivering business communication activities

5

Introduction

Having examined the ways businesses operate and seen the importance of relationships both within the organisation and to develop business with external stakeholders, it is clear that effective communication is vital to the delivery of most commercial objectives.

This chapter examines how communication activities can be planned and delivered to enable you to use both written and verbal skills to convey your ideas in a professional business context. It will examine different styles of communication as well as how to approach a variety of audiences.

ASSESSMENT CRITERIA

1 To understand how to plan business communication activities

2 To produce written business communications

3 To understand how to communicate verbally in a business environment

4 To be able to communicate verbally to others

CONTENTS

1 Communication in business
2 The communication process
3 Types of business communication
4 Written communication
5 Verbal communication
6 Marketing and client communication
7 Barriers to communication

1 Communication in business

1.1 What is communication?

Definitions

Communication is the two-way interchange of information, ideas, facts and emotions by one or more persons. It establishes relationships and allows for direction and coordination of tasks.

Non-verbal communication: Not all communication is verbal – a great deal of communication can take place without any words at all, through forms of body language. A raised eyebrow or frown can convey people's views or emotions, as can more obvious physical gestures such as the pat on the back or an arm around the shoulders.

1.2 Standard communication in business

In an organisation, communication takes many forms, including:

- giving or receiving information and instructions
- exchanging ideas
- announcing plans and strategies
- laying down rules or procedures
- comparing actual results against a plan
- manuals, organisation charts and job descriptions

1.3 Types of communication

Most communication within an organisation can be classified as either formal or informal.

Formal communication helps to provide management structure, so that individuals know what is expected of them and how they have actually performed. It could include plans, procedures, policies and performance reports and meetings, as well as the formal announcement and interpretation of management decisions.

Informal communication is a more casual way of interacting, using relaxed and interpersonal channels such as face-to-face or telephone conversations, e-mails and text messages. It does not follow the lines of authority, instead being a feature of co-operation between individuals.

Both types of communication are essential in an efficient and effective business organisation.

Example

Let us return to the example of Mainwaring and Sons, the fashion retailer looking to open new stores. The management of Mainwaring and Sons makes a formal announcement to the press about the opening and closing of stores on Thursday. However, most people had already heard about it, because the news had been 'leaked' on Tuesday and passed from person to person within the company and the media.

1.4 Formal communication

As mentioned earlier, this follows the procedural channels that are present within the organisation. It can therefore be:

- **Vertical** – downwards, from superior to subordinate, or upwards, from subordinate to superior.

  Downward communications can help management to convey key objectives and company-wide messages to employees at a lower level and therefore helps to link levels of the hierarchy. However, too much downward communication can cause those at lower levels to feel like they do not have a voice and become reluctant to make suggestions.

  For this reason, upward communication is essential. It provides management with feedback from employees and makes them aware of any problem areas.

- **Horizontal or lateral** – communication between people at a similar level in the organisation's hierarchy, whether they are in the same peer group or not.

  This form of communication helps different departments to share information, solve company-wide problems and co-ordinate their activities.

- **Diagonal** – interdepartmental communication between people of different ranks.

Example

Examples of different types of communication:

Vertical (downward) - The Head of Marketing sends a report and associated tasks to the junior members of the marketing team.

Vertical (upward) - A junior member of the sales department contacts a senior sales manager with customer feedback and a request for further information.

Horizontal - The Head of Marketing sends a report to the Head of the Human Resources.

Diagonal - A junior member of the accounts department sends a request for information from a senior sales manager.

Activity 1

Which of the following is not usually a purpose of lateral or horizontal communication?

A. Task co-ordination

B. Problem solving

C. Giving instructions

D. Conflict resolution

Information also flows into and out of the organisation.

- **Inflows** include market research and surveillance, allowing the organisation to identify and respond to external opportunities or threats.
- **Outflows** include advertising, marketing and public relations and usually involve the organisation trying to influence key stakeholders.

1.5 Informal communication

While the organisation will have a designated, formal communications network, it is inevitable (and not necessarily a bad thing) that there will also be a number of informal communication channels.

Informal communication:

- can move in any direction
- can skip authority levels

- is as likely to satisfy social needs as facilitate task accomplishments

Therefore, in a company being managed in a highly structured, authoritarian style, informal communication may not be as widely conducted.

Definitions

A grapevine refers to the network of social relationships that arise informally and spontaneously. It often carries more current information than formal communication and is subject to both rumours and gossip.

The grapevine tends to prosper when there is a lack of information being provided by the management or when employees feel insecure about their position or unjustly treated.

The grapevine can also be used by managers, seeking to get messages to their staff without formally discussing the matter.

Activity 2

Think of three examples of both formal and informal business communication activities from your own workplace.
(AAT Assessment criteria 1.1)

2 The communication process

2.1 The communication process

The communication process can be summarised as follows:

A Sender transmits a **message** through a **Channel** to a **Receiver**, who **decodes** the message and acts upon it.

Example

Rebecca is an estate agent showing potential buyers a newly built property. She needs to communicate to the customers why they should buy the property, even though it is very expensive. If she fails, she will not get sales commission this month.

In this instance, Rebecca is the Sender.

The message is the reasons to buy the property. It is transmitted by the channel of speech and perhaps also by gesture. She may reinforce the verbal message by providing some written information.

The potential buyers are the Receivers and they receive the message by listening and perhaps looking.

The message is successfully decoded by the buyers and they may decide to act on her advice when they have seen further properties.

In a business context, it is crucial to appreciate the importance of conveying the message in a way that it can be easily decoded. It is also vital to choose the right channel bearing in mind the needs of the receiver(s).

2.2 Communication patterns

A communication pattern illustrates how individuals communicate with each other within a group or organisation. Leavitt identified five major patterns of communication: wheel (or star), circle, all-channel, chain and Y. These are shown in the diagrams below:

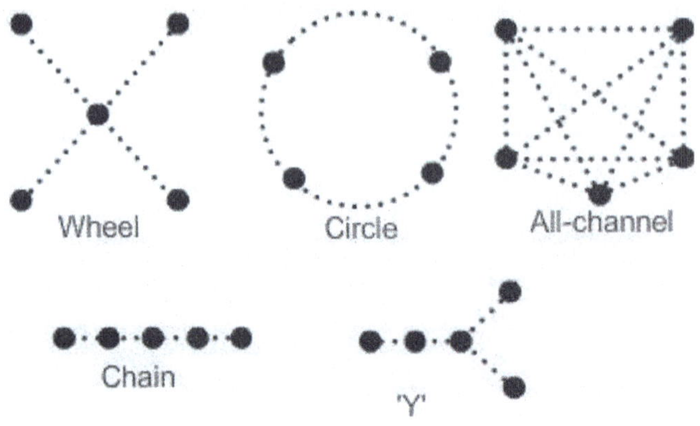

These patterns of communication can be grouped into two:

- Centralised networks – chain, wheel and Y – in these group members have to go through a central person in order to communicate with others. This can lead to unequal access within the group.
- Decentralised networks – circle and all-channel – information flows freely between members.

The wheel is the fastest way to reach a conclusion, making it ideal for solving problems.

For complex matters, the all-channel approach is best as it allows for a variety of viewpoints to be properly discussed.

The circle tends to lead to the highest level of satisfaction for the whole group, although leaders/central figures may prefer the wheel or Y. The circle however tends to lead to more indecision.

Activity 3

Think about your own workplace – which pattern does communication in your team or department follow from those identified by Leavitt?

3 Types of business communication

3.1 Forms of business communication

There are a variety of different ways business communications can be presented, depending on the purpose and intended audience.

Primarily the forms of communication will be

- written or verbal
- information-based or promotional
- internal or external

3.2 The intended audience and purpose

When deciding on the form of communication to use, consider the intention behind the activity (to inform or to promote) and the people you are addressing.

In terms of the audience, they could be classified as follows:

- Colleagues or customers (internal/external)
- Position within the company
- Social aspects – age, gender, cultural background

Although it is by no means an exact science, certain types of communication will work better for different groups.

In terms of the purpose of business communication activities, these can be split into three broad categories:

- **To inform** – crucial for internal updates, but also to keep clients up to speed with customer care issues
- **To consult** – communication is a two-way interaction and seeking advice and feedback is crucial to any business
- **To sell/promote** – conveying positive messages and seeking action and endorsement from consumers

Many communications will combine all three of the above.

Example

Windsor Electricals have developed a new loyalty scheme to reward customers who purchase their electrical appliances.

The marketing manager has been asked to communicate the new idea to the shareholders, company employees and existing and new clients.

In order to appeal to specific groups, he has decided to:

- Send a letter to the shareholders detailing the changes and also explaining the reasons behind them.
- Send an information-based e-mail to all staff and arrange a presentation during a training day where a director can explain the changes and take questions (this will get the key messages across in both verbal and written form and will not seem overly formal)
- Send a glossy brochure to sell this concept and reinforce the Windsor plc brand to all clients
- Write an online article about the changes and post links to it from various forms of social media to appeal to younger customers
- Send a press release to the local newspapers accompanied by a promotional competition

For each group, he has considered the best form of communication and the intended purpose of it.

Activity 4

For the following business communication activities, identify:

- The purpose
- The intended audience
- The desired outcome

A. A press release sent to local newspapers quoting the Managing Director of a company speaking about new environmentally-friendly policies.

B. An internal memo from the Head of Distribution to advise of a record-breaking volume of orders being despatched from the warehouse of a pharmaceutical company.

C. A training seminar including speeches from all departmental managers on annual progress of their departments.

D. An e-mail circulated to the decision-makers in the training departments of fifty leading financial institutions by a professional accounting body informing them of improvements to their assessment facilities.

E. A meeting of local employers held at a local school to discuss the benefits of work experience placements.

(AAT Assessment criteria 1.1 and 1.2)

3.3 Effective business communication

Effective communication involves ensuring that the right person receives the right information at the right time. It should therefore be:

- **Timely** – the speed of communication must be linked to the urgency of the issue being communicated. A report that a machine is out of action is of little use if it is delayed for hours or days, as it will increase the amount of production time lost.
- **Accurate and complete** – any information in the communication should be factually correct and all relevant facts should be stated to avoid wrong conclusions being drawn.
- **Relevant** – the message should not be excessive in volume as this will overload the receiver.
- **Directed to the right people** – care must be taken not to send information to the wrong people. This could cause confusion or even loss of confidentiality of sensitive information.

- **Understandable** – care must be taken with the presentation of the information, so that all recipients are able to comprehend its meaning.
- **Cost effective** – as far as possible, the communication must be achieved at a reasonable cost to the organisation.

Effective communication is essential for the organisation as it ensures that:

- instructions, rules and procedures are properly understood by all employees
- individuals know what is expected of them
- there is better coordination between individuals, groups and departments
- it is easier for managers to plan and control operations more efficiently
- forming, swapping and testing of ideas is encouraged, improving innovation
- there is increased trust and reduced conflict within the organisation

Activity 5

Your manager has asked you to inform the rest of the accounting department (eight other people) about three new products the company are due to launch in the next month. You have been given a written product briefing from the senior management meeting, which is incredibly technical and several pages long. Plan how best to inform your colleagues of the developments.

(AAT Assessment criteria 1.1)

4 Written communication

4.1 Forms of written communications

Examples of written communications include:

- reports
- research and Information
- promotional literature (brochures, flyers)
- letters
- e-mails
- memos
- press releases
- online blogs
- social media posts
- minutes of meetings
- findings from research

4.2 Effective written communications

Although there are many forms of written communication, all share the same requirements in order to convey the message.

- **Planning** – decide in advance what your are looking to say and list key points to ensure that they are not obscured by other information. Ensure the pattern of the communication is logical and the information is relevant prior to writing.
- **Accuracy** – errors in spelling and grammar can undermine the overall purpose of written communications so it is vital to check all documentation thoroughly. Checking should also avoid other clumsy traits such as repetition and using unnecessary words.
- **Structure** – whether writing a report for the directors or sending a brief memo to colleagues, written communications need to be clearly laid out with an introduction, main part and conclusion. They need to follow a logical sequence, and depending on their length should use signposts or headings to direct the reader.
- **Style** – largely dependent on the audience, the style of the writing will change. For marketing communications, a 'corporate voice' will

be more appropriate. Sentences and paragraphs should not be so long as to be confusing – a guide is a maximum of thirty words per sentence and ten lines per paragraph. Depending on the form of communication, the use of bullet-points, charts or images may help to break up more wordy documents.

- **Clear, specific and directed content** – the content should be purposeful, positive and constructive. Even information-based written communications should be upbeat and avoid a vast amount of information which could confuse the recipient.
- **Appropriate language** – most marketing will feature short, sharp statements and avoid wordy phrases so as not to complicate the brand message and maintain the audience's attention, whereas a detailed business report could be undermined by a lack of technical language. Likewise, if communicating via social media or mobile phone technologies, abbreviated forms may be more suitable.

Activity 6

Your company is due to launch automated e-statements to replace paper billing next month for all customers. You have been asked to communicate this to all of the clients you deal with regularly.

You should:

i. Decide which form of written communication would work best

ii. Plan your communication, including its structure and key messages

iii. Draft an initial communication

iv. Check and finalise the communication, noting any corrections

v. Write a brief description to your manager of the communication you sent and detail how you would keep records of both outgoing and incoming communications between you and clients on this matter

(AAT Assessment criteria 1.1, 1.3, 1.4, 2.1)

5 Verbal communication

5.1 Forms of verbal communications

Examples of verbal communications include:

- Presentations
- Speeches
- Meetings
- Telephone briefings/webinars.

5.2 Effective verbal communications

When communicating in business, it is important to remember that the process is a two-way interaction. Effective communication requires not only the skills to present effectively, but also the ability to understand the recipient's needs. Listening and questioning skills are therefore vital.

- **Active listening** – ensure the client is fully at ease and let them speak freely when the wish to, noting any crucial points which need further elaboration when you respond.
- **Effective questioning** – using a combination of open and closed questions to enable the other person to express their views whilst maintaining control. Open questions (e.g. How do you feel about...) enable broad and wide-ranging discussions, whereas closed questions (e.g. Do you think that…) add purpose and direction to the conversation.
- **Body language** – research suggests that up to 80% of communication is through our actions and the signals we show to others. A key to keeping people interested is to appear enthusiastic and supportive yourself, even by nodding and smiling. Equally if they start looking around the room, ensure you pick up on this and change the subject or your approach.
- **Relaxed atmosphere** – linked to the concept of body language, appear open and relaxed to encourage easy and honest interchanges. The other person is more likely to be honest if they are not being judged. Try to avoid physically crowding or rushing them.
- **Summarising** – this is a handy device for showing that you have listened and can empathise with the other person.

Bad listeners are those who do not allow the speaker to convey the whole story due to interrupting too often, jumping to the wrong conclusions and judging prematurely. Conversations can also dry up with too many closed questions or where the other person feels disheartened (if you are too easily distracted by your mobile phone or if you better their favourite claim to fame, for example).

Activity 7

Which of the following are signs of good active listening skills:

A. Becomes easily distracted

B. Maintains eye contact throughout

C. Shows constant curiosity and asks for examples

D. Listens for feelings as well as views

E. Completes the speaker's sentences before they have finished

F. Makes assumptions about the other person's views

G. Steers replies to get the answers they want

H. Checks understanding

To ensure your verbal communications and presentations are successful, many of the guidelines for written communications still apply. The following attributes are key:

- **Sustain interest** – vary the tone, volume and pace of your speech and include both 'light' and 'dark' to keep your audience interested. Enthusiastic body language also helps if communicating face-to-face.
- **Be clear and succinct** – there is a greater tendency to drift off the subject and become irrelevant when communicating verbally. Although improvisation can add colour to a public speech, it can also detract from the core message. Likewise, avoid jargon and use simple words and emphasise key points.
- **Persuade and negotiate** – in person, it should be more appropriate to more forcefully back up your key points with reasons.
- **Use an active, positive voice** – it is crucial to be encouraging or enthusiastic at least and entertaining at best. Even if meeting with colleagues to discuss policy, try to introduce some good news to keep spirits high and the atmosphere positive and productive.

- **Attempt interaction** – even when presenting, it is crucial that you engage the audience. Use both your verbal communications and body language to show you care, building respect and fostering a more open environment. Questions and interaction should also ensure the presenter does not speak too much.

Activity 8

Which of the following are signs of good verbal communication skills:

A. Gives opinions as if they are facts

B. Uses complicated technical jargon

C. Lacks clarity

D. Supports key points with substantial reasons

E. Appears aggressive

F. Shares personal experiences

G. Seems hesitant and self-doubting

H. Keeps control and attention

6 Marketing and Client Communications

6.1 The Marketing Mix

When referring to business communications, perhaps the most obvious activities are those, both written and verbal, directed at customers. As established in the previous chapter, a company's marketing strategy will determine how it communicates with existing or prospective clients. Rather than communicating as an individual, marketing activities allow business communications with a corporate or collective voice.

To examine the messages and methods companies use in their marketing, we will focus on the Marketing Mix. The Marketing Mix defines **7 P's**, which are 'mixed' to successfully achieve the company's marketing objectives and translate the brand identity to existing and new customers.

Product (what is sold)	The offering designed to satisfy the consumer's needs, whether physical products, services, people or conceptual property. Stresses the product's features, packaging, brand name, after-sales service and warranties.
Price (what is charged)	Includes the setting of price levels, discounts, allowances, payment terms and credit policy. Organisations can attack their competitors by reducing their prices or offering better value and entice potential customers using discounts.
Promotion (how it is sold)	Through advertising, publicity and special prize initiatives. Money-off coupons and similar promotion techniques enable better deals for consumers without cutting prices or entering into a price war. Direct sales, including personal selling and display merchandising, may be a better for some markets.
Place (where it is sold)	A choice of distribution channels for the products, stock can be managed, promoted and transported. Could include distribution outlets.
Process (how it is made)	The systems which enable products and services to be delivered in a timely, appropriate manner.
People (who provides/ uses it)	Both those responsible for producing, selling and supplying the company's offering and the consumers whose needs are being addressed.
Physical evidence	Testimonials and references

6.2 Product

There are two main product issues to consider:

- Product definition
- Product positioning

Product definition

The main issue is to define exactly what the product offering is for the customer. This can be done on three levels:

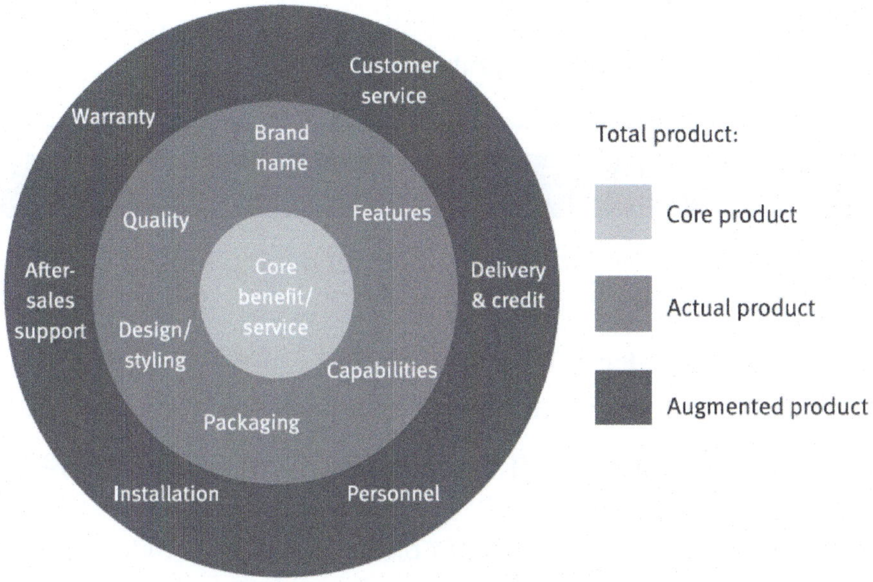

- **Core/generic product** – what is the buyer really buying? The core product refers to the use, benefit that the consumer is really buying when purchasing the product and the need that is being fulfilled e.g. a car is for personal transportation.
- **Actual product** - the tangible product or intangible service that serves as the medium for receiving core product benefits e.g. the car's engine size, different body shapes.
- **Augmented product** – consists of the measures taken to help the consumer put the actual product to sustained use, including installation, delivery and credit, warranties, and aftersales service e.g the car's manufacturer's warranty or dealer's discounted service contract.

Product positioning

This determines how the product relates to others available in the market, stressing the USPs for the product.

6.3 Price

There are four key considerations when deciding the price of a product. These are known as 'the 4Cs':

- **Cost** – the price must be high enough to make a profit (eg Cost plus pricing)
- **Customers** – what are they willing to pay? (eg Loss leaders and Price skimming)
- **Competition** – what do others charge for similar commodities? (eg Going rate pricing)

- **Corporate objectives** – what is the main priority? (eg. If to obtain market share at any cost: Penetration pricing; if to create a high quality brand: Perceived quality pricing)

Example

Using the above considerations, a number of pricing tactics can be employed. For example:

- **Cost plus pricing** – a mark-up is added to the cost per unit
- **Penetration pricing** – a low price is set to gain market share
- **Perceived quality pricing** – a high price creates the image of high quality
- **Price discrimination** – different prices are set for different markets for the same product
- **Going rate pricing** - prices set to match competitors
- **Price skimming** – after initially high prices, the price is later dropped to increase the demand amongst those unwilling to pay a higher rate
- **Loss leaders** – using products sold at a cheaper rate to lure customers in to buy other, more profitable items
- **Captive product pricing** – used where customers must make multiple purchases

Activity 9

Pear plc has created a new model of mobile phone. After several years of research and development, Pear are concerned that rival companies will quickly copy the phone's specification and sell their own versions. Pear have therefore decided to sell the phone at a high initial price per unit in order to recoup their development costs. Once rival versions are launched, Pear will drop the price in order to compete more effectively.

Which of the following pricing strategies are Pear plc employing?

A. Penetration pricing

B. Going rate

C. Perceived quality

D. Price skimming

E. Captive product pricing

6.4 Promotion

Promotion is essentially about market communication. In order to make consumers buy, companies move their target market through the AIDA sequence:

Awareness > Interest > Desire > Action

In order to do this, firms will use a combination of different techniques which form their 'promotional mix'. These include:

- Advertising (TV and radio, newspapers, online)
- Sales promotions (e.g. Buy one, get one free)
- Personal selling (e.g. field sales representatives)
- Public relations and sponsorship (eg sporting events)

6.5 Place

Companies have the option of either selling through direct channels (e.g. retail outlets, company e-commerce sites, direct mailings) or indirect channels (through distributors, wholesalers or selling networks).

Activity 10

Pike.com is an online retailer of games, DVDs and books. It is currently planning an upgrade to its website to make it easier for consumers to find the items that they are looking for.

Which element of the following elements of the Marketing Mix would this improvement relate to?

A. Price

B. Place

C. Promotion

D. Product

E. People

6.6 The strategic marketing process

Marketing functions have a direct impact on the strategic planning process of an organisation.

Strategic analysis:

- analysis of brand strength, product quality and reputation
- analysis of competition

- market research to determine consumer opinion (desk research, field research, product testing)
- detailed analysis of customer expectations and power

Strategic choice:

- decisions regarding which products to sell
- segmentation of target markets (eg geographic, demographic, socio-economic groups) and then focus on attractive segments
- developing strategies using Marketing Mix variables

Strategy implementation:

- setting budgets for promotion and advertising
- setting targets for sales revenue, market share and awareness
- monitoring and control

Activity 11

Which part of the strategic planning process would the following come under:

1. Setting budgets for a newspaper advertising campaign
2. Asking for public reactions to a new product
3. Classifying potential consumers by average income and deciding to target those earning over £20,000

For each of the above, choose from the following:

A. Strategic analysis

B. Strategic choice

C. Strategic implementation

7 Barriers to communication

7.1 Barriers to effective communication

Despite the need for effective communication, there are a number of barriers and breakdowns that can occur, causing problems within the organisation.

A barrier to communication is anything that stops information from:

- getting to its intended recipient(s)
- being understood by the recipient(s) and/or
- being acted on in the manner intended.

Typical communication barriers

- Professional status differences between receiver and sender can mean that more junior members of staff can be reluctant to pass information upwards for fear of criticism.
- Personal, social or cultural differences between the receiver and sender, such as age, education or priorities may mean that they interpret the information in different ways, causing confusion.
- Language differences or the use of technical or professional jargon can prevent understanding of communications.
- Distance between communicators can be a problem. Typically, individuals will respond more promptly to those nearby!
- Conflict between individuals within the organisation may lead to communication being limited or withdrawn between them.
- Overload – if too much information is communicated at once, the receiver may become overwhelmed and fail to understand what is expected of them.

Activity 12

Douglas has been working at Windsor Electricals from the age of 16. He is now a departmental manager in his early 40s. He sticks to a strict routine, arriving and leaving work punctually. He is married with children.

He has always worked in the department that he now manages and is the most experienced employee in his particular field. However, he is not familiar with latest developments in technology and feels swamped by an excess of useless information. He claims that he is, in any case, aware of the information he needs, but his subordinates worry because they notice that he ignores information that does not agree with his opinions.

Sally is a young accounting graduate who works in the management information department. She has been promoted quickly to supervisor level, having joined the company a few years ago straight from university. She is single and lives close to the office and often works late because she loves computers and is fascinated by their potential. She frequently tells anyone willing to listen that the company is old-fashioned and needs to be dragged into the twenty-first century.

Douglas hears this, disapproves but does not comment, and carries on in his usual way. Although Douglas and Sally are located in different buildings on the same site, their work requires them to co-operate regularly. Their relations are getting more and more strained and their work is suffering.

Identify and describe the barriers to communication between the two colleagues.

7.2 Consequences of ineffective communication

If the organisation fails to deal with the barriers to communication, its internal and external communications may become significantly less useful.

Lack of downward communication is likely to result in:

- poor awareness of corporate objectives at lower management levels
- poor understanding of working instructions and responsibilities
- poor morale of junior managers because they are not consulted about changes which affect them or their working conditions

Lack of upward communication, including 'feedback', has the following undesirable consequences for management:

- early warning of troubled areas is not received
- benefit of creative ability in subordinates is lost
- participation of subordinates is limited
- need for change is not appreciated because management is isolated from the operation areas
- control becomes difficult
- introduction of change is difficult

Lack of lateral communication often leads to:

- divisions in management teams
- lack of coordination
- rivalry between sections and departments
- lack of advice and involvement by staff specialists

Example

Perhaps the best way to think about the way in which communication can go wrong is to consider what good communication would be like:

- It would use appropriate language (e.g. no jargon; written so that the intended recipient can understand it).
- It would go only to who should receive it – not to everyone.
- It would use the right medium to communicate the information.
- The information would get to the recipient in good time for it to be used.

Using this, we can produce a list of how communications go wrong:

- Information is omitted or distorted by the sender.
- Information is misunderstood due to the use of inappropriate jargon or lack of clarity.
- Information is presented using an inappropriate medium (e.g. via e-mail rather than in a proper report, or via telephone when face-to-face is better).
- Information arrives too late, or is incomplete.

Activity 13

Which of the following is a likely consequence of a lack of downward communication within an organisation?

A. Rivalry between sections and departments

B. Difficulty when introducing change

C. Poor awareness of corporate objectives at lower levels

D. Early warning of problems is not received

7.3 Overcoming barriers to effective communication

In order to avoid these problems, management should first identify any barriers to communication within their organisation and then consider practical ways of dealing with them.

These could include:

- agree and confirm priorities and deadlines for the receipt of information
- spend sufficient time ensuring that the information is sent to all the right people
- keep communication as simple as possible, avoiding jargon
- confirm that the information sent has been received and understood
- avoid inconsistent verbal/nonverbal communication, as this tends to confuse the receivers

Example

Douglas is frequently accused of upsetting his colleagues with the tone of his frequent e-mail communications. Although largely popular with more junior members of his team, Douglas is aware that his written communications are leading to staff feeling demotivated.

What can Douglas do to resolve the situation?

Some suggestions would be:

- read e-mails sent by other managers to compare and contrast the tone and content with his own
- try to communicate in different ways rather than sending so many e-mail memos – face-to-face meetings and speaking to staff individually could get a better reaction

- ask staff informally if he could improve his communication in some way and why they respond as they do to his e-mails
- make it clear to any staff with serious criticisms that he is not meaning to cause offence
- attend training on man-management or communication skills.

Ultimately, successful communication depends on continuous feedback and monitoring of existing communication systems. Information received from monitoring should be evaluated and findings acted on swiftly. If difficulties are identified these need to be corrected before further damage can occur.

Sometimes failings in the communication process are caused by external or unexpected difficulties. These include:

- Unexpected breakdowns of technology or equipment.
- A communication method may be inappropriate for a particular message.
- Receiver(s) may not be either unavailable or not in the correct frame of mind to accept a message.
- Messages may be delayed due to a variety of factors, causing mistrust and suspicion.
- An official message may be received before a manager has the opportunity to discuss an issue informally with his staff.

Activity 14

Five possible barriers to communication are as follows.

a. The people communicating might come from very different backgrounds, in terms of work experience and expertise, or socially. Substantial age differences, and lifestyles, can also create barriers to communication.

b. The message might be distorted in transmission, e.g. if it has to be transmitted to several people before it reaches the end user.

c. In a multinational organisation employees might have to overcome a language barrier to communicate with each other.

d. If there is information overload, an individual might be given too much information, and be unable to understand the message.

e. Where there is conflict within the organisation, and two individuals or departments are hostile towards each other, communications from one to the other will be treated with suspicion or disbelief.

How could each of these barriers to communication be overcome?

Activity 15

Returning to the example of Pike.com from Activity 10, you have been recruited to work for the company as their new accountant. Following the improvements they have made to their website, they have decided to promote their products and services more widely to consumers.

You have been asked to act as a staff representative and put forward a marketing proposal for how the company might promote these developments. You will need to establish an idea of how best to communicate with potential customers and the sort of messaging you think may prove worthwhile. This will then need to be presented to the board of directors in a meeting.

Required:

1. You have been asked to represent the staff in the meeting, so determine the best ways to communicate with your peers across all departments to get their input.

   a. Explain the methods of communication you chose to consult your colleagues

   b. Draft your written or verbal communication with them

   c. Detail the records you would need to keep and other considerations

2. You need to decide a marketing strategy and some messages to present to the board of directors in the meeting.

   a. Consider the elements of the Marketing Mix and decide the pricing strategy and core messages for the company to promote

   b. Draft key communications which would form part of the message

   c. Detail the records you would need to keep and other considerations

3. You have been asked to present your ideas in the board meeting, but can provide your ideas by whichever verbal or written forms you feel will serve your purpose.

   a. Explain the methods of communication you chose to present ideas to the board

   b. Draft your written or verbal communications and how you would approach them

   c. Details the records you would need to keep and other considerations

(AAT Assessment criteria 1.1, 1.2, 1.3, 1.4, 2.1, 2.2, 3.1, 3.2, 4.1, 4.2)

Answers to chapter activities

Activity 1

The correct answer is **C.**

As lateral communication refers to communication between individuals at the same level, they would be unlikely to give each other orders.

The other main purpose of lateral communication is information sharing.

Activity 2

The answer will depend on the individual's working environment, however common answers would include forms of :

- Formal communication – meetings, reports, company policies, tenders
- Informal communication – e-mails, conversations, gossip and rumours

Activity 3

If the team leader prefers to have communication coming through them, it is likely to follow the Wheel, Chain or Y. If the department allows for more free communication between members, it would be either the Circle or the All-Channel patterns.

Activity 4

A. Purpose: To promote the company's policies and enhance their reputation within the community.
Audience: The general public.
Desired outcome: Increased sales.

B. Purpose: To inform and motivate staff.
Audience: All employees of the company.
Desired outcome: To continue with successful operations.

C. Purpose: To train and inform staff.
Audience: Junior members of staff.
Desired outcome: A more knowledgeable and effective workforce.

D. Purpose: To both inform and promote their qualifications.
Audience: The decision-makers/customers.
Desired outcome: More students taking the qualification.

E. Purpose: To inform and discuss the placements.
Audience: Both the local employers and the school.
Purpose: To see mutual benefits and ensure more students are seeing benefits from the scheme.

Activity 5

It is crucial that the information is broken down to make it understandable and accessible for your colleagues. As you are primarily seeking to inform them of a policy, the e-mail should be simple and to the point. Probably the best angle would be key points listed in bullet-points.

The e-mail maintains some formality, whilst also making the policy more 'friendly' and would be appropriate for peers and colleagues in the same team. If you seem overly 'corporate' they may switch off or take offence.

In addition to the e-mail, it could then be suggested that individuals ask questions if they have any queries, through informal chats in the office.

If you have access to website links or videos these could also be a good way to break up the dry topic.

Importantly, keep a record of the communications for your manager.

Activity 6

The actual nature of the draft communication will depend on the individual, but the following approach would seem beneficial:

As the launch refers to electronic innovation it is also probably most apt to use electronic rather than paper based written communications on this occasion. E-mail would be the most straightforward way to achieve this, although more sophisticated and media rich links or video content could be incorporated if the clients seem susceptible to such things.

The structure of the communication would need to be suitable for the recipients. Therefore for customers you know prefer the personal touch, you may precede the e-mail with a telephone call. Likewise, for those with a short attention span, the e-mail should be brief. For some less technologically aware customers, you may even have to apologise!

The key message would most likely incorporate some core CSR messages and stress the benefits to the client. Promoting environmentally friendly policies like paperless billing can be of great commercial advantage as discussed in Chapter 3. There is a strong customer care element to this development also, so it is a good opportunity to show your business looks to meet customer needs and make their lives easier. Technological advancement is also implied by the initiative, so it is a good opportunity to show your business as being modern and innovative.

Importantly, do not be scared to say different things to different people! Consider the age and working ethos of your clients and judge the situation for each separately.

In terms of content, as the customers are people you know relatively well, there is no need for anything overly pushy, but ultimately this communication is a marketing exercise designed to enhance value and therefore act as a promotional tool. Therefore, you need to 'sell' the idea as well as merely inform them of why it is happening.

It should be sharp and snappy but informative and respectful. Every feature mentioned should have a benefit alongside it. The content should be clear and easy to understand.

After you have drafted the communication, it is necessary to check for mistakes. Clients may dwell on an embarrassing error in spelling rather than reading the content if there are mistakes.

It is vital to keep records of all communications so that you can both prove they have been sent and use them later in your discourse with the customer. They may provide feedback that can inform future business decisions and allow you to be more sensitive to their needs. This should be recorded in a structured way, such as a spreadsheet or CRM software if available.

Activity 7

The following are signs of good active listening skills:

B Maintains eye contact throughout

C Shows constant curiosity and asks for examples

D Listens for feelings as well as views

H Checks understanding

Activity 8

The following are signs of good verbal communication skills:

D Supports key points with substantial reasons

F Shares personal experiences

H Keeps control and attention

Activity 9

This is an example of **D Price skimming**

As high prices are set on launch with the intention of lowering them under competition.

Activity 10

This would relate to **B Place**

As the website is the main place where Pike.com's business is conducted.

Activity 11

1. **C Strategic implementation** as budgets are being set for advertising
2. **A Strategic analysis** as market research is being conducted
3. **B Strategic choice** as the market has been segmented and the attractive segment determined.

Activity 12

Analysis of the case reveals that there are a variety of reasons for the barriers in communication that exist between Douglas and Sally.

The major reasons are:

- Differences in social background - for instance, age, education, marital status, etc. These might result in a failure to understand each others' point of view, values and priorities or to even listen to the information the other person is giving. They could be stereotyping each other (Sally may have decided Douglas was a technophobe from their first interaction).
- As they are in different departments, they might not often have a chance to see each other face-to-face and either build a relationship or settle their differences. If their contact is limited to phone calls, for example, they will not benefit from non-verbal messages and this could cause further issues between them.
- Personal barriers seem to exist between them. Douglas may resent Sally's quick promotion and she appears to view him as unambitious and stuck in a previous era. His family may restrict his ability to devote the time she feels he should to work and learning new technology. Likewise, her attitude and methods of expressing her displeasure have caused a lack of trust.

If the problems persist, it seems likely they will cause further personal conflict between the pair, who could become increasingly antagonistic towards each other and start to see problems where they do not exist.

Activity 13

The correct answer is **C Poor awareness of corporate objectives at lower levels.**

A tends to be a problem without lateral communication and B and D are both problems caused by a lack of upward communication.

Activity 14

a. When individuals communicating with each other come from different backgrounds, they should be encouraged to show consideration for the other person. When an engineer communicates with an accountant, the engineer must be wary of using engineering jargon without explaining it, just as accountants must be careful of using accounting and finance terms that non-accountants are unlikely to know. A highly educated person, when communicating with someone less educated, should choose his words carefully, so that his message is clear and understandable.

b. Communication flows should be organised so that there are as few links in the communication chain as possible between the sender of the message and its eventual recipient. Lateral communications should replace unnecessary upward and downward communication flows. Electronic communication systems should contribute towards this aim.

c. Language difficulties can be reduced in two ways. First, employees should be given language training as appropriate. Secondly, the organisation should select an official language for all its meetings at a certain level of management and above. In many global corporations, English is the official language.

d. Information overload can be reduced by improvements in reporting systems. For long reports, there should be a much briefer summary containing all the essential points and recommendations. Control reports should use reporting by exception, and draw attention to performance of an unusual or unexpected nature (such as large variances). Narrative can be summarised into tables and diagrams.

e. Attempts to resolve conflict between individuals or departments should be made by the management in charge of them both. A solution to the problem of conflict is partly an improvement in communications. Management should arrange for more direct contact between individuals in different departments, and should use their interpersonal skills to try to overcome misunderstandings and disagreements.

Activity 15

The response will dependent on the experience and views of the student. They should however include the following key distinctions:

- The different nature of communicating with peers and with management in terms of style and content, with a different tone for the first and third parts of this exercise
- In terms of modes of communication, it may be best to try something more informal with peers, as this is a consultative exercise. It could even be an opportunity to use social media. The presentation to the board will need to be more structured and respectful of their position. It will probably allow an opportunity to verbally present the ideas, using presentation methods discussed in the next chapter, but accompanying reports and analysis would be expected, which would probably best in written form.
- Accuracy is key when speaking to people at a higher level so the contents of the presentation (written or verbal) to the board should be carefully checked.
- The Marketing strategy should identify the main messages and means of promotion, with reference to the Marketing Mix and a pricing strategy. In terms of product, the position and definition should be clearly shown and in addition to physical product, intangible benefits (the augmented product) should be referenced. Promotional methods should also be considered.
- Some indication of the student addressing weaknesses in their communications (e.g. self-doubt when speaking to the board) and trying to overcome barriers is required.

6 Presentations and Presentation Software

Introduction

Having established some of the necessities of effective business communications in the previous chapter, we will now look in more detail at two types of verbal communication common in the workplace, presentations and meetings.

This chapter focuses on the tools an individual can use to deliver worthwhile presentations to a range of audiences. Presentations are one of the most feared aspects of daily business operations, but without them crucial messages could not be imparted and potential revenue streams may be left untapped.

ASSESSMENT CRITERIA

Deliver a presentation

1 Understand the purpose of preparing for and evaluating a presentation

2 Understand the techniques used in enhancing a presentation

3 Be able to prepare for the delivery of a presentation

4 Be able to deliver a presentation

5 Be able to evaluate a presentation

Presentation software

1 Input and combine text and other information within presentation slides

2 Use presentation tools to structure, edit and format presentations

3 Prepare interactive slideshow for presentation

CONTENTS

1 The nature and purpose of presentations
2 Preparing for your presentation
3 Writing your presentation
4 Delivering your presentation
5 Presentation software and visual aids
6 Contingency planning
7 Assessing your presentation

1 The nature and purpose of presentations

1.1 Introduction

Presentations are not just important for managing directors seeking to inspire and inform their staff or salespeople looking to sell products or services to their clients. All parts of a company's business function may need to present their ideas and views to others in a way that their audience will respond to.

For the accountant, presentations can make an enormous spreadsheet or two hundred page report more digestible for others. Likewise, as your career progresses and you partake in project teams or start to fulfil non-accounting managerial tasks, presentations will be increasingly expected.

Unquestionably presentations add to the kudos of the presenter. If they work well, career opportunities and recognition follow, awarding the presenter a sense of expertise and authority amongst their peers. If speaking to external clients, the ability to negotiate with a large group of decision-makers concurrently, and to entertain them, can make effective presenters a vital asset to the business.

1.2 The requirements of presentations

It is firstly worthwhile to establish the unique nature of presentations when compared to other forms of verbal communication.

Presentations rely on a sense of performance and whereas in other forms of business communication acting naturally is predominantly advantageous, presentations require something different. The presenter needs to exhibit particular, specialised skills. For example, elements of dramatic performance are particularly useful. Voice projection, using props and developing characters are not necessarily seen as being career skills, but such stage techniques can be found in meeting and conference rooms and are in fact necessary to bring some topics to life.

Due to this, there is an element of self-analysis and awareness involved in presentation that does not necessarily sit easily with many professionals in less creative roles. There is a considerable advantage for the company in an individual promoting products and services to rooms filled with hundreds of people, but for the individual spokesperson concerned this can be a daunting experience.

It may not necessarily be the volume of people which the presenter finds intimidating, but instead the status they encounter. This is one aspect we will address in the planning of Presentation 1 in this chapter, which requires a presentation to the senior management of a company. The fact that either this, or speaking at a national conference in front of hundreds of others with strong views on a subject, may cause extreme nerves is not necessarily a cause for concern. Presentations, to a greater extent than meetings and other such interaction, rely on momentum and as such, adrenaline can be a valuable aid.

1.3 Types of presentation

In a business context presentations can be categorised as follows:

Type	Audience	Purpose	Advantages	Challenges
Business – Internal and Informal	Peers or colleagues	To impart information, but to also offer something new.	Likely to have a high degree of control and the audience on your side.	Can take audience for granted due to familiarity with them.
Business – internal and formal	Colleagues at all levels	To impart information, but also to offer something new. If the presentation is to an annual conference or similar, motivation or inspiration may also be expected.	Likely to be familiar with the surroundings and the audience. This is an opportunity to shine and have some authority over your peers.	Greater scrutiny as the audience is likely to be knowledgeable and some will be at more senior levels. Due to the formality, expectations will be higher and the audience may be more difficult to control.
Business - external	Decision-makers at other companies	To sell products or services, either directly or by exemplifying expertise.	The personal opportunity is enormous – if you win, you will be a hero! Business rules apply to this presentation, so although most audiences will be polite, some may just want to negotiate.	Vast preparation is required, ranging from research of your company and the client to studying the ergonomics of the room. Difficult questions could result.

Guest speaker	This may not be in a professional context, as it could be at a social club dinner or wedding. If it is professional, it is likely to be when acting as a facilitator or speaking at a conference.	To exemplify expertise and/or entertain the audience.	The audience are likely to be polite and respectful. There is an opportunity to practice for more heavy corporate events, knowing that the audience are fairly relaxed.	Audience expectations may be higher. If your personality is not normally extrovert or entertaining, this could be out of your comfort zone.

Activity 1

Explain why presentations are so widely used in business.

(AAT Assessment Criteria 1.1)

2 Preparing for your presentation

2.1 Preparation

A commonly used statistic is that 90% of the success of presentations is determined before the presenter stands in front of their audience.

There are five essential elements to the preparation of a presentation:

1. Research and profile the audience
2. Structure and shape the presentation
3. Design visual aids to support this
4. Rehearse and familiarise
5. Plan for every possible problem

Ideally, these elements should be addressed in this order. For example, creating visual aids before considering the needs of the audience or deciding on the structure can lead to a presentation which is both inappropriate or irrelevant, or merely narrates written information which could be handed out anyway.

Before starting this process, it is good practice to get the basics of the presentation in place. Presenters should therefore ascertain:

- the title of the presentation
- the objectives of the presentation
- the audience
- the time allowed
- the venue and its possibilities and limitations

2.2 The audience

For a successful presentation, knowledge of the audience is essential. The audience should be seen as a group and their collective needs should be considered at all times. The presentation is for their benefit, rather than the presenter's, and as such they should be the main priority.

Having researched and identified the audience's needs and the questions they would be keen for the presenter to answer, the start of the presentation should aim to hook the audience and the remaining sections should relate back to them. Therefore it is crucial that the audience feel the presentation is relatable and are able to establish from the start why it is of benefit and interest to them.

A presenter needs to establish how knowledgeable the audience might be on the topic they are due to present and pitch their subject matter accordingly. For example, if presenting a session on commercial awareness to a room of dentists, it is to be assumed that they will know about dentistry and the workings of the NHS, but may know less about marketing, ethics and organisational culture.

The presenter will also need to consider the most suitable approach in terms of pitch, content and the level of interaction. Every audience will be different and whereas a presentation on the monthly CSR activities for peers could take a fairly relaxed and light hearted tone, presenting to the board or delivering a presentation on poor financial performance may require a more serious and focused approach. This will be covered when we look at the presenter's role in the next section.

The positioning of the audience also matters. When addressing the use of visual aids later in the chapter, it will become clear that their viewing conditions are crucial. The seating arrangements for the room can both aid and harm presentations. The most commonly used alternative room formats are:

- Theatre Style – in this format, the participants sit in rows as they would at a theatre or in a lecture hall. The rows are typically straight, with a central aisle.

- Classroom Style – this is similar to the theatre model above, but typically involves larger desks and people sitting in pairs.
- Cabaret Style – this involves sitting in groups around a table. It is most suitable therefore where group discussion or interaction is required.
- Boardroom Style – this is only appropriate for smaller groups, as it involves all participants sitting around a long table. Usually the chair or speaker would be at the top of the table, with their main supporters on either side. If able to determine where people sit, it is important for the presenter to mix departments and mentalities.
- Horseshoe Style – this format allow the presenter to be surrounded by the audience and therefore have their full focus. Again more suitable for smaller groups, it is seen to be more open and friendly than the boardroom model, especially as the 'hole' the presenter is in gives them easier access to their audience.

Researching the audience is vital to keep the presentation relevant. If presenting to decision-makers, the focus needs to be on their requirements and the specific decisions they are looking to make. It is crucial for any presenter to remember not to present based on their view of what the audience wants to hear, but what they actually need to hear.

Example

Wonderstuff Ltd is a provider of nutritional supplements. The company was invited to pitch for an opportunity to supply its nutritional products in a large supermarket chain. The supermarket chain did not want to stock a vast number of different products in this line as they were unsure of the ethical implications of some of the marketing messages in the market, especially for the student population. Therefore this was a vital one-off opportunity.

The Managing Director and Head of Marketing delivered a one hour long presentation to the buying department at the supermarket chain. Their assumption was that, given the reputations of these businesses, price would be the most important consideration. Therefore they focused on this aspect and ensured they would be cheaper than their competitors and offered a variety of monetary incentives to the supermarket chain.

Much to their surprise, Wonderstuff Ltd did not win the contract with the supermarket chain. When they contacted them for feedback, the customer informed them that their main concerns were how the image of the product would fit in with their own and how it would be marketed to allay some of their ethical doubts. Marketing, promotion and CSR considerations were given less than a slide and no more than two minutes in the presentation from Wonderstuff Ltd whereas other nutritional food suppliers covered this topic more extensively.

Therefore the business was not won because the audience's key concern was neither identified nor addressed.

Activity 2

Think of three presentations you have attended, with different audiences. Considering the audience's requirements, explain how the presentations differed in the following ways:

- Style
- Content
- Use of visual aids

(AAT Assessment Criteria 1.1, 1.2)

2.3 Planning and Structure

There are various theories about dealing with and channelling nervousness, but being prepared, with a clear plan and a disaster checklist will go some way to addressing many of these concerns.

The timing of the presentation is crucial here and when adding structure to the presentation, the time allowed and therefore allocated to each section needs to be clearly in the presenter's mind. For example, if the presentation is to last 30 minutes and covers three main topics, it is likely that the introduction and conclusion will be around 2.5 minutes each, therefore allowing around 8 minutes per topic. The presenter should also be aware of whether any questions and answers should be covered in this time or if extra time will be allowed.

Presenters often fail because they assume that the content is in their head (that is ultimately where it came from) and therefore do not familiarise themselves with it prior to the presentation. Cue cards listing key points remain a great tool to solve this particular problem, although PowerPoint has to some degree replaced this, as the Slides and accompanying notes act as both prompts and the background context the audience is not party to.

The standard structure of a presentation could be described as follows:

- tell the audience what you are going to tell them
- tell them
- tell them what you told them

This structure will prove worthwhile in most presentations and ensures a strong start and finish which is vital for the maximum impact to be achieved.

Let us consider each step of the presentation in turn.

Activity 3

Presentation 1 - Effective Teams

Let us return to Activity 21 in Chapter 4. This required a presentation on effective team work, under the title 'Effective Teamwork – Skills and Behaviours Required'.

The following seventeen activities will refer back to this presentation.

Make a thorough plan for the preparation of the presentation, explaining the benefits of this process for the eventual outcome.

(AAT Assessment Criteria 1.3, 1.4)

3 Writing your presentation

3.1 The presentation: Introduce and hook

It is crucial that the start of any presentation sets the tone for what is to follow. Unlike the start of meetings to be covered in the following chapter, presentations need to commence with something which will grab the audience's attention, so apologies, administrative announcements or informal introductions are not appropriate. Unlike in a meeting, the audience do not need or require a lengthy agenda, they require a hook. In other words, it is crucial for a presenter to establish instantly how the audience's questions are about to be answered.

In a business context, setting the tone is usually to assert expertise or purpose straight away. For this reason, if presenting, latecomers can be ignored and the flow needs not be interrupted.

There are two parts to the start of the presentation, the introduction and the hook. It may not be necessary for introductory lines if the speaker has been adequately introduced or the atmosphere in the room implies it is best to get underway instantly. If this is not the case, introductions may be necessary. If the audience is relatively new or the location is novel, such as would be the case if pitching for business at a client's site, a reference could be made to the location of the meeting. As long as the sentiment remains sincere, there is no harm in repeating the comedian's phrase that 'it is a great to be back in (Town X)' and to perhaps compliment the host on their facilities. If overseas, cultural difference could be noted. For example, a reference to the hotel's cuisine or local sightseeing attractions could create genuine warmth from the audience. It is crucial to judge sensitivities if trying to instil humour into such an introduction. Do the locals agree that their transport network is inefficient? If so, a joke at its expense would create empathy. If not, offence could be caused.

Presenters need to introduce themselves and the purpose of their presentation as soon as possible. Even if they start with an attention-grabbing rhetorical question or quote, they need to establish the basics and clarify the purpose. This said, although the audience would want to put their presenter into a context, too much self-promotion can be counterproductive

The hook is the first **point of engagement** with the audience. They need to understand what is about to addressed and why it is relevant to them. It is vital that the presenter appears business-like, focused and in full control. This is not to say his or her introduction should be dull or without personality; it should be sharp, to the point and interesting. A flavour of what the presentation will address, perhaps with a 'teaser' of a key opinion, is usually an effective way to start.

One common tip for successful presentations is to 'start at the end' – in other words, to present the key point or argument in the introduction and then back it up with interesting facts and sub-theories and specifics throughout the presentation. This approach is likely to hook an audience and prepare them for the journey to follow.

Example

Where presentations go wrong…Poor beginnings

If you say: "Hello, can everyone hear me at the back?"
If you say: "There are still a few latecomers arriving, but we might as well get started now."
If you say: "I am so sorry if…"
If you say: "I'm not very good at this sort of thing"
If you say: "I am not sure why they asked me to do this"
If the audience start messing around with their notes or are not settled.

Activity 4

Presentation 1 - Effective Teams

To start writing this presentation, compose a three sentence introduction. This should follow the advice above and be learnt prior to the presentation being delivered.

(AAT Assessment criteria 1.3, 4.3)

3.2 The presentation: Key Points

A good presentation should be clearly divided into sections. Not only does this provide the audience with a structure they can follow, but it also helps the presenter to remember the contents easily.

There is a 'rule of three' which is widely followed for the main part of presentations. In other words, splitting the contents into three clearly distinguished subjects. This of course may not always be possible depending on the brief, but it will typically enable a presenter to focus on the most important aspects and to use a structure the audience will be familiar with.

To add cohesion to the presentation, many presenters will use simple tools such as alliterative or repetitive titles. For example, for a presentation on customer service could be sub-titled Communication; Client Care; Creating Value or How we speak; How we listen; How we act.

There are five common ways the following and main part of the presentation can go wrong:

1. Irrelevant information – even if an introduction focuses on the audience, sometimes they are forgotten the more the speaker elaborates

2. Inappropriate language – whether using too much jargon or just saying in three sentences what could be said in three words
3. Data overload
4. Lack of structure and cohesion
5. The power of PowerPoint

There are several devices used to structure presentations effectively, but perhaps most importantly, the presentation should tell a story. It should take the audience by the hand and walk them through the key points. Anecdotes and illustrations are particularly worthwhile to add some reality and a human perspective into business presentations. If this can relate to the presenter's own experience, this can also add to how people in the room relate to them. People tend to remember and share anecdotes, so a good one can really add value.

We will address the issue of humour here. If the presentation is a Best Man's Speech, a gag reel will be expected. However, in a business context, humour should be carefully utilised. Even for a fairly serious presentation, there needs to be light and shade to maintain interest and develop a sound relationship between the presenter and the audience.

Humour is obviously risky. If it works well, it will add an enormous amount to the presentation and how it is viewed. It must however be appropriate to the audience, in good taste and topical rather than personal. Lifting the mood of the room adds to the momentum of the presentation, but waiting for a laugh or showing the mannerisms of a stand-up comedian could be counterproductive.

If a presenter is uncomfortable telling jokes, quirky facts or statistics, tailored content to the audience or inserting a video clip could have a similar impact.

It is important that no presentation becomes too heavy and data-driven. Where statistics are used, it is crucial that they are done so with purpose and to make them digestible to the audience. When looking at presentation software, this will be addressed in more detail.

Example

Where presentations go wrong...Inappropriate or irrelevant content

If you say: "The next section is a bit boring too be honest"
If you say: "I am not sure why I included this"
If you say: "This bit might not be relevant to most of you"
If you say: "I am now going to cover these statistics in great depth"
If the audience appear bored due to data overload
If the audience do not respond well to your style or humour
If the audience cannot understand what your are saying
If the audience are simply staring at the slides.

Activity 5

Presentation 1 - Effective Teams

Returning to Presentation 1, identify your three big ideas which will form the main part of the presentation and under each topic come up with five sub-topics which will be covered.

(AAT Assessment criteria 1.3)

Activity 6

Presentation 1 - Effective Teams

Describe how the presentation will link key topics together and how pace, volume and different elements of the presentation can enable that key points are made effectively.

(AAT Assessment criteria 4.4, 4.5)

3.3 The presentation: The grand finish

One of the most common problems presenters face is that due to either poor timing or external factors (such as the previous contributor running late or a power cut), they run out of time to be able to express themselves effectively in their concluding section. This can have a seriously detrimental impact on their presentation, as the audience will be waiting for a key point or two to 'take away with them'.

If time is limited or the speaker is tired or flustered by the end of the presentation, it may well either be rushed or fizzle out completely. This will lead to an ineffective presentation as for most audiences, the last point is the point they will remember the most. Better practice would be a tight, thought-provoking finish, expressing a clear opinion or signposting an element of the presentation which requires further contemplation. A sound bite or a big rhetorical question are popular ways to achieve this.

Passion is important in the concluding section – if the presenter needs their audience to believe them and to adopt their viewpoint, they need to stress it in a convincing way. This will also enable them to end on a high. Where this is the case, the following process can be achieved:

Momentum of the presentation

↓

Passionate, tight conclusion

↓

Action points or thought processes initiated

↓

Applause and acceptance from audience

↓

Positive energy in the room

↓

Action points occur

Example

Where presentations go wrong…ineffective endings

If you say: "Sorry guys, we have run out of time so won't be able to cover the other things"

If you say: "Well that's about it from me really"

If you say: "Sorry to have taken up your time"

If you say: "Anyway, it is all covered in the pack so read up on it there"

If the audience have already started to clear away their things before you have finished speaking

If the audience cannot remember anything you said when you try to talk to them about it later.

Activity 7

Presentation 1 - Effective Teams

Returning to Presentation 1, compose the following:

a) Summaries you could include throughout the presentation – note the purpose of these

b) Your concluding section.

When completing this exercise, it may be a good opportunity to revisit the introductory section also.

(AAT Assessment criteria 2.4, 4.7)

Example

Let us consider how the above structure can work in three instances:

Mainwaring and Son's Conference – Chairman's keynote address
Introduction/Hook: Recently things have been going well but there are some areas for improvement moving forward.
Three key areas:
Good news: Things that have worked well recently in the stores.
Bad news: Things that have not worked well.
Future news: How things could look moving forward.
Conclusion:
If we follow the plan of action, we will go from strength to strength. The key is new staff training.

Windsor Electricals Sales pitch to Mooney Homes
Introduction/Hook: We have the solution that will make your business work better and save money in the meantime.
Three key areas:
We understand your problem.
We have the solutions.
We want to work with you.
Conclusion:
If you sign up for a long-term contract, we will ensure that your properties are better equipped for less money and in a quicker time than anyone else.

"How I made my first million" – Geoffrey's story of rags to riches in the restaurant trade
Introduction/Hook: Anyone can make a fortune with the right business plan.

Three key areas:
Understanding local culture.
Understanding local food.
Understanding local business.
Conclusion:
If you do enough research and embrace the market, you can make a fortune from a local hospitality.

3.4 Rehearsal and familiarisation

Having written the majority of the presentation, it is crucial to rehearse its contents to ensure that the timing, pace and delivery work effectively.

Most advice suggests that rehearsing the presentation as often as possible will lead to a better presentation on the day. This should be out loud, timed and as close to the real conditions as possible. If software is being utilised, this should also be part of the rehearsal as if the Slide content does not fit into the allowed time limit for the presentation, it is better to remove it in advance rather than rushing to get through them all or being forced to skip sections.

Given the importance of the start and end of a presentation, the opening and closing parts should be learnt and practised repeatedly to ensure the pace and tone are right. These aspects are critical for getting the audience's attention and making key points.

Familiarisation is also important, not just with the content but also the room and other conditions. Knowing the facilities available and how they may be utilised is crucial and this will also help to identify potential risks and problems and have a solution for each in turn (see section 5 for more detail on this).

Activity 8

Presentation 1 - Effective Teams

Rehearse your presentation at least three times under timed conditions. At the end of each trial run, make notes of what requires improvement and which parts did not flow properly. Explain any changes you made during the rehearsal process.

(AAT Assessment criteria 3.3, 3.4)

4 Delivering your presentation

4.1 The presenter

For the reasons above it is therefore the presenter's responsibility to keep the content relevant and give their audience reasons to listen to them.

The presenter's persona is crucial to the success of any presentation. The Mehrabian study looked at the factors which engage an audience with a presentation or speaker and therefore have the greatest impact on them.

The study found that 55% of the factors considered most important by the audience were from non-verbal indicators, such as body language. The audience was particularly responsive to confident speakers, who appeared knowledgeable and had the demeanour and posture to make them listen. 38% of engagement was attributed to verbal factors such as tone, pace and delivery. Only 7% of the impact came from the actual words spoken. For this reason, presenters need to be very aware of how they come across – 93% of the audience's positive responses were down to how they presented rather than what they said.

There are five key attributes any presenter should demonstrate in order to be effective:

- **Professionalism** – it is crucial to appear professional both in terms of attire and how the presenter conducts themselves. Appearing flustered by questions or mishaps or seeming ill-prepared or poorly equipped will cause the audience to lose faith in their expertise.
- **Passion** – in some business communications, a calm and considered approach is deemed appropriate, but in presentations this is not necessarily the case. Passion means that you genuinely care what you are talking about and without showing such enthusiasm for the topic, the presenter cannot expect others to have an interest either. Having said this, being too loud or forceful can cause the audience to object to the presenter's style, so the passion needs to have a cause.
- **Personality** – charisma and wit play a large part in sustaining interest and keeping the audience on side. To appear charming and funny will encourage an audience to listen and feel more comfortable.
- **Performance** – confidence is pivotal to the success of a presenter imparting their message. Some presenters are relatively quiet people away from a conference room but take on an alter ego when required. Presenters need to be energetic.

- **Personal expertise** – it is important for the presenter to add value and provide new knowledge or analysis in order to justify their status and win the audience's trust.

The value of alliteration will be covered later in the chapter in terms of helping to remember key points, but a further 'P' could be added to these five - the name of a software tool covered in the third section of this chapter.

The presenter's voice is vital. Although it is possible to change this and training can enable regular presenters to modify their standard tone (as has been the case for several high profile politicians and actors), presenters must be careful not to adopt a fake voice or start to mimic others. This is the equivalent of the so-called 'telephone voice' where people (whether consciously or subconsciously) try to sound more eloquent. In an informal setting, this could cause derision rather than concentration.

As a general rule, the presenter's voice needs to be strong and assertive, clear and well-paced (many people have a tendency to speak too quickly when under pressure and therefore others struggle to comprehend them). As with all aspects of the presentation, audiences will respond well to variation in tone as a means of direction – volume and intensity should therefore rise and fall accordingly.

As suggested by Mehrabian's 55% score, body language is also important. Audiences typically respond well to passion – they need to know that the presenter wants to be there and to engage with them. As with all communication, eye contact is essential. It has been said that presenters should be like lighthouses, revolving to have eye contact with the entire room. For this reason, those relying too heavily on looking at notes or their slides on a screen will lack a crucial connection with the audience. One of the largest criticisms of presenters who focus too closely on their visual aids is that their body language implies a lack of interest in their subject and focus on their audience.

The way a presenter stands and how they move their arms and legs is also important. Movement should be with purpose, rather than dancing around the area and distracting the audience. They should also ensure that they appear approachable – for this reason, it is often best to stand during presentations to larger groups, whereas sitting down will be better where the audience is smaller and more personal, informal approach would be effective. The main concern when deciding whether to stand or sit is how the sound will project to the audience – for this reason, added height may enable greater coverage across a large space, whereas a more directed approach from a lower angle can prove better if seated around a table or when the audience is in close proximity.

The final point on the presenter is that even if they are nervous (and some degree this is inevitable), they cannot risk being be too self-aware, as this can make the situation worse. Mark Twain said “there are only two types of speaker in the word: 1. The nervous and 2. Liars” and this quote has some credence. Nervous energy may not be wholly negative and can be controlled and used for the better, as we will see below.

4.2 Audience Interaction

Questions and Answers

To judge the reception of the presentation and ensure that the audience’s needs have been met, it is common to open the floor to questions at the end of a presentation. Only the most experienced presenters permit audience-created questions during the presentation, as these can be distractions and ruin the flow and thread of the presentation itself.

Presenters should anticipate and prepare responses to possible questions in advance and create some of their own to offer to the room should the audience fall silent.

Audience Participation

Depending on the brief of the presentation, in most cases, some form of audience interaction should have occurred prior to the Questions and Answers at the end. This can both keep the audience interested and check that the presentation is on track. Presenters can either ask questions and for a show of hands or vote, use rhetorical questions or make empathetic observations to keep their audience involved. It is important that the relationship with the audience remains respectful though and for this reason any humour directed at them as a group or as individuals must be carefully considered.

Social media has also allowed an extra dimension to audience participation at larger events. Using a conference-specific hashtag (e.g. #csrevent14) can allow direct communication from the audience and be utilised on the presenter’s terms. This could be used for suggesting topics or adding to a mini-debate from an issue raised.

Such audience interaction also allows seemingly natural break points for the presenter, if the presentation is particularly long. Asking a question for brief discussion or playing a video clip can add variety, enable the speaker to assess where they are up to and also give their voice time to recover.

Feedback forms have been commonplace at the end of seminars and conferences involving a series of presenters, so they may be a worthwhile exercise.

Activity 9

Presentation 1 - Effective Teams

Explain the purpose and benefits of giving the audience a chance to ask questions and participate throughout the presentation.

Think of:

a) Three ways you could involve the audience in the presentation

b) Three questions they might ask you

(AAT Assessment criteria 2.3, 2.5, 4.6, 4.10, 4.11)

5 Presentation software and visual aids

5.1 The role and purpose of visual aids

The remaining factor in the preparation of a presentation is the use and design of visual aids.

It is firstly worth noting that presenters have always had visual aids to enhance their speeches. As will be discussed later in the chapter, the cause for concern is that these aids can take over the presentation to the point where the audience is focusing on them and not the presenter. Of course, this is counter-productive and it must be remembered that they are there to help the presenter, not to replace them.

Visual aids are to support rather than dominate and if used effectively can:

- provide structure and prompts
- enhance the speech by adding colour to it
- create a brand image for the presenter or reinforce that of his/her company

5.2 Presentation software

The three most popular forms of presentation currently available are:

- PowerPoint
- Prezi (a cloud-based storytelling tool to enable information to be drawn from a variety of locations)

- Keynote (Apple's presentation package)

PowerPoint remains the most popular of these, so therefore this chapter will focus on this software, but the general ideas and guidelines will remain the same for any slideware.

The majority of this section will cover the software available to produce professional, sophisticated slide presentations which will wow your customers and colleagues. The ability to create mini-adverts on our screens and show these to others has undoubtedly added to fuel to face-to-face negotiations.

Microsoft has estimated that there are around 30 million PowerPoint presentations happening every day, with at least 1 million occurring at any given moment. This does not account for all of the other types of presentation software which can be used or other forms of visual aids.

Slides should have:

- Uniformity (for example, colours and fonts should be consistent)
- Clarity (for example, dark backgrounds or pastel fonts can make the slides unintelligible)
- Simplicity (for example, it is better to have lots of slides with less content as these will add to their impact and to overuse the 'bells and whistles' will only confuse or annoy an audience)
- Story (they should add to the storytelling)
- Purpose (for example, they could pose a question and then resolve it)
- Variety (they should use a number of different visual devices, animations and interactive elements)

There is no rule for the perfect PowerPoint Slide, but successful slides tend to feature pictorial or animated content and text in the form of questions or snappy statements. They are also created from scratch by the presenter. Slides which are text-heavy tend to alienate or bore the audience, especially if they are simply used as a script for the presenter to read from the screen.

If the words spoken in a presentation are identical to those on the Slides with no variation, this is an ineffective use of the software. Where this happens, not only will the presenter not be looking at the audience, but their perceived laziness will not be appreciated. Presenters are there to speak, not to read and if they rely on the latter, audience interaction will be limited.

Likewise, it is worth remembering that slides and handouts are different presentation tools with contrasting purposes. Slides are for visual impact and support, not for further reading. Therefore if the slides are also the handouts, the audience could question why they needed to personally attend the presentation, if the notes could have simply been sent to them.

It is important that the presenter does not have too many slides, as this can add extra pressure of the presentation. Trying to get through fifty slides will seem like climbing a mountain and the presenter can resort to merely trying to get to the end rather than imparting information and views passionately or effectively.

When referring to preparation, the content of the slides needs to be carefully considered. Sometimes presenters will start their preparation by opening up a software programme and typing random thoughts into slides without consideration for the overall presentation's message or purpose. Dumping such information into slides like will most likely result in too much data and tangential content. Likewise, using existing presentations or presentation templates as a base can lead to inappropriate or off-topic distractions for the audience.

A final cautionary note is that having a good slide presentation does not mean that rehearsal is not necessary. Although the computerised presentation can act as a prompt, if it is effective, it will not have enough detail to maintain interest and for this reason it is vital that the presenter establishes how to talk around the slides in advance.

5.3 Slide and slideshow creation

As discussed above, it is important to ensure that presentation software is used selectively and carefully. There can be a temptation to use the many functions on offer to entertain or amuse the audience, but it must be remembered that the presentation's objective is unlikely to be 'to show what PowerPoint can do'.

There are many different types of information which can enhance a presentation, in addition to text. Therefore, the following should be assessed in terms of their suitability for the audience:

- Text animations
- Slide transitions
- Images
- Charts and tables
- Video and animated sequences
- Sounds and audio clips

If used methodically, the above can all add colour and credence to a presentation.

Animating text – by using text animations, the presenter can reveal the contents of the slides sentence by sentence or section by section. This allows the slide to develop and for the content to be fed to the audience in the most effective way, with impact. If all text is always visible, the audience may read this as soon as the slide is shown and then stop listening. Different effects can be used to make these reveals more exciting.

Typically these effects are split into three groups: entrance, emphasis and exit. Examples of these include:

- Entrance: Appear, Fade, Fly in, Float in, Shape, Swivel, Wipe, Bounce.
- Emphasis: Pulse, Spin, Bold
- Exit: Fade, Wipe, Shrink and Turn

Slide transitioning – when moving from slide to slide, there are also a number of animation options.

The most popular are:

- Checkerboards, Blinds, Boxes, Ripple and Flash

Use of images – these should be appropriate and with purpose. Irrelevant images can seriously distract and detract from the content of the slide. For example, if the slide is addressing cost-saving measures, an image involving money or a light bulb to denote ideas may be appropriate, but a picture of a doctor would not be.

Charts and tables – the slides are a visual tool and therefore when presenting statistics, it is often best to do so using graphs or diagrams to provide an overall summary. These will grab the audience's attention and help them to comprehend and remember more complex analysis.

Video and audio – both video and audio clips provide great variety in a presentation and can break up long presentations by giving the presenter a rest and changing the audience's perspective. Client testimonials, for example, are often used. Animated sequences can have a similar impact, if professionally created. These allow for concepts to be translated often in a novel and therefore thought-provoking way.

5.4 Slide templates and themes

When creating new slides, there are a variety of different slide templates and themes which are set as standard and can be chosen from to save the user designing their content from scratch.

The layout template of the slide provides the structure into which content will be entered. There are a number of options available, including a Title Slide (suitable for the start of the presentation), Title and Content formats (to be used throughout the majority of the slideshow) and other more specific templates, for example the Content with Caption slides. As long as the slide format is appropriate to its content, a variety will probably be required.

Themes can also be established, using the Design tab. These enable the user to have a set background with options to change the colour, font and effects present. Mixing themes on the whole will confuse the audience, but these are useful tools if your company does not have its own template.

More likely than not, in a corporate context, the company will have a branded PowerPoint slide background and established format, which should be followed especially when presenting to external clients.

5.5 Text in a presentation

As indicated previously, it is important that presentations remain consistent in terms of their style. Therefore the presenter may not wish to radically alter fonts or colours in a presentation too often. Where this does happen, it should be for maximum impact. For example, different font sizes could be used to show the relative importance of different factors or different colours could be used to classify data.

At all times, consider:

- The font being used and if it is appropriate for the audience (if trying to appear serious and professional, a quirky or childish font will not work)
- The size of the font (it needs to be visible to everyone in the room)
- The colour of the font (which colours have the most impact or represent the point being made the best?)
- Whether forms of WordArt or SmartArt may help.

Due to their summative nature, presentations will include more bullet-points than many other forms of communication. These can be used effectively to structure the presentation and convey its key content. The format of the bullet-points is also important. For example, using a tick instead of a dot can show a productive and confident approach to the subject.

Using effects and animating text can bring topics to life. Examples of the sort of effects which can be used both within slides or part of slide transitions are listed above and rather than going through each individually, it will suffice here to say that these functions can make a real difference to a presentation. They can add an energy and tone to the content and if appropriately used, increase the professional appearance of it. This said, if there are animated effects the presenter must be careful that they do not take centre stage and therefore where possible should remain silent while they develop. Again, the audience must be considered carefully – over-use and effect overload can cause them to switch off and using some of the more novel effects (for example, bounce) could seem out of place with more serious or analytical content.

Crucially, the presenter will need to decide how to time the use of effects and the presentation as a whole. Timings can be introduced when the animation or effect is being added, so that content will automatically appear after a given time period. This is a useful device if the presentation has been well timed during rehearsals, but can be risky should the slides outpace the speaker (making them rush to say everything before the next slide or bullet-point appears) or vice versa. Most presenters will prefer to use a remote control as their trigger, as this allows greater control and some flexibility should the presentation veer slightly off track.

Activity 10

Presentation 1 - Effective Teams

Before creating your final presentation using software, see if you can create a shorter version where every slide simply contains one word. How might this be of use in terms of both preparation and delivery of the presentation?

5.6 Charts, tables and images in a presentation

There are many alternatives if the presenter wishes to add more graphical content to their presentation. For an accountant, most presentations are likely to include some statistical data and therefore pie charts, bar or column charts, scatter graphs, organisational charts, flow charts and doughnuts are all available and should be used to show content in a pictorial manner. To do so, use the Chart button on the Insert tab of PowerPoint.

In terms of images, options include actual photos, corporate brand images, clip art, screenshots or scanned images. Again, the Insert tab has a variety of image options available.

5.7 Video and audio in a presentation

To get the audience's attention or to further illustrate a key point in the presentation, the use of video or audio can be particularly effective. The Insert tab has a Media option, which allows both to be inserted.

The content here may have been recorded by the presenter in advance, for example from interviews with colleagues and clients. It could also have been downloaded from or linked to websites or media libraries. It is important that before using any video or audio from another source, that the copyright implications of doing so are considered.

Activity 11

Presentation 1 - Effective Teams

Detail how the following elements were included in your presentation and why/when you included them:

Content	Slide(s) where this appears	Reasons for inclusion
Main heading with impact		
Text		
Questions/quotes		
Numbers		
Animated text		
Graphics inc images		
Charts, tables, graphs and analytic diagrams		
Corporate style/messaging		
Sound		
Video		
Animation		
Weblink		

(AAT Assessment criteria (Presentation software) 1.1, 1.2, 1.3, 1.4, 2.1, 2.3, 2.5, 2.6)

5.8 Editing and saving a presentation

Even with the use of templates, many of the slides will required editing to ensure that they appear correctly in front of their audience. This can be particularly crucial if other sources are being used or previously created slides are being reworked. Resizing, repositioning and combining content will be required and all animated sections require thorough checking. As with all files, it is also essential that the presentation is saved according to company guidelines, ideally password protected to add to security.

5.9 Associated technology

Other associated technology includes remote controls and pointers. These can add to the effectiveness of a software presentation, but where limited use will impress the audience, overuse may frustrate them.

Activity 12

Presentation 1 - Effective Teams

One of your colleagues was asked to create a similar presentation in a previous role and has provided you with four slides from their presentation. Give at least one reason why each slide does not seem appropriate without amendment:

1.

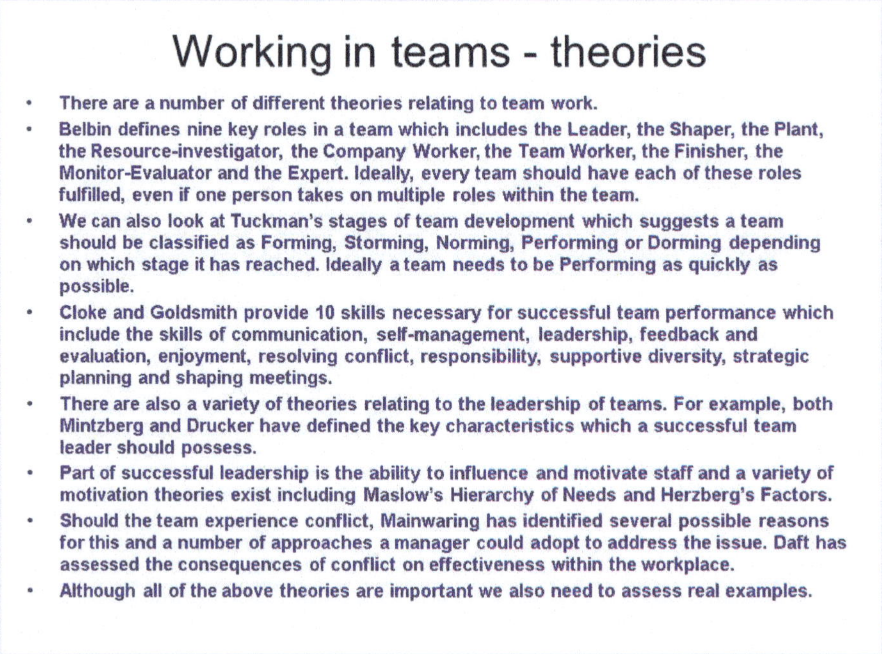

2.

Successful teams

- What makes a successful team?
- How can we achieve this?
- Where do we start?

3.

Successful teams - measurements

- Staff feedback
- ✓ Absenteeism
- ❑ PRODUCTIVITY
- ❖ *Knowledge of objectives*
- ▪ Collective spirit

4.

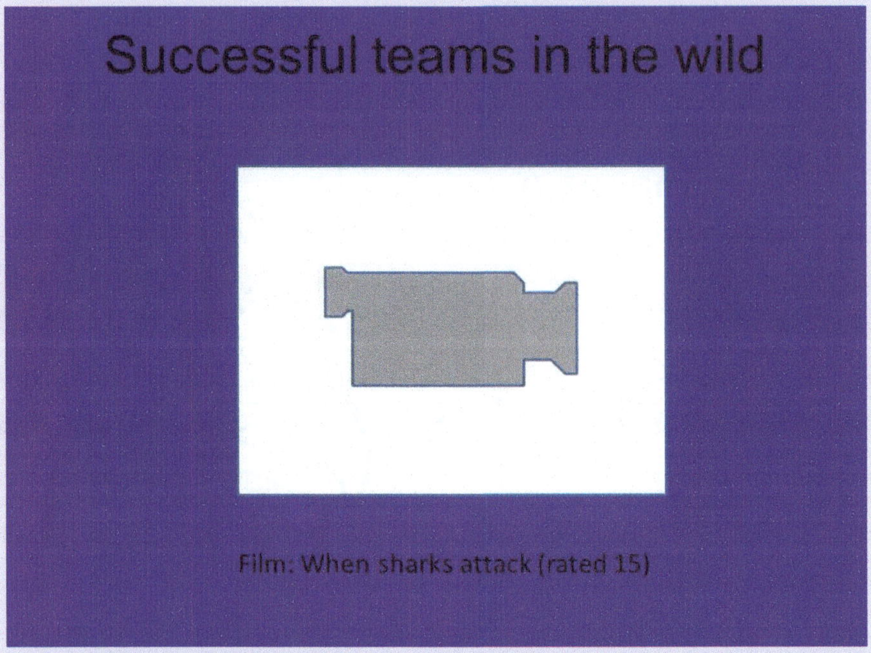

Using the above, explain some of the crucial elements that any slide template or background should contain.

(AAT Assessment criteria (Presentation software) 2.2)

5.10 Other visual solutions

However, more traditional methods should not be forgotten as they can be equally effective when used correctly.

These include:

- Flip charts – the paper-based alternative, more commonly used in meetings and workshops (as discussed in the next chapter), but equally useful for some parts of presentations. They may seem humble, but little can wrong. They can be reused and also prepared in advance if desired, although one of their other major advantages is that they can record interaction with the audience as it happens. One tip if writing flip chart notes up during the presentation is to mark the key points in small pencilled wording in the top corner prior to the presentation as a prompt the audience cannot see. One major drawback of flip charts is that larger audiences may struggle to read them and they rely on neat handwriting.
- Whiteboards – similar to the flip chart above, they allow for ideas to be noted and ordered as they happen and for the presenter to take a step-by-step approach to their explanations. Interactive whiteboards,

more commonplace in the training environment, can allow a mixture of these functions and the use of software above.

- Overhead Projectors – these allow the presenter to put up the equivalent of slides using transparent sheets. The presenter can then annotate throughout the presentation. This option can be seen as a little old-fashioned in a commercial context, but enables a good combination of the pre-prepared slide and the ability to make notes throughout, similar to an interactive whiteboard.
- Autocues – Perspex screens with a scrolling script are now often found surrounding a lectern in lecture halls and have their place in the commercial environment also. These allow the presenter to appear to be speaking to their audience, when in fact they are reading information on the screen. There is however some skill to pacing these speeches correctly so that the speaker and their speech on the screen stay synchronised. For this reason, they do not allow for ad libs or flexibility.

Example

Where presentations go wrong...unproductive visual aids
If you say: "I'm not sure if you can read this"
If you say: "Sorry, there is too much information on this slide"
If you say: "Let's skip the next twelve slides"
If the audience say: "Can you make the information bigger"
If the audience do not even look at the slide
If the audience seem so preoccupied with the slide they are not listening
If equipment does not work

Activity 13

Presentation 1 - Effective Teams

Create the final PowerPoint slideshow for your presentation. Make a record of how you made amendments to the presentation over time (including formatting, resizing and changing of animated content/images) and how you designed the interactive slideshow to link the slides together.

Include accompanying speaker notes for the presentation, hand-outs if applicable and timings/effects.

(AAT Assessment criteria (Presentation software) – 1.6, 1.7, 2.2, 2.4, 3.2)

Activity 14

Presentation 1 - Effective Teams

Imagine that the presentation was actually for a group of GCSE Business Studies students – how would the content differ and why?

(AAT Assessment criteria (Presentation software) 3.1)

Activity 15

Presentation 1 - Effective Teams

Provide an example of another type of visual aid which could used in addition to slides and design or plan the content or context accordingly.

(AAT Assessment criteria 1.2, 2.1)

6 Contingency Planning

6.1 The disaster checklist

Due to the reliance on different forms of equipment to deliver the presentation, a key part of preparation is the creation of a so-called disaster checklist. This should be an honest risk assessment of all factors associated with the presentation and involve a series of last-minute checks.

The exact nature of the checklist will depend on the individual, but typically the following twenty elements would be checked.

1. The date, time and location of presentation is known
2. The room facilities and layout are clear
3. The audience's nature and objectives have been identified
4. Presentation structure is in place
5. Start and end are learnt
6. The content has been well rehearsed
7. Slides are prepared to include required content and timings
8. Spelling and grammar on handouts and slides is accurate
9. Separate speaker's notes are to hand

10. Technology is working – laptop, projectors, electricity, internet access, microphones, lighting
11. Files and internet links are easily available
12. Associated technology is present – pointers, remote controls
13. All visual aids have been tested
14. Non-technological equipment is in place and working – paper, pens, handouts
15. Questions and answers have been prepared
16. Back-up slides and content is ready
17. Previous feedback has been considered
18. Other elements to the day's agenda are known
19. Water and refreshment are available
20. Key audience members and audience sensitivity are established

Having a contingency plan to address issues is vital. For example, what would happen if something went wrong with the PowerPoint presentation? A back-up is required: as a minimum ensure the presentation is saved in at least three places (e.g. on your laptop's hard drive, on a USB stick and in a file-sharing area such as your company's network drives or a virtual data storage facility such as The Cloud. Experienced presenters go so far as to have a spare laptop or their own projector. Likewise if there is no electricity, ensure that you have a print-out of the presentation so you can replicate it on a flip chart or whiteboard.

It is not only technology that can fail. For example, pens can run out of ink, presenters can lose their voices and lunch could have been unavoidably late – as the presenter, all such events should be planned for.

The more experienced you become at presentations, the more worthwhile it is to keep notes of the standard material that worked well previously – this can be perfect to fall back on should the presentation not be going to plan.

Activity 16

Presentation 1 - Effective Teams

Create a checklist and contingency plan in preparation for the delivery of the presentation above.

(AAT Assessment criteria 1.5, 1.6, 3.2, 4.1), Presentation software 3.3, 3.4)

7 Assessing your presentation

7.1 Important questions for the audience

It is crucial that when assessing your presentation, you focus on the quality of the communication rather than the quality of the information. Not all experts are necessarily great presenters and just because you may have shared some excellent and thought-provoking points does not mean that the audience listened or understood them in context.

As suggested above, the most important people in the presentation are the audience and therefore it is important to gauge their reactions throughout the presentation as well as their final analysis at the presentation's conclusion. Although informal feedback could be provided through conversations with the audience afterwards, it is crucial to establish some key questions on which the presentation may be judged and could form a feedback questionnaire. Below are some examples.

1. Was the audience engaged?
2. Was the presentation easy to follow?
3. Could the presenter be clearly heard and seen throughout?
4. Did the presenter introduce themselves and the topic?
5. Were the audience hooked from the start?
6. Did the audience understand the key points?
7. Did the audience relate to the presenter?
8. Did the presenter use appropriate body language?
9. Were audience interaction and/or questions encouraged?
10. Did the visual aids show information in a clear and concise manner?
11. Were animations and images used with purpose and impact?
12. Was the balance between information and presentation correct?
13. Did the presenter summarise throughout the presentation?
14. Did the presentation end with strong conclusions?
15. Did the presentation leave key questions unanswered?

Feedback is important to any presenter as it allows them to identify the strengths and weaknesses of the presentation and look to improve for future presentations. Sometimes presenters feel that they have conveyed their message in a convincing manner but later find out the audience failed to respond to any of their calls to action. Without feedback it can be difficult to judge why this happened. For example, the presenter may not be aware of issues with sound or display when in full flow or may have misunderstood the brief.

As suggested above, it is also crucial that the presenter seeks to engage the audience or accurately gauge their reaction throughout so that negative feedback can be avoided. Encouraged interaction may highlight audience reaction, as may body language or actions such as relentless fidgeting, chatting amongst themselves or focusing too closely/obsessively on either hand-outs or the screen. Relaxed and open body language, nodding heads and laughter are all good signs and as such imply the presenter can continue as planned. Should the audience however seem distracted, hostile or bored, the presenter should react accordingly and use a backup plan.

Activity 17

Presentation 1 - Effective Teams

Design a ten question audience feedback form for your presentation.

Make a list of three benefits of this exercise.

(AAT Assessment criteria 1.7, 5.1)

7.2 Self-assessment and evaluation

As indicated above when referring to the ability to change approach should the audience's reaction not be as desired, it is crucial to self-evaluate throughout the presentation.

At the end of the presentation, it is also important to assess how the presentation could have been better. Part of this process will involve elements of which the audience may be unaware. For example, there may have been gaps in the preparation or arising difficulties were not addressed by the disaster checklist. Likewise, the presentation may have been entertaining but not necessarily informative, which could be a problem is this was the primary objective.

Activity 18

Presentation 1 - Effective Teams

Give three benefits of evaluating your own performance in a presentation.

After the presentation, complete the following self-assessment:

Element	Strengths	Areas for improvement	Mark out of 10
Preparation and research			
Rehearsal			
Introduction			
Aims / objectives			
Language and eloquence			
Use of voice, tone and pace to emphasise points			
Body language and gestures			
Use of visual aids, software and equipment			
Hand-outs and other information			
Response to arising issues			
Audience participation and reaction			
Informed responses to questions			
Summaries and links throughout			
Strong, passionate end			

(AAT Assessment criteria 1.8)

(If all of the above have been incorporated, AAT Assessment criteria 4.2, 4.3, 4.4, 4.5, 4.6, 4.7, 4.8, 4.9, 4.10, 4.11)

From this evaluation, it is important to look at ways to improve for the following presentation. This could involve the creation of new resources, a different approach, or a change in the style and/or format of the content. In some cases, communication training may help.

This is not to say that if, for example, humour failed it should not be attempted again and likewise with interactive or animated elements. Extra rehearsal and preparation may however be required.

Activity 19

Provide a written evaluation of the presentation, listing points of strength and areas for improvement. Identify at least five points to enable future improvement and development when making presentations.

(AAT Assessment criteria 5.2, 5.3)

7.3 A further example of a presentation

Activity 20

Butterworths have been asked to provide a speaker at the National Garden Exhibition to present to a group of one hundred retailers in the garden equipment sector.

Nataliya, who is responsible for marketing within the company, needs to write an internal memo to ask for suitable candidates. Which key requirements and personal attributes should Nataliya stress to interested employees?

(AAT Assessment Criteria 2.2)

Activity 21

Let us return to the garden exhibition where a representative of Butterworths was due to present to trade buyers. Nataliya had selected Henrik to undertake the task and received the following feedback from the audience.

A. The presenter was very passionate

B. The audience were able to check their e-mails and talk between themselves during the presentation

C. The presentation told the audience things they already knew

D. There were lots of opportunities for the audience to be involved

E. The presenter provided good hand-outs to take away

F. The presenter seemed modest and unsure of himself

G. The presenter told a lot of jokes which seemed out of place

H. The presenter made personal comments about members of the audience

I. The presenter used lots of images to make the presentation more exciting

J. Sometimes the images on the screen seemed quite strange

K. There was a thought-provoking video which really explained the way the company works

L. I was not sure what the point of the presentation was

M. The last few slides seemed to be totally ignored as he ran out of time

Required:

a) Which of the comments suggest that the presentation was effective?

b) On the whole, should Henrik be asked to present again based on this feedback and how could he improve his performance?

c) When asked about his performance, Henrik told Nataliya, "I am the best person at using PowerPoint and that is the only thing that matters in presentations." Discuss whether this view is correct.

Activity 22

Presentation 2 – Project Finances

At the end of Chapter 11, you will be required to present your analysis of the project. Make notes on what worked well and what could be improved with your experience on Presentation 1. Provide analysis of audience feedback and your own self-assessment.

Answers to chapter activities

Activity 1

Presentations are so widely used in business because they allow the presenter to convey a message to a wider audience than other verbal communication and also to add colour to this message. They are particularly useful where a lot of data needs to be translated for an audience or for any form of negotiation or persuasion.

There are different types of business presentation, including informal, information-giving presentations and external pitches to win business. Different audiences will present varied challenges to the presenter, but there are definite career and personal benefits to being able to communicate effectively in this environment.

Activity 2

This answer will be dependent on the individual's experience, but should, without stereotyping the audience, show how different types of presentation require alternative approaches. For example, typically younger audiences or peers will respond well to a more relaxed, humorous style and perhaps be more open to interactive elements and video/animation. This said, those who are not as technologically aware may appreciate the effects more as they will have greater impact.

Activities 3-19

Presentation 1 - Effective Teams

The completion of these activities will enable the successful preparation, delivery and evaluation of the presentation above. Largely therefore no specific feedback can be provided, however where questions incorporate some theory or explanation, this is below.

Activity 9

Involving the audience not only adds variety to a presentation, but it also provides a crucial way to ensure they are engaging with the content and that their needs are being met and questions answered. Presentations are not one-way communication and it is vital that the presenter seeks both explicit and implied feedback (such as body language) throughout.

Questions can be seen as tests of the presenter's knowledge and therefore it is vital to prepare for these adequately. In many ways, this may be the most constructive and practical element of a presentation as the audience are likely to want to put key ideas to the test and see how they could work in reality.

Activity 12

The following criticisms apply to the colleague's slides:

1) This is far too text heavy and as a result is both boring and difficult for the audience to read. It also is written in full sentences and so could easily form a script for the presenter, possibly meaning reduced interaction with the audience.
2) In this instance, the image is totally inappropriate for either a business presentation or for the subject matter.
3) The inconsistency in colours, fonts and styling is a distraction in this slide. Most likely given this haphazard approach, animations would also be random and therefore provide a lack of consistency which would cause confusion rather than impact.
4) There are two main issues with this slide, the background colour is too dark for the text to be visible. Also the video content does not seem relevant or appropriate to the audience.

Therefore some of the crucial elements which should be addressed would include:

- Easy to read text – in terms of size, font, background colours
- Appropriate video and images
- Consistent formatting and awareness of corporate bland
- Variety and interesting content

Activity 14

For a group of school students, more animations and images may be required to keep their interest. Also any 'heavy' or more serious content or theories could be removed.

Activity 17

Benefits of this exercise include:

- The audience's understanding can be evaluated – did they

comprehend the key messages and get the answers they required

- They presentation style can be assessed to see if there is room for improvement – for example, did the audience pick up on points being emphasised and how did they feel about the presenter's body language
- Depending on what went well, the presenter will know which strengths to play to moving forward
- Areas for greater preparation can be noted for the future
- Follow-up from the presentation can be adjusted to cover any gaps
- A comparison can be made with self-evaluation to see how accurate this is

Activity 18

The benefits of self-assessment include:

- To inform planning for future presentations
- Evaluation of whether the audience responded as desired
- Establishing things that worked well and could be utilised again
- Highlighting areas for future improvement (possibly to organise relevant training)
- Creating audience profiles for future use to enable effectiveness

Activity 20

Nataliya should focus on the five P's for successful presenters:

- Professionalism
- Passion
- Personality
- Performance
- Personal expertise

She could therefore ask for someone who is:

- A good communicator, who is outgoing and confident
- Has a passion for a particular subject or the company itself and therefore would like to share their ideas
- Is used to speaking or performing in front of large groups of people

- Is able to communicate in a clear and concise manner
- Is knowledgeable
- Enjoys discussing ideas with others
- Is able to use the relevant equipment
- Is looking for career development

When deciding on who would be best for the role, she should also consider who has the time required to prepare and rehearse effectively.

Activity 21

a) Positive comments included:

A The presenter was very passionate

D There were lots of opportunities for the audience to be involved

E The presenter provided good hand-outs to take away

I The presenter used lots of images to make the presentation more exciting

K There was a thought-provoking video which really explained the way the company works

b) On the whole it seems that Henrik's presentation had considerable problems. Despite his passion and embracing technology, it seems that some of his humour and the images he used were not appropriate to the audience. Nerves may have had a detrimental impact, as his modesty was noted and could have caused the inappropriate and personal use of humour.

The presentation also seems poorly practiced and prepared as he ran out of time and seemed to be lacking a clear structure, message or objective.

All of these factors could have been part of the reason the audience seemed so distracted.

c) Henrik's reliance on the software could in many ways explain the problems he encountered. As some of the images were strange and confusing and the message was not clear, it seems he forgot the audience's needs and relied too heavily on the visual aids. Where deviating from the slide content, he also seemed to fail to engage the audience and may have even offended some. Therefore, although he used a good video and the slide content may have been good in places, Henrik's example shows the importance of a confident, well organised and charismatic presenter who the audience can relate to.

It should also be stressed that there are other forms of visual aid other than PowerPoint and for variety, he could have maybe used a whiteboard or flip chart to record the interaction with the audience, for example.

Activity 19

Presentation 2 – Project Finances

See Chapter 11.

Organising and facilitating meetings and workshops

7

Introduction

Whereas presentations enable individuals to convey corporate information or promotional messages to an audience, other forms of internal and external communication allow for greater interaction.

The participative nature of meetings and workshops allows for greater discussion, the sharing of ideas and the setting of priorities. If these activities are well organised and effectively led, they can be valuable tools for the daily running of the business and the successful negotiation of new contracts.

This chapter will look at the different forms of meeting and workshop and explain the process behind their planning and content.

ASSESSMENT CRITERIA

1 To understand the responsibilities involved in arranging meetings and workshops

2 To assess how to facilitate and structure meetings and workshops to ensure that objectives are met

3 To assess the different forms of communication and presentation within meetings and workshops

4 To be able to lead meetings and workshops and be aware of requirements during and after their facilitations

CONTENTS

1 The role and purpose of meetings and workshops
2 Planning and scheduling
3 Structure and content
4 Group participation
5 Leading meetings and workshops
6 Summary

1 The role and purpose of meetings and workshops

1.1 Definitions

Definition

A meeting is a gathering of two or more people that has been convened for the purpose of achieving a common goal through verbal interaction and the discussion of one or more identified topics.

Crucially therefore, meetings are characterised by the common goal the participants share. This will be examined in more detail in this chapter, but the three most common objectives of meetings are:

- to share and appraise information
- to discuss viewpoints
- to reach a conclusion or negotiate agreement

Definition

A workshop involves a small number of active participants meeting in order to share ideas and generate plans in a specific context.

Whereas some meetings are dominated by senior participants, workshops are very much a meeting of minds and as such interaction and the exchange of ideas are vital.

Like all forms of communication, meetings and workshops can be formal or informal and can involve both internal and external stakeholders.

1.2 The role and purpose of meetings

Meetings are crucial to ensure the continual exchange of information and participation of those required to deliver objectives.

Intracompany meetings

These are internal meetings, usually only attended by employees of the company. The following are typically formal, but could be held informally depending on those involved and the matters being addressed (for example, environmental or social responsibility issues may be appropriately handled in a less corporate manner).

Types of internal meeting include:

- Board meetings (to decide strategy from higher level discussions)
- Committee meetings (tend to address serious corporate governance issues and as such are formal and often investigative)
- Cross-departmental management meetings (horizontal communication to implement board level decisions across the organisation)
- Operational meetings (similar to the cross-departmental meetings, but involving lower level, day-to-day decisions)
- Staff meetings and briefings (usually departmental, these feature specialised, vertical communication from a manager to their reports)
- Performance-related meetings (for individuals and departments to maintain accountability and a line of command)
- Investigative meetings (often for disciplinary reasons or issues relating to human resources)
- Team or project meetings (for special interests, more likely to have more of a mixture of participants involved)
- Off-site meetings (sometimes known as 'away days' in the UK, these meetings give a different dimension)

Intercompany meetings

- Conferences and Seminars (companies or professionals with shared interests across industry sectors or geographical boundaries meet to decide common policies)
- Pre-bid meetings (prior to the business development meetings below, these enable constructive research and for all concerned to establish and overview of mutual objectives and working practices)
- Business development meetings (where one company 'pitches' for business from another or seeks agreement on terms of agreements)
- Performance-related meetings (to discuss how the commercial partnership and any productivity/service level agreements are working in action)
- Team or project meetings (relating to a particular project and discussing the responsibilities and activities of the two or more companies involved – see below example)

One of the greatest criticisms of meetings is that they can be a waste of time. To challenge this belief, it is important that meetings have a clearly defined purpose. As with any form of communication, if the meeting or workshop does not have clear objectives, it is unlikely to prove productive. Where the meeting involves several people with varied interests, irrelevant content may take precedence if the purpose is not known or enforced.

Examples of the purpose behind meetings include:

Intracompany meetings

- to form strategy by making and implementing decisions – particularly evident at the top of the management hierarchy, but the process can also involve more junior staff in companies where participative management is encouraged
- to share ideas and accountability – meetings are essentially a democratic process and promote collective responsibility and decision-making
- to inform staff of developments – it is often more effective to convey the latest news in person and meetings allow direct communication to a group of feedback, as well as an opportunity for them to respond
- to oversee and assess progress – sometimes it can be difficult to judge how previously determined goals are being delivered without sitting down to analyse this
- to discuss internal and external threats and opportunities
- to assert structure and control - managers can use meetings to co-ordinate activities and exert influence over their team
- to manage and develop staff – one-on-one meetings are particularly valuable to monitor performance
- to develop a team or group ethic amongst the participants
- to motivate those involved – managers can use meetings to ensure their team 'buy in' to ideas and are inspired to deliver

Intercompany meetings

- to establish customer and client needs
- to negotiate terms
- to analyse performance and progress
- to promote the brand and policies
- to provide information
- to solve emerging issues
- to add a personal dimension to written communications
- to share good practice and market intelligence
- to develop team ethics and mutual motivation

Example

To show how meetings can be used throughout a project, we can return to the example of Mainwaring and Sons, the men's clothing retailer who are looking to open new high street stores.

A series of meetings are held throughout the course of the project:

- **Senior Management Strategy Meeting** - the board of directors and senior managers met to decide the policy of opening new stores. During this meeting, more informal sub-meetings were agreed, as well as an overall objective for the project and the creation of the project team.
- **Internal Kick-off Meeting** – this was the first meeting of the project team at Mainwaring and Sons. It enabled the team members to introduce themselves, discuss the objectives for the project and clarify their responsibilities for the early stages of research and recruitment.
- **External Stakeholder Initiation Meeting(s)** – these meetings sought feedback from those who could either play a role in the project (e.g. suppliers such as construction companies) and those to be affected by it (e.g. local government).
- **Operational Meeting** – this meeting was chaired by the project manager, establishing the organisational structure and culture of the team and guidelines for future activities and meetings.
- **Informal Project Team Meetings** – held on almost a daily basis, these meetings were sometimes held across the office and without the structure of formal operational and progress review meetings.
- **Internal Progress Review Meetings** – these periodic meetings (typically monthly but on a more frequent basis towards the end of the project) were typically formal in structure with an agenda and members of the team reporting on their function. At Mainwaring and Sons, the progress in terms of finances, technology, human resources, community liaison, logistics and marketing were reported at each meeting.
- **Bidding Meetings (including Pre-Bid Meetings)** – hosted by the project manager, these meetings allowed contractors to familiarise themselves with the services expected and then to bid for the business. Mainwaring and Sons made attendance at these meetings mandatory for those interested in bidding.
- **Sub-contractor Progress Review Meetings** – similar to the internal meetings above, the project manager and key members of

the team frequently met with suppliers to review their individual and collective progress in terms of key points of action. Typically, these meetings were formal and with one sub-contractor per meeting and included weekly updates from the construction company and infrequent meetings with others such as the signage company, EPOS provider and solicitors.

- **Emergency meetings** – arranged only when the project ran into extreme and unforeseen difficulties, these meetings involved internal and external participants. The main focus was to seek the resolution to emerging problems rather than to inform. Issues caused by the refusal of planning permission and therefore needing to find a new site at short notice led to an emergency meeting being called at Mainwaring and Sons.
- **Sign-off meeting** – at the conclusion of each major stage of the project (e.g. refurbishment and refit of retail premises, local media marketing and promotions), a meeting was held to sign-off the task. This included the payment of suppliers for satisfactory work.
- **Completion meeting** – after the conclusion of all sign-off meetings with individual suppliers, this meeting was held for the project manager to seek the final agreement of the board to the project.
- **Review and Reflection meetings** – these meetings were held to allow all parties to learn lessons from the process. Feedback was exchanged and, with the stores now operational, the project team what they could have done differently and future strategy.
- **Community meetings** – these meetings were held shortly after the store openings. By open invitation, these allowed local government officials, the general public and other secondary stakeholders to seek information and have their say.

Activity 1

Kenneth is the Managing Director of Windsor Electricals. He is becoming increasingly concerned that every time he walks through Douglas' departmental office the team seem to be having a meeting in their conference room.

Douglas is asked to give five reasons why he feels the need to meet with his team so regularly.

Suggest the types of meeting Douglas could be holding and provide five different purposes he could be seeking to achieve in the meetings.

1.3 The role and purpose of workshops

Although workshops are a form of meeting, they are different in their structure and purpose.

As defined above, workshops tend to have a smaller and more specialised set of participants. They are often similar to focus groups in that they have a very specific purpose but a fluid structure to allow free-flowing communication between participants. Workshops engender a different mind-set to other standard meetings due to their encouragement of several different viewpoints and a team-based approach.

Workshops are often run by facilitators, who are sometimes neutral with no stake in the workshop's outcome. They empower expert participants to share their ideas, often by working through scenarios, activities or questionnaires in small groups. Although there is a place for facts and statistics, workshops tend to focus more on analysis and opinion. Those involved can be creative and the unorthodox can be considered.

Workshops can either make recommendations to the business or be tasked to achieve instant results. If the latter is the case, they can be an extremely efficient and quick way of making team-based decisions.

Their collaborative nature results in instant buy-in from those involved due to a feeling of mutual responsibility. As such, the inclusion of workshops in decision-making can change the organisational culture of a company.

Example

Mainwaring and Sons have decided to implement a brand new training programme for the additional recruits required for their new stores. During their management meeting, Farhan (the Project Manager) and Nataliya (Head of Human Resources) have been tasked to create the programme using the expertise of all departments in the business.

In order to get input from a variety of departments and across all levels of the organisational hierarchy of the company, the two managers decide to set up a workshop.

The main objective of the workshop is to use collective experience to form a new training programme and recommend changes to the company's staff development policy and mechanisms.

The workshop will include eight participants:

- Nataliya – the Head of Human Resources, the department responsible for implementing the training
- Sian – a member of the accounts team who has been with the company for twenty-five years

- Steve – although he has only been with Mainwaring and Sons for a short time, the Head of Operations and Logistics has worked for a number of other well-known retailers
- Darren – an Assistant Manager at one of the flagship stores who is known for his creative thinking
- Graham – a Store Manager from a different store known for his expertise in staff training and attention to detail
- Maninder – a Marketing Assistant who is young and dynamic, with a degree in business strategy
- Kasper – seen as an innovator, he is an integral part of the team Farhan has been managing. He looks to improve systems and will revert to a quality assurance role when the project is completed
- Belinda – the company's Social Secretary who is also a trained counsellor

Although Nataliya will participate as a key internal stakeholder, it has been decided that an independent, outside facilitator would be better to provide impartiality and focus on the mechanics of the day. This will be Jean-Claude, a local businessman who has worked with Mainwaring and Sons extensively in the past, as the owner of a company specialising in recruitment and employment law.

Farhan will act as the scribe and recorder and will not participate in the actual discussions in order to concentrate on providing reliable and accurate records of the decisions reached.

This workshop possesses:

- A clear purpose and reason
- A good mix of participants (varied status, skills, expertise, experience and departments)
- Structured and constructive leadership.

1.4 Advantages of meetings and workshops

Meetings and workshops therefore have many advantages. They bring people from different perspectives together to make decisions and discuss issues for the greater good of a company or business partnership. This can lead to fewer rash decisions and a sense of genuine acceptance due to the involvement of diverse business interests. This said, they can cause slow decision-making, a lack of individual accountability for poor performance and are often vulnerable to unnecessary compromise and members pushing their own agenda.

2 Planning and scheduling meetings and workshops

2.1 Key considerations

Like all forms of event management, meetings and workshops require careful organisation and a sound awareness of the people, locations and systems involved. A rule of thumb of facilitation is that successful meetings are 80% preparation and 20% execution.

When facilitating meetings, it is therefore crucial to look at the criteria for effective meetings above and ensure that all are met throughout the process. To plan a meeting effectively, the organiser must firstly ascertain:

- Why is the meeting being held?
- Who is attending?
- When should it need to be held?
- Where should it be held?

Activity 2

Douglas is a manager at Windsor Electricals. He has asked his administrative assistant, Priya, to arrange a cross-departmental meeting to discuss the implementation of the new guidelines for operational efficiency as the board feel some departments are not implementing the guidelines correctly. This is deemed a key business policy.

Priya contacts all members of the company and asks them to attend a meeting, although she does not specify the reasons for it. Although she indicates that the meeting will be the following Wednesday in the company's conference room, she does not give any timings or provide any further information.

Give three reasons why Priya's actions are unlikely to result in an effective meeting.

2.2 Determining the participants

It is essential that the correct people attend the meeting. Some meetings and workshops lose their sense of direction and prove ineffective because those involved in the issue are not present and those whose interests are peripheral start to dominate.

The participants of most meetings are obvious, with attendance being inherent to their roles within the organisation. For example, a board meeting will automatically include all board members and a marketing meeting will necessarily involve managers in the marketing department.

Where this is not the case, the person calling the meeting will usually have decided who should be involved when reaching the conclusion a meeting was required in the first place. However, it sometimes falls to other staff to schedule meetings without sufficient guidance.

There are five key aspects to consider when deciding the invitees:

- The purpose of the meeting
- The strategic level of the meeting
- The role of the meeting in terms of general business activities
- The areas of expertise and knowledge required
- The timing/location of the meeting and personal/social considerations

For example, if the purpose of the meeting does not indicate high level decisions will be made, there is no need for a member of the board to be invited. And if the meeting is regarding financial planning for the production of materials, there would be little requirement for someone from the marketing team to attend.

If the meeting is not integral to the delivery of the business objectives (for example, if decisions are likely to be made via e-mail at a later time), it may not be a priority for potential invitees. Likewise, if the meeting is fairly routine, inviting outsiders (especially from higher ranks in the company) would be inappropriate.

Participants therefore need to be appropriate, available and adding value in terms of their expertise and personal characteristics. The commonly held view is that for effective meetings, the number of people needs to be reduced to only those necessary to accomplish the goal.

Activity 3

Priya is an administrative assistant at Windsor Electricals. She has been asked to schedule two meetings for next week:

1. The monthly board meeting to determine the organisation's strategy moving forward
2. A meeting to discuss an unhappy medium-sized client who believes their orders are always delivered late

Who should Priya invite to the above meetings?

2.3 Scheduling

In the modern world, most of the planning of meetings can be achieved using technology. With synchronised calendars operating through internal computer systems, mobile devices and the company's CRM system, it is possible for schedules to be viewed concurrently and events and information to be co-ordinated from conception to conclusion.

Having identified a list of potential attendees, although it is possible to invite them to attend using a normal conversational telephone call, memo or e-mail, this can be a time-consuming and complicated process. Even if the organiser has a date and time in mind, the personal approach is reliant on people responding quickly and allows for negotiation, causing conflict if participants feel that their needs are not being acknowledged.

Although there is no 'correct' way to schedule a meeting, it is sound practice to identify the two or three key participants first and offer them a choice of times. If the meeting is internal, most likely the senior manager(s) will take priority, if an external client is involved, they will most likely be most important. This hierarchy is crucial to determine because a business development meeting without a client or a management meeting with only junior staff are pointless. Priorities of others will need to be changed and diaries adjusted if necessary.

It is crucial to keep a record of all confirmed attendees and any special requirements (a spreadsheet or diary being the norm). If the meeting is a significant period in the future, a confirmation or reminder is often advisable via e-mail if desired.

With computerised calendars, it should be easier to suggest times based on a knowledge of availability, but the bigger the group, the fewer options that should be presented. Even where key attendees are given respect and priority, it is crucial for the organiser to set the options for them to decide from. Asking for everyone to suggest convenient times is too ambiguous.

Although the above process is more personal, scheduling meetings and workshops can now be automated for increased efficiency. Most IT systems have file sharing systems and meeting proposal facilities are now part of standard e-mail setup. These allow an organiser to propose a meeting to everyone collectively. Having accepted or declined this invitation, the attendee will consequently find the appointment in their calendar, with an optional reminder scheduled. This approach enables greater co-ordination and the recipient can be aware of the other confirmed attendees. If we were to take the use of technology to its extreme, the event may be even logged via social media.

When scheduling meetings, the following points should be considered:

- the method being used (personal or automated)
- the calendar/diary system (paper-based or computerised)
- the tone of communications (informal or formal)
- the nature of proposed timings (rigid or open for negotiation)
- the level of information (a simple Yes/No or more detail)

> **Activity 4**
>
> Consider your own work experience and think of a meeting or workshop you feel would be worthwhile to improve the performance of the business.
>
> Required:
>
> 1 Decide on a list of participants and give appropriate reasons for their inclusion.
>
> 2 Plan how you will invite the participants to attend the meeting and give reasons for your approach.
>
> 3 Draft an e-mail or memo to all of the proposed participants to provide them with the information they require prior to the meeting.
>
> (AAT Assessment criteria 1.1)

2.4 Timing and frequency

Having determined the participants, the timing and venue need to be decided. For an effective meeting or workshop, conditions need to be conducive to productive work and convenient for the participants.

Meetings can be one-off events (usually the case if discussing something short-term or specific) or recurring (usually the case if delivering strategic objectives). One-off meetings are ad hoc in nature and therefore the mix of people in attendance will vary from meeting to meeting.

If recurring, meetings are typically be weekly, fortnightly, monthly or annually and often on the same day and time for ease of planning. Usually arrangements for the next meeting are a final point of discussion at the previous one.

In terms of productivity, ideal times to meet would be:

- when most key people are available
- when the participants have something worthwhile to say (often frequently held meetings can prove repetitive)
- when everyone involved can focus on the meeting and individuals

are not preoccupied with other concerns

- when minds are active and relationships are positive (late on a Friday afternoon for example may not be a good time to meet, some suggest 9am or 3pm as optimum times)
- the start of a week/cycle/year is often a good time for a meeting to energise and cover a lot of ground
- the end of a week/cycle/year is often a good time for a meeting to reflect and analyse

2.5 Locations

The setting for a meeting or workshop can help to define its tone and have an impact on the behaviour of those involved.

For example, a formal boardroom would typically be used for high level discussions between senior management, whereas a staff meeting can be held in the middle of the office as long as the manager maintains control. For more creative meetings, quirky or colourful locations may be used, whereas for reflection or analysis, the venue will normally be the opposite.

For the reasons above, it is vital that those in the meeting feel comfortable and happy to express themselves. This would normally mean that it is best to conduct meetings in quiet surroundings without interruptions.

If meeting with a client or supplier, there is some importance as to whether you are on 'home ground'. There can be some comfort and control from having meetings on your premises, as well as the knowledge of technology and other factors in the building. However, a client may appreciate the effort required to visit them and the experience can also add value to your arguments by showing empathy in relation to their working environment (for example, making reference to a gymnasium on the premises or an office charity effort you have witnessed).

There may be a strong case for an off-site meeting. This is where the meeting is located outside the company premises, either at a conference centre or somewhere less orthodox. Productive meetings can be held over breakfast or lunch, especially if building client relationships is an important objective of the meeting. Likewise, the senior management of a company might see a week-end at a rural retreat as an opportunity to bond in a social context as well as to discuss key business decisions.

There are two primary reasons to take meetings off-site:

- They remove participants from the office environment and therefore allow clear thought and focus on the meeting itself
- A change of environment can stimulate the participants to be more productive or free thinking and their shared experience can bring them closer together.

Given advancements in technology, the tendency is now for many meetings to be held virtually, with participants accessing the meeting remotely via telephone or websites. Videoconferencing and conference calls via telephone have allowed people unavailable to attend in person to participate fully in meetings remotely. These methods have also allowed for more frequent transnational meetings, without the need for travel.

The telephone conference call is especially popular where businesses operate over a number of sites and it is difficult for the managers to leave the workplace. For example, store managers in retail chains often have regional briefings and phone in sales figures every day to avoid needing to leave their shop. This saves on the travel costs of the regional manager and allows an easy exchange of shared ideas from managers across a larger area.

Key benefits of videoconferencing and telephone conference calls include:

- Geographical barriers to attendance are removed
- It is usually relatively cheap if compared to specially organised events
- They can be arranged at short notice if participants have access to mobile devices
- The contents can often be recorded for later use
- It is easier to integrate visual or multimedia aspects
- Remote meetings fit in closer with the culture of working from home
- People can feel more relaxed if they are home, as meetings in the boardroom can be too rigid and formal

Key disadvantages include:

- A heavy reliance on technology can cause problems where mobile device signal or broadband strength is unreliable. Failing technology can risk interruption or cancellation of the meeting.
- The lack of interaction and inability to pick up and benefit from others' body language. For example, without eye contact participants struggle to perceive others' reactions, intent or attention levels as well as they would in person.
- The meetings can be more difficult to control and lack co-ordination and moderation as the call initiator may not 'chair' the meeting as they would in person.
- Participants can become daunted by a lack of familiarity with the protocols and technology/equipment used.
- Appearance consciousness can cause some participants to feel

uncomfortable, as they are too preoccupied with how they sound on the loud speakers or appear on the screen. Lower level workers in particular are said to feel anxious about these methods of communication and silence can be easier if you are not seen.

- There can be too many surrounding distractions and disturbances, leading to a lack of concentration for the participant and unhelpfully loud background noise heard by others.
- There are considerable set-up costs such as purchasing the equipment required.

Activity 5

Kenneth, the Managing Director of Windsor Electricals, remains concerned about the lack of adherence to the operational efficiency policy and has asked Douglas to address the issue again.

Kenneth has identified three key issues:

1 The international offices do not seem to understand the cultural aspects of the policy

2 Individual managers in the UK do not appear to be working well together to deliver this and other policies and hostility between departments is starting to develop

3 Junior staff do not understand how the policy applies to them and require more information from their managers.

Kenneth has asked Douglas to set up meetings to ensure these problems are addressed.

For each of the three problems above, which of the following types of meeting would work best to ensure the right audience are present and the objectives are met:

A. A meeting in the office's conference room

B. An off-site meeting

C. A remote meeting via videoconference

2.6 Meeting resources

Whether the meeting is at the office or off-site, the organiser will need to ensure that the attendees have all the equipment to hand and that the resources are in place to facilitate a smooth-running session.

In addition to providing the attendees with the information they require to attend and participate in the meeting, most meetings require some or all of the following to be available:

- Writing equipment, including pens and paper
- Flipcharts, whiteboards, smartboards and other means of making notes for the group
- Laser pointers, board pens and other means of highlighting information on the above boards
- Media display equipment – multimedia projectors and screens
- Computer and internet access – may include devices themselves, but at least sources of power and connectivity
- Food and drink throughout the day
- DVD player/TV/radio
- Teleconferencing equipment
- Speakers, headphones and microphones

When considering these requirements, there are further aspects of the room which the organiser may wish to assess:

- Lighting
- Windows and air conditioning
- Alarms, health and safety and access
- Seating arrangements

For off-site meetings, further considerations will include:

- Travel and accommodation for participants travelling a long way
- Entertainment should it be an all-day event.

Due to these direct and indirect costs, the budget for an off-site meeting would be considerably higher than one held in the office. Off-site meetings will also often take more time to organise, as they necessarily involve greater liaison with the venue and resource specialists, for example those providing equipment, technology or catering.

Example

Farhan is the Project Manager responsible for the Mainwaring and Sons new store development project.

He has decided to hold the Kickoff meeting for his project team as an off-site one day event to allow the team to spend some time getting to know each other better.

At the end of the day, Farhan studies the costs of the event:

- Room hire
- Coffee and early morning refreshments
- Display equipment for presentations (Including projector)
- WiFi access for the day
- Stationary and writing pads for all participants
- Lunch
- Charge for use of equipment for army-themed teambuilding exercise
- Afternoon tea
- Prizes to reward outstanding ideas
- Parking permits for all participants
- Overnight hotel stay and evening meal for two team members who work remotely and have travelled a considerable distance

Although the day proved worthwhile and the project staff seemed happy, Farhan will still need to justify his expenditure to the management.

Activity 6

Returning to the meeting you proposed in Activity 4, all of your invitees have confirmed they will be able to attend and it has been suggested to you that the meeting is held at a local conference centre.

Required:

1 Suggest three reasons for and three against hosting the meeting off-site.

2 Create a venue checklist to list all of the resources needed and any outside specialists you need to contact.

3 Draft an e-mail or memo to one of the resource specialists to confirm your requirements.

(AAT Assessment criteria 1.2 and 1.3)

3 Structure and Content of Meetings

3.1 Pre-meeting Organisation

The key to effective meetings is organisation. As we have seen, many of the more complex organisational activities occur prior to the meeting, to co-ordinate commitments and ensure that key players or potential customers are able to attend.

Some logistical planning will also be required in between the confirmation of attendees and the meeting itself. This may be as simple as reminding people of the time and location or providing a map to the car park.

Depending on the nature of the meeting and the formation of the agenda (see below), the organiser may have lengthy communication with the participants during this time period, asking for suggestions for content or responding to requests for further information to enable the delegates to prepare. If such conversations are taking place via e-mail, all communications should be kept to avoid any confusion at a later date.

As with any event management, potential risks should be identified at this time. For example, technology could fail on the day making the core PowerPoint presentation seemingly unavailable or inadequate supply of food and drink for those with particular requirements could create an unproductive atmosphere.

Many such issues cannot be planned for, but it is essential to give yourself the best chance of succeeding and problems which could be solved could be added to your meeting checklist.

3.2 The Agenda

The Agenda is perhaps the most important aspect of the pre-meeting organisation. It should be circulated to all participants prior to the event to set the tone well in advance. The Agenda should highlight the purpose of the meeting and provide it with a structure. It will also allow participants to adequately prepare questions or responses.

Although there can be some benefit to a similar structure for regular or recurring meetings, no two agendas should be the same. Were agendas to be repeated in this way it would suggest that the meetings are starting to lack clear purpose and becoming mere routines.

A typical agenda will be broken into administrative aspects and discursive elements. For example, apologies for absence, reading previous minutes and making corporate announcements tend to be more administrative and are often referred to as 'housekeeping'. If off-site, these parts of the meeting can even extend to health and safety information and lunch orders! Although such content may seem like unnecessary distractions from more pressing or serious business matters, they can provide relief from in depth discussions and foster a sense of community in the group.

The items for discussion should be clearly listed on the agenda, often with sub-headings to further detail the specifics. The source of these items can vary, depending on how participative the meeting is intended to be. If it follows a more democratic structure and the main participants are equals, agenda items will often be suggested and determined by the whole group. This can lead to negotiation with the organiser and the chair/leader of the meeting, as colleagues strive to have their concerns given priority. In deciding whether items should be included, it is crucial to look to the timings and the purpose and see whether the suggestion fits.

Agenda items should be allotted times to keep the meeting on track and ideally each item should have a presenter or topic leader to act as a chairperson for that section (this would be the person who suggested its inclusion if following the democratic model above).

To determine the timings, consider how long was spent on similar agenda items in the past. One popular approach is to split the agenda items into six parts, spending two-thirds of the meeting covering the current, one sixth following up on past issues and actions and the final sixth preparing for the future. If timings can be fairly confidently determined, it is best to warm up with easier issues and move on to those more difficult to resolve when the meeting has momentum. This said, if there is a particularly pivotal and complex issue, it may be best to schedule this first to give it ample time and attention.

If agenda items look to be too substantial or information-packed, data and reports can also be sent prior to the meeting so that time is not wasted with participants rifling through documentation. Agenda items requiring technology and/or extra information to be provided should be noted ready for the day.

Even remote meetings should have an agenda. It is much easier for attendees via conference call to speak for too long in an irrelevant or irreverent fashion and the agenda should enable others to force them back on topic.

Activity 7

Returning to the meeting you were looking to organise in Activity 6, you have now been asked to compile the agenda and liaise with the attendees to ensure their points of interest are being addressed in the meeting.

Required:

1 Draft an agenda for the meeting, annotated with timings and other requirements.

2 Your colleague Sunil has suggested an agenda item that you are happy with. Include this item on your agenda and send Sunil an e-mail to confirm this and detail your expectations of him for his part of the meeting.

3 You have received an e-mail back from another colleague, Courtney. Courtney is unsure of the purpose of the meeting and needs clarification on why she is attending and what she needs to do in advance.

(AAT Assessment criteria 1.3, 2.1 and 2.3)

3.3 Presentation and discussion

The contributions of participants typically combine presentation and active discussion in most worthwhile meetings. One of the traditional criticisms of meetings is that they take too long and become uninteresting and uninspiring. A crucial reason for this is the habit of the senior participants to dominate and speak for the majority of the meeting without interruption or consultation, so the blend of informing and discussing is crucial to overcome these problems.

Variety in the modern meeting can also be easily created by incorporating different forms of information, utilising technology and having interactive, participative elements. This enables a sense of empowerment for attendees and also keeps them interested.

For example, the presenters may choose to use the following during their part of the meeting:

- PowerPoint presentations (see Chapter 6)
- Graphs and charts to analyse statistical data
- Videos to illustrate a key point in action
- Notes and information packs
- Group activities and discussion to act as an introductory exercise.

Activity 8

Priya has been asked to liaise with the board of directors to arrange their next meeting at Windsor Electricals. Kenneth is due to report back to the directors on the recent sales trends and has been given the relevant data from his sales department.

In recent meetings he has picked up that some of the board members are getting bored with endless statistics being presented and therefore wants to liven up his twenty minute stint.

Kenneth asks Priya for three ways he could present the information differently. What should she recommend in this instance?

(AAT Assessment criteria 2.2)

3.4 Workshop Activities

Due to their nature, workshops often feature more developed and interactive group exercises, allowing the participants to work through a problem or issue together and complete a series of tasks to reach their conclusions.

For example, rather than attendees merely discussing the way to introduce new environmentally-friendly policies into a business as an agenda item, in a workshop the participants could:

- Split into groups and focus on specific areas
- Carry out audits on other companies' policies
- Work through scenarios and case studies of either real or simulated companies facing similar dilemmas
- Complete questionnaires or mind maps in small groups and then feedback collectively
- Conduct conference calls with experts in the field

These sort of workshops are more task-oriented, but often can yield a greater number of ideas than conventional discussions.

Activity 9

Using the meeting you have planned in Activities 4, 6 and 7, redesign the meeting agenda to work as a plan for a day-long workshop. Map out the content and tasks involved in each session and the equipment required.

(AAT Assessment criteria 2.2)

3.5 Minutes and Points of action

Minutes are essential for most meetings. Minutes can take two forms – minutes of narration (descriptive) and minutes of resolution (which include agreed outcomes).

Their function is to:

- serve as a record of discussions
- confirm decisions
- record agreed actions and responsibilities
- prompt action from those who attended the meeting
- inform those who did not attend the meeting.

A designated minute-taker or scribe should be appointed. The minute-taker's role is vital, as they must follow the discussion and articulate the contents clearly and concisely in writing. This not only involves close concentration on the proceedings but also an ability to process and disseminate information effectively.

The role also allows other participants, who maybe lack some of these skills, to concentrate on items on the agenda where they have a valid contribution to make. In committees, this would typically be the role of the Secretary, who provides all administrative support prior to, during and after the committee meeting.

In addition to recording what is said in the meeting and therefore summarising the content, the minutes should also note all of the action points assigned during the meeting – without such plans being made and responsibilities being allocated for the future, the outcomes may not be delivered. Ideally the plan of action should be created throughout the meeting or workshop, rather than waiting until the end.

Whether you provide the notes by e-mail or photocopied hand-outs, it is crucial that they are circulated to all those who attended and those who will be affected by any decisions taken at the meeting.

Activity 10

Obtain a set of minutes or meeting notes from a recent meeting at your workplace. If possible, try to compile the minutes for a meeting yourself.

Identify within the minutes the following:

1 The overall purpose and nature of the meeting

2 The level of participation of the attendees

3 The key questions discussed and how they were handled

4 The action points decided during the meeting

(AAT Assessment criteria 2.3 and 2.4)

4 Group Participation

4.1 Group dynamics

Having established the agenda, it is important that the issues are discussed in a purposeful, positive manner. The group dynamic is therefore integral to meeting's success. It relates to how people interact, their feelings towards each other and their hopes, aspirations and beliefs. Part of meeting preparation is to identify the other attendees and determine your relationship with them. Attendees will have a different approach to interaction with a board member in comparison to their peers.

4.2 The meeting environment

To achieve this, a certain structure and ethos is required and the following three aspects need to be promoted by the key players in the meeting:

- **Rules and procedures** – boundaries and expectations need to be clear from the start to keep the meeting on track. In most meetings, the clock plays a crucial role, keeping to time and avoiding spending too long on one topic. If the meeting starts to lack purpose or direction, the clock needs to have the final say.
- **A healthy, positive atmosphere** – although participants should be encouraged to share their views truthfully, it is equally essential that personal issues and conflict do not disturb the flow or damage the purpose of the meeting or workshop. Negative discussions could harm morale and if dealing with suppliers or customers, negative energy could harm your company's reputation.
- **The participation of everyone** – group pressure or strong leadership can sometimes lead to meetings being dominated by larger personalities and therefore it is crucial that everyone involved feels valued and motivated. If the agenda is effectively constructed, they should be able to prepare and contribute effectively.

4.3 Key Participants

There are certain key roles and responsibilities which should be apparent in every meeting:

- **A Chairperson or Leader** – to chair and steer the meeting towards its objectives.
- **A Facilitator or Moderator** - to set the agenda and keep the atmosphere positive and productive, ensuring that certain personalities do not have a detrimental impact (for a Workshop, this

person would normally also assume the leadership role, for many meetings it would be the manager's role)

- **A Scribe** - to keep detailed and accurate notes for future use.
- **A Timekeeper** – to enforce the agenda timings.
- **Presenters** – to introduce ideas.
- **Participants / Contributors** – to listen to content and question or discuss.

As well as these common roles, other roles in meetings include:

- **Listeners and Talkers** – there is likely to be a mixture of both in any meeting, but it is important that a few Talkers do not dictate proceedings and marginalise the Listeners.
- **Protagonists and Antagonists** – there will also be a mixture of those supportive and those disruptive to the agenda
- **Innovators** – contribute novel ideas and solutions.
- **Scientists** – analyse the suggestions of others in a clinical manner.
- **Entertainers** – keep spirits high and lighten the tone.
- **Dreamers** – lack perspective and a grasp of reality.
- **Self-propagandists** – focused on proving their own worth and sometimes compete with other participants in doing so.

Some of these participant behaviours can have a negative impact on the dynamic. For example, the entertainer's behaviour can make important decisions seem trivial and deflate lively debate and the self-propagandist's efforts to promote themselves can lead to focus on their personal performance rather than factors influencing the business.

As well as the roles above, which are specific to meetings, we can also return to Belbin's team roles identified in Chapter 4 as one blueprint for the sort of mix of characteristics a productive meeting requires.

Activity 11

The off-site meeting at Windsor Electricals is due to take place next week and Douglas has agreed to chair proceedings. Given that the management team are not currently working well together, he fears that the meeting may become subjected to personal issues and therefore be difficult to control.

In the absence of a facilitator, Douglas is aware that he needs to establish ground rules to keep matters under control. Give five examples of ground rules or other actions Douglas could adopt for the meeting.

(AAT Assessment criteria 3.1)

5 Leading meetings and workshops

5.1 Leadership in meetings

Every meeting requires leadership. Although the content of meetings can be extensively delegated, it usually falls to one person to determine the schedule, participants, agenda and responsibilities. The most obvious chair is the person who called the meeting or the most senior ranking participant. If they are of board level, it is likely an administrative assistant will however perform some of the organisational tasks listed under their guidance.

Leading the meeting is as much about setting the right example as it is about enforcing rules or speaking more than anyone else. In some cases, especially with workshops, the person chairing the meeting may well deliberately disengage from the issues prior to the meeting, knowing that they need a clear mind and true objectivity to effectively sit in judgement and draw conclusions.

The meeting leader should ensure they adhere to the schedule, arriving and starting the meeting on time to show the importance of the meeting and the expectations of those in attendance. It is their responsibility to guide the participants through the purpose of the meeting and explain the relevance of and links between agenda items. By introducing each agenda item during the course of the meeting, the leader maintains standards, keeps control and endorses the presenter of each part.

5.2 Leadership responsibilities

The key responsibilities of any leader in a meeting are as follows:

- **Keeping the meeting on time and on track** - steering discussion and encouraging participants to contribute in a way that fulfils the meeting objectives. If the objectives are fulfilled before the scheduled close of the meeting, it is better to end it early to show the overwhelming purpose.
- **Assigning roles** - Items that surface and must be addressed should be assigned during the meeting discussion. Assign a particular individual or group to follow-up on each action item. A deadline and priority level should also be assigned for the action items.
- **Managing conflict** – there are likely to be some difficult personalities and opposing views in a room and this can be challenging for the meeting leader. Although meetings are best where ideas are expressed honestly and constructively, if the atmosphere becomes

particularly heated this can be to the detriment of the objectives. It has been known for some companies to hire professional facilitators to deal with high-conflict meetings. Leaders should not be scared to intervene and ask anyone causing trouble to leave or remain quiet.

- **Summarising**– even where the leader is not sitting in judgement, they will still be the person to either have or encourage the final say on each issue. To enforce this, it is common for the meeting leader to take personal responsibility for recording the essential notes from the meeting, whether on an interactive whiteboard, flipchart or in a notebook. By co-ordinating the team's efforts in this way, the leader is reconfirming the productive nature of the meeting and their own role. Summing up throughout enables the meeting to stay on course and clarifies the key points as they are raised and make sure all parties are aware of decisions as they are made and commitments as they are allocated.
- **Recognising and managing different views** – it is important that the leader listens effectively to the other participants and identifies similarities and differences between the opinions expressed. The leader needs to be open to different perspectives and provide feedback impartially and tactfully and to be able to negotiate to reach conclusion on complex issues. The leader may also serve as a moderator in the absence of a Facilitator and as such needs to understand the assumptions and bias of others. If successful, they develop trust.
- **Concluding and reviewing** - at the end of the meeting, the leader should review the action items and reflect on what the group did well during the meeting and which areas need improving. The leader's responsibilities also go beyond the meeting itself, as they need to direct future plans agreed during it. Personally sending the meeting information to participants is a good way to do this.

Activity 12

Which of the following suggest sound leadership of a meeting:

1 Some participants are allowed to dominate and suppress the views of others.

2 The meeting jumps from item to item with no logical order or links.

3 Participants do not have clear roles.

4 Notes are made by the whole group with no co-ordination.

5 All agenda items run late.

6 Everyone is offering an opinion.

7 Debate is honest to the point where some people are upset.

8 Drinks have not been available all day.

9 The leader offers a summary at the end of each agenda item.

10 The leader declared at the start of the meeting that the purpose would be clear by the end.

11 People are telling jokes.

12 No one wants to leave at the end of the meeting.

5.3 Meeting follow-up

Meetings and workshops will inevitably result in a list of decisions and recommendations from which a plan of action can be formed. This is especially crucial for workshops, which typically propose changes to policies or procedures within a business.

It is part of the leader or faciliator's responsibility to ensure that such proposals and actions are followed up on, to make the meeting or workshop worthwhile.

The following devices can be used to check the progress of a meeting or workshop's action points:

- For this update to be included as the first item on the next agenda
- Informal checks on progress could be arranged by the leader via e-mail, with calendar reminders if desired
- A progress review meeting for individual action points
- Written reports could be provided by the person allocated the task for circulation and feedback from the leader/group
- Telephone conference calls and other short, remote meetings could keep communications open

Activity 13

At Windsor Electricals, Priya has been asked to send the follow-up information for today's board meeting, including the minutes she compiled and the action points, which Kenneth has confirmed. One of these action points is for Phil, the Operations Director, to provide weekly productivity statistics to the board.

Suggest two ways Priya can ensure Phil fulfils this requirement.

6 Summary

6.1 Effective meetings and workshops

In conclusion, effective meetings and workshops rely on the following:

- A clearly defined purpose
- The correct attendees
- A suitable time and location
- An established agenda
- Good leadership and the right people in key roles
- The involvement of participants
- Healthy discussion
- Clarification and summaries throughout
- A constructive plan of action
- Detailed and published minutes.

They are a crucial mechanism for participation in the business and the effective sharing of ideas and collective formation of strategy. Although they should be used carefully and selectively, if communication is effective and the participants act as a team, they are essential to the running and development of any commercial enterprise.

Activity 14

Which of the following is an advantage and which is a disadvantage of using meetings and committees rather than individuals making decisions?

A. Increased accountability for the quality of the decision made

B. Increased speed in decision-making

C. Reduced conflict in the decision-making process

D. Increased acceptance of the decision made by the rest of the organisation

Activity 15

Bentley Books is a leading provider of pet care guides.

Craig, the Managing Director, has asked you, as head of the Accounts Department, to look at the company's CSR and community relations policies and has suggested using meetings and workshops to get feedback and ideas from internal and external stakeholders.

Although you are not restricted in terms of budget, given your role as an accountant, it is expected you will not be too flamboyant in your planning!

Required:

1 Given the brief above create a plan of action indicating

   a. The meetings and workshops you feel will work best
   b. Who will attend them
   c. Their purpose and structure
   d. Extra considerations and costs for each meeting.

2 Explain how you will schedule the meeting and ensure most participants attend – give examples of relevant communications.

3 Create an agenda or workshop plan for each of the meetings you have identified.

4 Define your own role and those of key participants in the meetings.

5 To prepare for the meeting, note down how you will communicate your ideas and the different forms of media you will use.

6 Establish the rules and objectives for each meeting (will these differ from meeting to meeting?), including a guide for participants on how and when to contribute to the discussion.

(AAT Assessment criteria 1.1, 1.2, 1.3, 2.1, 2.2, 2.3, 2.4, 3.1, 3.2, 3.3)

Activity 16

Following on from the example of Bentley Books above, Craig has asked you to attend the monthly managers' meetings. He has however confided in you that in his view these meetings are increasingly unproductive and suggests the following reasons:

- Lack of participation – some managers seem to keep quiet in the hope the meeting may end earlier.

- Non-attendance – not all managers turn up, with some sending junior staff in their place.
- Decisions are rarely made at the meetings as the managers don't know what will be discussed and rarely come prepared.
- The manager of the Distribution division is a formidable character and often takes over the meetings, insisting that he is correct on all issues.

Required:

Having attended the first meeting, you realise that all of Craig's beliefs are correct. He suggests you send him a brief memo to detail why you think things are going wrong and to suggest improvements.

Activity 17

Think of a company or staff meeting you have recently attended.

Required:

1 Assess your own contribution in the meeting – what was your role and how much did you contribute? How could you improve your own involvement?

2 Assess the way the meeting was handled by the leader (if this was not you) – how did structure and run the meeting and how could their approach by improved?

3 Assess the contributions of the participants – how and why did they get involved?

4 Provide a summary of the key five points discussed and the action points identified in the meeting.

5 Detail how progress of the five action points you identified was monitored after the meeting's conclusion.

(AAT Assessment criteria 3.2, 3.3, 3.4 and 3.5, 3.6)

Answers to chapter activities

Activity 1

Douglas' meetings are all with his own team so therefore are likely to be primarily staff meetings and briefings and performance-related meetings. Their frequency also would fall in line with the idea of them being progress review meetings for a project nearing completion. As the whole team appear to be involved and Kenneth, as a board member, is unaware of the reasons, it is unlikely they are meetings for investigative reasons or to discuss any more advanced or cross-departmental issues.

Reasons for these meetings being held could include:

- to inform staff of developments
- to assess the progress of the team on special projects (as the meetings are so frequent, these seems likely)
- to share ideas and promote collective decision-making
- to assert structure and control (Douglas has opted for more formal meetings so these seem likely)
- to develop staff
- to promote the idea of team work
- to motivate staff

Activity 2

Reasons why Priya's actions are unlikely to result in an effective meeting include:

- She has not invited the correct attendees – only departmental managers are required for this meeting and she has invited those with no interest in or ability to influence the issue being discussed
- There is no stated purpose to the meeting – even the participants who should be there do not understand why they have been asked.
- There is no established agenda – without timings, no one is aware of the issues to be addressed or how long the meeting will take. They do not know if they need to prepare anything in advance.

Activity 3

1. The monthly board meeting will be for the directors and senior management of the company only. Although sometimes departmental heads may be invited to brief on a particular issue, this regular meeting is usually for the board of directors only.
2. This meeting is more at the operational level of the business and it is not a large client so no senior management would be required. All individuals responsible for the client's orders should be invited. Most likely the Sales, Customer Service and Operations/Logistics departmental managers would attend this meeting, as well as those responsible for the day-to-day running of the account, including Account Managers and operatives in the Customer Service and Packing and Distribution departments (these people may however be selected by departmental managers). The meeting population should not be too large to allow efficient problem-solving.

Activity 4

The answers to the activity are reliant on the individual's experience and working environment. As guidelines, answers should include:

1. A clear list of individuals by job title. Depending on the issues to be discussed, the appropriate level of decision-maker should be identified and whether or not individuals from different departments would be required. If the purpose is to discuss new ideas, a workshop for a smaller group may be suitable.
2. This is a matter of personal choice and will be dependent on the company's technology. The modern view would be to use scheduling software and shared calendars to propose the meetings – this is certainly more efficient. This said, where calendars are more complex and a variety of needs must be met, the personal touch and negotiation may be better for the purpose.
3. The draft e-mail should include:
   - A polite introduction
   - The purpose of the meeting
   - Suggested times and a place if appropriate
   - The required preparation or when this will be sent
   - A call to action – perhaps including a date for the latest reply.

Activity 5

1 The international offices who do not seem to understand the cultural aspects of the policy would be best served by

C a remote meeting via videoconference.

This would allow overseas participants to be involved without the expense and hassle of travelling to the UK.

2 Individual managers in the UK do not appear to be working well together to deliver this and other policies and hostility between departments is starting to develop would be best served by

B an off-site meeting

This would allow the managers to get away from the office hostility, focusing on the issue and developing better personal relationships with each other in a changed social environment.

3 Junior staff do not understand how the policy applies to them and require more information would be best served by

A a meeting in the office's conference room

This would save on any travel costs and if the meeting is quite brief, people can get back to work quickly if they are at the office. As this would be the usual setting for staff and team meetings, it makes sense to hold this meeting on-site.

Activity 6

The answers to the activity are reliant on the individual's experience and working environment and can be used to inform thinking on the work-based evidence element of assessment.

As guidelines, answers should however note the following:

1. The three reasons in favour could include:
   - Increased focus from being out of the office
   - The social and teamwork benefits
   - Novelty value of a change of environment
   - The expertise and specialist support of the conference centre

   Three against could include:
   - Extra costs – to hire the room, equipment and added service
   - Time-consuming nature of liaising with the venue and others
   - The need for travel and possibly accommodation

- Data would be more easily to hand in the office

2. The venue checklist could include:
   - Equipment: Pens, Pads, Flipchart, Projector, Wifi Code, Laptops
   - Catering: Coffee at 9am, Lunch, Afternoon Tea
   - Parking Permits/Instructions
   - Information Packs for attendees
3. The memo should clearly state the date of the meeting and the name of the company. It should clearly indicate the service or equipment required, including cost.

Activity 7

The answer is reliant on the individual's business idea and working environment. As guidelines, answers should include the following:

1 An agenda could be as follows:

9-9.30am Introduction and Meeting Admin (Person A)

10-11.30am Topic One: Marketing (Person B)

11.30-1pm Topic Two: HR Systems (Person C)

1-2pm Lunch

2-3.30pm Topic Three: Operations (Person D)

3.30-5pm Topic Four: Corporate Goals (Person A)

5-5.30pm Summing up and plans for action (Person A)

In this example, the topics are building from the easiest to the most heavy. Extra notes are also with the Agenda to state where extra information or equipment is required.

2 The e-mail would inform Sunil of the item's inclusion and tell him when it would be discussed and state the purpose of the section in the context of the whole meeting. Extra equipment required would be mentioned. The e-mail would most likely seek clarification on any activities or presentations Sunil wishes to include. This communication can also stress the importance of timings and following the procedures you have put in place.

3 This is not unusual as the meeting approaches and people believe they have better things to do. Clearly state the purpose of the meeting (relating this specifically to Courtney and her role) and give an overview of your plans.

Activity 8

Priya should recommend any of the following ways to make the statistics more interesting:

- Putting the agenda item's contents into a short, colourful PowerPoint presentation or similar
- Using graphs and charts to show and compare data
- Handing out colourful booklets to summarise the key data which can be read later

If Kenneth wishes to be more inventive, he could play a video with customer testimonies or the sales team providing their analysis.

Activity 9

The answers to the activity are reliant on the individual's business idea and working environment and can be used to inform thinking on the work-based evidence element of assessment.

As guidelines, the answers should include the following:

The main difference between a meeting and a workshop is the highly interactive element. Therefore the workshop plan should be much more detailed and involve lots of participation. The group should be small and focused on specialist issues. Scenarios, tasks and more hands-on analysis should be included as well as the usual discussion of key issues.

Activity 10

The answers to the activity are reliant on the individual's business idea and working environment and can be used to inform thinking on the work-based evidence element of assessment.

As guidelines, here is an example for a departmental staff meeting:

1 The overall purpose and nature of the meeting could be to determine departmental objectives for the next month

2 The attendees largely listened to their team manager providing updates on company policy, but were frequently asked for their opinions. One team member provided a ten minute update on the new computer system and included a couple of slides to do so.

3 Key questions were largely about the forthcoming Christmas

holidays and working expectations for the period. One team member appeared to ask a lot of questions regarding the company bonus. The manager appeared to handle these queries concisely.

4 The team member working on the computer system was asked to provide a memo to staff on a weekly basis to keep them informed. The manager agreed to hold individual meetings regarding the bonuses. The manager asked for e-mailed feedback within a week to include customer views on current promotions.

Activity 11

Ground rules are likely to relate to the following key aspects, so Douglas could use one or more examples of each:

- **Time-keeping** – fines for late arrival or return from refreshment breaks; limits on how long people can speak for continuously
- **Respect others** – people should make business issues personal
- **Interaction** – do not dominate or speak over each other. A rule could be to wait until invited to speak by the session presenter or leader
- **Contribution** – all participants should contribute to discussion
- **Being Positive** – participants must not criticise without good cause

Activity 12

The following suggest sound leadership of a meeting:

6 Everyone is offering an opinion

9 The leader offers a summary at the end of each agenda item

11 People are telling jokes (as long as this is not as a serious debate is going on, it implies a good atmosphere)

12 No one wants to leave at the end of the meeting (although meetings must keep to time this implies a level of enjoyment and enthusiasm which has been encouraged by the leader)

All other factors suggest poor leadership.

Activity 13

Priya could either suggest that Phil sends the data via e-mail to the other members of the board and could create a reminder on his e-mail and mobile devices to support this. She could similarly set up a file-sharing group to enable others to view Phil's data.

Another alternative would be to book weekly conference calls for Phil to explain the information to others.

In the long-term, the success of Priya's idea could be topic for discussion in the next meeting.

Activity 14

The correct answer is **D. increased acceptance of the decision made** as the meeting or committee could be made up of people from different departments or across varied levels.

In terms of the other options, meetings can lead to less accountability due to the idea of collective responsibility, they tend to cause slower decisions and can actually cause further conflict where there are differences of opinion.

Activity 15

This answer will be down to the individual's preference, as long as answers are detailed and decisions are informed.

This said, it seems that given the brief a mixture of workshops and meetings could be used given the company's desire to create new policies and encourage a fresh approach.

Initial workshops could be held on each of the three areas to work through scenarios and real-life examples and share practice from all levels and departments in the business. Then meetings would be held with at either board level or with relevant managers to decide the policy.

The purpose of initial meetings or workshops is therefore to research and gain an understanding of how things could be improved, whereas the later meetings will focus more on creating policies and commercial improvement and benefit.

All agendas should include varied discussion and opportunities to participate within clear boundaries and a time structure. All meetings and workshops need a Leader, Facilitator, Note-taker and mixture of participants.

The level of communication/participation will rely on body language signals from those involved and the progress of the meeting and it is recommended that if presenting, a variety of media is used. This could be more clearly codified in the rules, which should also include time management and the maintenance of a healthy discussion and positive environment.

Activity 16

MEMO

Accountant > MD (Craig)

Having attended the meeting, it seems that there are several problems with the management meetings. However, I think all can be easily resolved.

It does not seem the managers take these meetings seriously – this is why they do not attend or participate. As the company continues to grow we need to stress how important it is to co-ordinate activities across departments and ensure we learn from each other. As the meetings become more effective, hopefully more will realise the need to attend.

To be effective and ensure managers give them priority, the managers should only address important issues and be limited to senior staff. An agenda would help with this – at the moment, managers are not prepared to either add items to an agenda for discussion or bring along documentation of importance for other matters.

Linked to this, we need to ensure that the meetings centre around decision-making and therefore we need minutes and action points to be noted, by a secretary. We all need to be reminded of what has been decided and provide updates at later meetings.

The agenda and focus above should ensure that the distribution manager does not dominate the meeting as much and that all voices are heard and only relevant issues are discussed. Perhaps we need a more clearly defined chair and some rules to support this.

I hope this helps.

Accountant

Activity 17

The answer depends on the individual's working environment and can be used to inform thinking on the work-based evidence element of assessment. As guidelines, here are some key points to be addressed:

1 This assessment should include an analysis of personal contributions and when the individual felt it right to get involved during the meeting. Some analysis of their role in comparison to other participants would also be worthwhile.

2 In terms of leadership, the methods of control and setting the tone should be included, along with any rules put in place. Also it should be noted how they dealt with conflict or awkward moments or participants.

3 For the participation of others, consider the modes of communication used as well as the content of their discussions and any general rules for how and when they contributed.

4 The five key points from the meeting should have a corresponding action point. For example, if it was decided that more school-leavers should be recruited, an action plan could be to promote the business at local school careers events.

5 Some of the ways that progress could be monitored are:

- Sending a report to all other attendees
- Providing an update via e-mail to the leader the next week
- Updating company records with a new policy
- Holding a conference call to briefly go through findings
- Putting data on a shared drive or document for all to view.

Managing Project Finances

8

Introduction

Although accountants will be required to utilise their financial and non-financial skills on a daily basis to perform their role within the finance department, on occasions they will also be required to work on special projects outside of their usual scope.

The chapter both provides an overview to the nature of project work in comparison to the functions of everyday business, highlighting why projects are unique in their requirements and structure. As successful management of project resources is often the responsibility of the accountants on the project team, this will then be addressed in detail.

ASSESSMENT CRITERIA

1 Be able to develop a budget for a project

2 Be able to manage costs against a budget

3 Be able to complete financial transactions and evaluate project costs

4 Be able to comply with the standards of financial management

CONTENTS

1 The nature of projects
2 Project initiation
3 Project planning
4 Project implementation and control
5 Project completion
6 Project evaluation
7 Compliance

1 The nature of projects

1.1 Introduction

A project is a unique undertaking to achieve a specific objective. Consequently, projects have defined schedules and their own allocation of resources, including staff and funding.

Projects are time-sensitive and have a unique set of stakeholders, all of whom have an interest in the outcome of the project specifically. These stakeholders include the customers who authorise the project, the project sponsors who invested in it and the suppliers whose goods and services formed part of the project's delivery.

Due to their unique nature, projects often involve a group of specialists, taken from diverse areas of a business. As project costing and control are so integral to the project's success, the accounting function of the business usually has a large part to play, and often project managers or their most trusted team members have a financial background.

1.2 Successful projects

For a project to be successful, it requires:

- consideration of the project stakeholders
- the setting of SMART objectives throughout the process
- identification and planning of resources
- clear time-scales and milestones
- quality requirements to be identified and managed
- a carefully constructed and continually reviewed financial plan
- risk assessment and scenario planning
- good leadership
- a strong team ethic within the project group

The following threats can throw the project off course and therefore should also be conquered:

- poor planning
- few control mechanisms
- specification changes
- unrealistic deadlines
- under-resourced budgets
- poor management

Throughout this chapter, each of these will be addressed to ensure that knowledge of how to counter the threats is established.

Activity 1

Which of the following does a project always have:

A. Considerable paperwork

B. A budget unlikely to cover its costs

C. A unique objective and stakeholders

D. The involvement of the IT department

1.3 Constraints

Every project has constraints and factors which can prevent or regulate the activities of the project team. The 'project triangle' identifies the main constraints to any project:

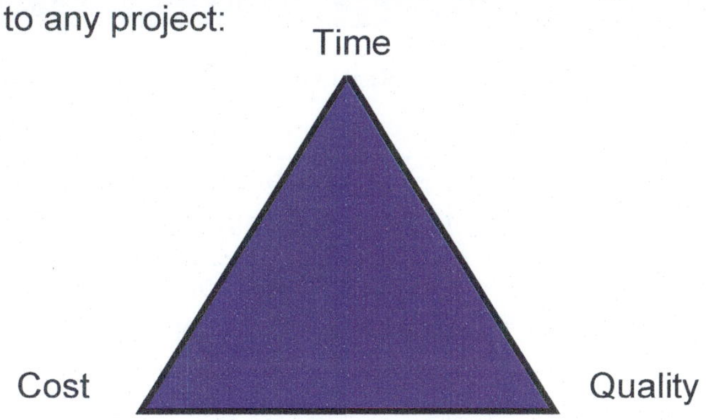

When managing the finances of a project, the conflicting interests of these three factors will present frequent challenges.

1.4 Project stakeholders

As stated above, projects have a unique set of stakeholders. Their roles can be described as follows:

- **Project sponsor** – they initiate and provide the resources for the project, including the appointment of the project manager and signing off the project plan.
- **Project owner** – this is the person for whom the project is being carried out and as such they are interested in the ultimate outcome of the project. They are usually a departmental manager or similar and may take a steering role.
- **Project customers/users** – they are the group of people whose needs the project should satisfy as they are the end users likely to be left with the project's legacy.

- **Project manager** – they are responsible for the successful delivery of the project and the regular and routine management of resources, including staffing and sub-contracting. As the leader of the project team, they make many of the daily decisions and act as key communicator within the entire chain of command.
- **Project team** – they are responsible for achieving tasks set by the project manager to time and to budget. They tend to have a varied range of skills, with many of the key business functions represented.
- **Project steering committee/board** – they oversee the project and make high level decisions regarding its progression. This board is often chaired by the project sponsor.
- **Project champion** – this largely supportive and informal role gives a voice to the project at the highest levels of the organisation.

Activity 2

There are a number of people involved in a project. Match the people below to the correct description.

Project sponsor	Responsible for all high level decisions relating to the project
Project owner	Responsible for the successful delivery of the project
Project manager	The person for whom the project is being carried out
Project board	Provides resources for the project

1.5 The project life cycle

The Project Management Institute has defined 5 Project Management Process Areas which breaks down the process involved in delivering projects from start to finish (known as 'the project life cycle'):

- Initiation
- Planning
- Execution/Implementation
- Evaluation
- Completion

We will now consider each of these in turn.

2 Project initiation

2.1 Reasons to initiate a project

Projects are initiated when a need or objective is defined.

As such, there are a number of reasons why a project could be initiated:

- to help meet the company's long-term goals and objectives
- to enhance or improve products, services or processes
- to solve problems identified internally or externally
- to take advantage of new opportunities resulting from SWOT analysis
- statutory or legal requirements

Activity 3

Which of the following is **not** likely to require the implementation of a project?

A. The accounts department's procedures are seen to be in need of serious reform through a comprehensive review.

B. A SWOT analysis has shown that there a significant grants on offer for companies who have environmentally friendly policies in action and your company has none in place.

C. A new law has limited the number of hours a driver can be on the road for commercial purposes and a haulage company is facing serious operational issues.

D. It seems that payments are not being made on time due to a poorly organised administrator in the accounts department and as a result a few previously happy customers have complained.

2.2 Assessing feasibility

In order for a project to be deemed worthwhile, the feasibility of the project and its associated requirements and risks should be assessed. When judging the feasibility and risks involved, the question which should be asked is whether or not the project is worthwhile when the associated costs and other effects on the business are taken into consideration.

To assess feasibility, a SWOT analysis will most likely be utilised. Within this, technical, operational, social and environmental feasibility will be analysed, as well as financial considerations.

In terms of economic (or financial) feasibility, a cost-benefit analysis will identify and evaluate the costs of the proposed project over its anticipated life and of the eventual outcomes resulting from the project.

Benefits can be classified as being either tangible (those which can be evaluated financially e.g. reduction of labour costs when systems are automated) or intangible (those which are not as easy to quantify e.g. the impact on management information and team working patterns of a new computer system). To assess the tangible benefits will typically require assessment of the payback, positive net present value or internal rate of return likely from the initiation of the project through to completion.

When performing the feasibility and risk assessment analyses on the proposed project, it is equally important to consider the benefits to the company of the project.

Below is a SWOT analysis to identify the potential strengths, weaknesses, opportunities and threats to enable assessment of whether a project would prove worthwhile.

Example

For the Mainwaring and Sons new store development project, the following SWOT analysis was performed:

Strengths	**Weaknesses**
Knowledge of the local retail market Past experience has shown an ability to open stores successfully	No strong relationships with suppliers in the construction industry The company is not as technologically advanced as competitors
Opportunities	**Threats**
Local government incentives to fill the high streets in certain areas There are many good quality candidates for employment The identified sites are locations where retail is enjoying a period of prosperity and the company has a proven track record	Other retail stores have publicly complained about the level of bureaucracy involved and poor local workmanship Competitors are looking to embark upon price wars The project requires finance borrowing and associated risks

2.3 Other considerations

Even if the economic feasibility test of the project does not seem convincing, there are many other benefits to why a project could prove worthwhile for the company, such as the social opportunities identified above. Therefore in addition to cost feasibility, the following should also be assessed:

- Time feasibility (can the project be delivered in a timely fashion and to deadline?)
- Resource/technological feasibility (can the company actually deliver the more complex aspects of the project or can they outsource these parts if not?)

2.4 Project Initiation Document

If having assessed feasibility and risk, the decision is made for the project to go ahead, a Project Initiation Document (PID) is produced to act as a base document for initial approval of stakeholders and continual assessment. This document serves to:

- define the project and its scope
- provide background to the project, including its objectives
- identify the key project deliverables and desired outcomes
- explain the roles and responsibilities of project team members
- provide cost and time estimates for the project
- clarify the benefits for potential stakeholders and investors
- state the methods of control and communication
- detail any project constraints or links to other projects

The PID therefore ensures that all stakeholders are aware of the reasons behind the project and the approach to be taken.

Activity 4

At an initial project meeting, one member of the team claims that the Project Initiation Document is a useless piece of paper.

Write one sentence to convince them otherwise.

2.5 Developing a budget for a project

Budgeting is key to successfully planning any business operation and to be able to run an effective, efficient project, it is essential that all resources and costs associated with the project are clearly identified and budgeted in a realistic, achievable manner. A project's budget needs to be researched, designed, implemented and often modified.

Budgets are useful for several reasons, which can be summarised using the acronym CRUMPET:

- **C**o-ordination – the budget ensures staff are all working towards the same goals and for the good of the company
- **R**esponsibility – the budget authorises staff to make expenditure, hire staff and generally follow the plans laid out in the budget.
- **U**tilisation – budgets help managers to get the best out of their business resources
- **M**otivation – the budget can be a useful device for motivating people to perform to meet business objectives
- **P**lanning – budgets encourage decision-makers to look ahead and analyse potential opportunities and threats
- **E**valuation – whether or not budgets have been met is a key performance indicator for the business and individuals
- **T**elling – budgets help to communicate expectations over a given period to all stakeholders.

Once the objectives of a project are clearly defined, research for the project is required. Data should be collated using both internal and external information. For example, salary costs, raw material availability and cost and market information. If there are limiting factors involved, such as the availability of skilled staff or a shortage of raw materials, these will require consideration and contingency or alternative plans should be put in place.

Key factors for the successful budgeting of a project are:

1. Clear objectives and timescales of both the project and the budget-setting
2. Collate all relevant cost information
3. Ensure any capital expenditure is evaluated
4. Identify and address limiting factors
5. Present options to the project team for consideration

2.6 Collating cost information

When considering project cash flow, a number of different types of project costs should be considered. For example:

- **Capital costs** – costs incurred by the acquisition of assets such as land, buildings, equipment
- **Labour costs** – costs incurred by the human capital involved through a payroll system, including overtime rates
- **Materials costs** – costs incurred by the need for extra consumables purchased to ensure that key aspects were delivered
- **Overhead costs** – costs incurred by the organisational and administrative support required on the project, including rent and energy supply for buildings used
- **Supplier costs** – costs incurred by sub-contractors or agent employed on the project
- **Financing costs** – these are usually incurred as interest charges but could include other sources of finance such as grants and subsidies.

Example

Let us return to the Mainwaring and Sons new store development project covered in previous chapters and consider the costs involved.

These would include:

Capital costs – the building or refitting of new stores and associated planning permission

Labour costs – the initial cost of specialised staff to ensure project delivery and then the recruitment and training of new staff to work in the stores

Materials costs - the cost of new equipment to fit the stores and then ensure they could function

Overhead costs – the cost of any rent which is needed, plus the administrative costs of local government planning and the need to ensure community buy-in

Supplier costs – the cost of construction and legal companies required for outsourced parts of the process

Financing costs – the interest from the business loan the company organised to fund the development.

For further analysis of costs, the AAT Level 4 Financial Performance and Budgeting Combined Text/Workbooks provide detailed content relating to all of the above.

Activity 5

Consider a project you have been involved with in the workplace. Assess and explain the costs involved with the project using the categories identified above.

(AAT Assessment criteria 1.1)

2.7 Evaluating capital expenditure

When each decision regarding project expenditure is made, it is vital to consider as many options as possible. For example, is it more cost-effective to lease equipment rather than purchasing it?

This type of decision has been covered in the AAT Financial Performance unit. The activity below revisits make or buy decisions in this context.

Activity 6

Yarrow Limited has discovered that instead of buying a machine outright it could lease it instead. You are required to complete the following tasks to establish whether the company should lease or buy the machine.

The discount factors you will need are shown below:

Year	*Discount factor 10%*	*Year*	*Discount factor 10%*
0	1.000	3	0.751
1	0.909	4	0.683
2	0.826	5	0.621

Calculate the discounted lifecycle cost of purchasing the machine based upon the following:

- purchase price of £700,000
- annual running costs of £50,000 for the next five years, paid annually in arrears
- a residual value of £200,000 at the end of the five years.

Year	*0*	*1*	*2*	*3*	*4*	*5*
Cash flow						
DF						
PV						
NPC						

Calculate the discounted lifecycle cost of leasing the machine for five years based upon the total annual costs of £200,000 paid annually in advance.

Year	*0*	*1*	*2*	*3*	*4*
Lease costs					
DF					
PV					
NPC					

Based on the calculations it is best to [ ] (insert LEASE or BUY) the machine, in order to save £ [ ]

2.8 Limiting factors

A limiting factor is when the shortage of one resource means that that resource limits the entire capacity of the operation.

Example

Barbecue Limited manufactures two products for which the following details are available.

	Product X		*Product Y*
Selling price	£38		£38
Direct materials 8 units @ £1	£8	4 units @ £1	£4
Labour 4 hours @ £2	£8	6 hours @ £2	£12
Variable overhead 4 machine hours @ £3	£12	3 machine hours @ £3	£9
Fixed overheads	£5		£7

Maximum demand for X is 2,500 units.

Maximum demand for Y is 2,000 units.

Required:

Calculate the optimum production plan for Barbecue in each of the following two situations:

(a) Labour in the next period is limited to *16,000* hours, with no limit on machine hours.

(b) Machine hours in the next period are limited to *12,000* hours, with no limit on labour hours.

Solution

We would like to produce Xs and Ys up to the point where maximum demand is reached. (There is no point producing beyond this, because customers do not want any more.) So ideally we would like to produce 2,500 X and 2,000 Y. To do this we would require the following resources.

	Labour hours	*Machine hours*
2,500 X	10,000	10,000
2,000 Y	12,000	6,000
	22,000	16,000

If labour is limited to 16,000 hours we will not have enough labour hours to achieve this. Similarly, if machine hours are limited to 12,000 our production will be restricted.

To tackle this problem we begin by calculating the contribution earned per unit of each product.

Contribution for each unit of X = £ (38 – 8 – 8 – 12) = £10 per unit
Contribution for each unit of Y = £ (38 – 4 – 12 – 9) = £13 per unit

(a) Labour is limited so we calculate the contribution earned per labour hour for each product.

X = £10/4 = £2.50 per labour hour

Y = £13/6 = £2.17 per labour hour

You get more contribution per labour hour for X than for Y so make as many Xs as possible.

Available hours = 16,000 2,500 Xs require 10,000 hrs

The remaining hours are all used to make as many Ys as possible.

Remaining Ys will take six hours each to make so produce 6,000/6 = 1,000 Ys.

Contribution = (2,500 × £10) + (1,000 × £13) = £38,000

(b) In this case, machine hours are the scarce resource so we calculate contribution per machine hour.

X = £10/4 = £2.50 per machine hour

Y = £13/3 = £4.33 per machine hour

Now it is better to make Ys. Making 2,000 Ys requires 2,000 × 3 = 6,000 machine hours. That leaves us a further 6,000 machine hours for making Xs.

6,000 remaining hours for X means making 6,000/4 = 1,500 Xs

Contribution = (1,500 × £10) + (2,000 × £13) = £41,000

Note that, in the assessment, if you are told the maximum demand for a product it is a big hint that this method should be used.

2.9 Recommending a budget

When recommending a budget, at least two techniques need to be considered in terms of their advantages and disadvantages, not only financially but also in terms of motivational or qualitative aspects.

Let us consider some of the different techniques and approaches which could be taken:

- **Top-down** – the budget is imposed by the senior management
- **Bottom-up** – the budget is initially prepared by the managers responsible for the department and operational decisions and then reviewed by senior management
- **Ideal budgets** – this is a perfect-world scenario and often therefore proves unachievable and demotivates staff
- **Attainable budgets** – designed to be achieved in reasonable conditions
- **Zero based budgeting** – each cost element is justified and this approach does optimise resources, however this can be a time-consuming approach
- **Rolling budgets** – continuously updated.

Example

The advantages and disadvantages of Top Down compared to Bottom Up Budgeting:

Top-down (imposed)

Advantages	Disadvantages
Quick	Lack of local knowledge
Decision-makers are experienced	Lack of local ownership
Greater awareness of corporate strategy and external factors	Organisational goals may not be accepted
Improved co-ordination between plans and objectives	Management initiative may be stifled

Bottom-up (participatory)

Advantages	Disadvantages
Ownership of the budget	Budgetary slack built in
Increased motivation due to this input	Can be time-consuming
More realistic budgets determined by those responsible for them	Managers may not co-ordinate their own plans with those of other departments
Greater co-ordination and co-operation between budget setters	

2.10 Contingency planning

Contingency plans need to be also considered regarding availability of resources and time constraints to ensure any overspend or project overrun is within an acceptable level. A contingency reserve is controlled by the project manager and is usually an accurate cost estimation of a possible issue that may arise.

Management reserve is built into budget preparation for parts of the project that cannot be predicted. For example, major disruption to one aspect of the project. This figure tends to be a fixed percentage (for example, 5% of the project) for emergency funds to be available and usually controlled by management outside of the project.

Activity 7

Returning to a project from your workplace (from Activity 5), recommend a budget, including sub-budgets with classified costs and incorporating a contingency and management reserve.

In a short written report to your manager, explain the reasons behind your budget recommendation, making reference to how you reached key decisions and evaluated costs and expenditure. You should also show that you have considered at least two types of budget and justify the approach you took.

(AAT Assessment criteria 1.2)

3 Project planning

3.1 The purpose of a project plan

Project plans provide the framework for the future control and ultimate delivery of the project. They allow project managers and financial controllers to keep the project on track by presenting clear and measurable objectives for both the staff working on the project and the external stakeholders involved, the customer and sub-contractors and suppliers. Both the customer and the suppliers will want to be aware of whether the project is running to time and to cost to ensure that it is deliverable within reasonable boundaries for them.

Project plans should therefore be open, realistic and clearly broken down. It is also advisable to allocate responsibilities and deadlines or provide a structure for doing so within the plan. When setting targets for the completion of work, it is important to not only focus on the physical, tangible deliverables such as completed products, as the provision of reports, designs and management information are equally important in terms of time-sensitivity.

A well written project plan will allow the members of the project team to know:

- the key objectives of the project (the earlier chapter on Working in Teams focused on the importance of setting objectives for smaller business groups and this would include project teams)
- the roles and responsibilities of both the internal project team and the external stakeholders
- the budgetary framework for the project
- what the critical success factors are (i.e. those to be prioritised in terms of delivery)
- whether the project is on track (this can be achieved using milestones or goals)
- the ultimate success or failure of the project

The project plan is also important for the 'customer', in other words the person or organisation who requires a successful conclusion of a project. This may not necessarily be another company, as the same procedures would apply for an internal project reporting to the board of directors (for example, the implementation of an office move).

3.2 Elements of a project plan

A number of separate, detailed plans will be incorporated:

- **A detailed time plan** – this lists all of the activities and how long they are expected to take. This may be in the form of a Gantt chart (see below).
- **A financial cost plan** – this shows the planned expenditure listed by activity or work package, as identified in the time plan above. This plan will also include the costs from the resource plan and contingency plan below.
- **A quality plan** – this identifies the key outcomes expected by all stakeholders and especially the users/customers. It may also include safety and security and auditing measures. For most projects this takes the form of a Project Quality Plan.
- **A resources plan** – this shows all of the human and other resources required to deliver the project and lists the purchases of labour and equipment/services required.
- **A contingency plan** – this would typically be in the form of a risk register and should include associated costs and further issues.
- **A communication plan** – this clarifies the organisational structure of the project team and how communication between key participants will occur throughout the process.

3.3 Work Breakdown Structures

Work Breakdown Structures (WBS) break the more complex tasks involved in a project into manageable pieces. From these, Work Packages (WPs) and Statements of Work (SOWs) are then created.

The WP specifies the work to be done for each package identified in the broken down WBS and the SOW describes the deliverables and outcomes expected from that WP.

This allows a clear framework for the project to be managed according to and establishes the responsibility for each part of the project. It also allows for costs to be more easily identified and risk to be more easily assessed.

Example

The Mainwaring and Sons Project WBS was as follows:

1. Market Research and Promotion
2. Store Location and Construction
3. Community Impact

4. Human Resources
5. Operational Resources

Within each, packages of work were created with clear objectives for each identified in the SOWs.

3.4 Gantt Charts

A Gantt Chart is used to help control the schedule of a project, using bars. It provides a horizontal timescale and as such enables both the budgeted and actual timescales to be seen alongside each other.

Example

An example of a project undertaken to examine the current procedures in the accounts payable department is provided below. The project manager's first step is to break the project down into phases:

Phase	Task	Estimated time to complete task
1	Document current procedures	3 days
2	Produce flowcharts	3 days
3	Summarise paper flow and methods for receiving, processing and sending information	4 days
4	List problem areas and develop initial recommendations	3 days
5	Develop improved processing procedures	2 days
6	Track sample transactions for one week under existing procedures	5 days
7	Track sample transactions for two weeks under new procedures	10 days
8	Deliver a final report to assess findings and provide recommendations for changes	3 days

This could be expressed in a Gantt chart as follows using a bar chart method where the budgeted times and the actual durations are both shown (actual being underneath in darker bars on this chart).

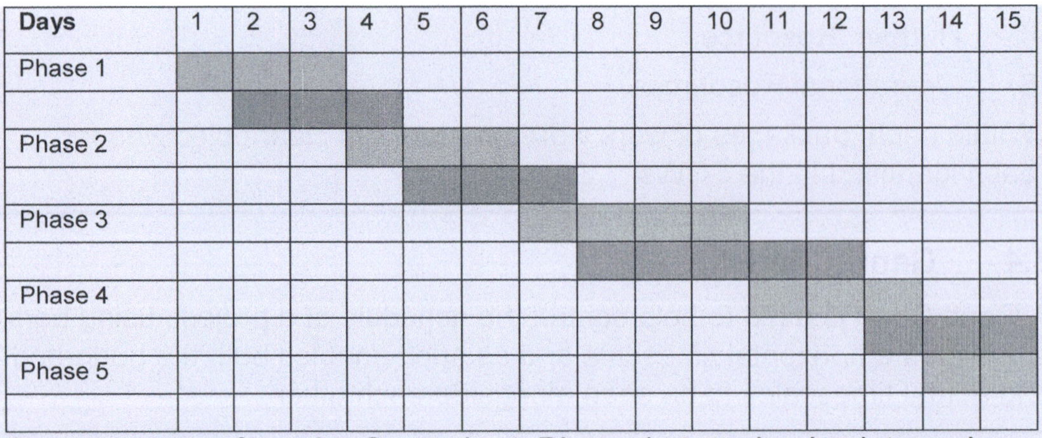

As can be seen from the Gantt chart, Phase 1 started a day late and Phase 3 overran by a day. Therefore by the time the project had reached Phase 5, by the time the phase was due to be completed, it had not even commenced.

A Gantt chart can also incorporate critical timings. For example, if testing scheduled in Phase 6 had to begin by Day 20 regardless of other circumstances.

(Note that for most projects, Gantt charts would use actual dates rather than numbered days as in the example above).

3.5 Critical Path Analysis

Critical Path Analysis allows the project management team to assess which activities are deemed to be critical and therefore given priority. CPA identifies tasks which need to be completed before others can begin and positions certain activities on the critical path. These activities cannot overrun without causing serious damage to the progress of the project.

The CPA network diagram will show the duration of a project, where there is slack time and where there is flexibility. This process can be a complex one and does not require further explanation here.

Activity 8

With reference to a project you have been involved with (used in Activities 5 and 7), explain the planning mechanisms used to 'budget' the following factors:

- Time
- Quality

Give three reasons why these elements may also have an impact on the financial budget for the project.

(AAT Assessment Criteria 1.2)

4 Project implementation and control

4.1 Project execution

Once the project plan has been developed and agreed by both the customer and the project team itself, the project can commence. During the execution of the project, the financial aspects of it will focus on emerging changes and deviations. If either occur, it is vital that the project manager and those responsible for the finances of the project respond accordingly to keep the project on track.

Constant reviewing, monitoring and evaluation of the project are therefore required and revisions require implementation as appropriate. Most likely any revisions will focus on or impact on costs and therefore the finances of the project will be both under scrutiny and likely to change.

4.2 Control in projects

Effective project control requires a system to regularly gather project data and to compare the actual project progress with the plan. If deviations are discovered, corrective action must be taken:

- report the deviation
- obtain authorisation for changes
- take corrective action

A successful control system should therefore have many positive outcomes:

- to prevent deviations
- to correct deviations
- to prevent future deviations by revising plans, targets, measures and expectations
- to ensure that improvements are effectively implemented

The control stage of the project includes three key elements:

- Change control – as new factors emerge during project execution, it is essential to ensure that changes to the PID and scope/costing of the project are communicated. Budgets, objectives and processes which have been altered must be authorised, recorded and communicated to all stakeholders to manager both daily operations on the project and the expectations of its ultimate delivery.

- Financial/cost control
- Performance control

In terms of performance control, time and quality are the most important factors. Time can be controlled through milestones and targets as described above. Quality can be controlled and assessed using a Project Quality Plan (PQP) which defines acceptable standards.

During the course of the project, it is not just the scale of expenditure which requires analysis, but the timing of it. For example, if expenditure on the project is generally later than originally planned, this will often mean that the project is behind schedule and therefore could be a cause for concern.

Controlling costs can be achieved through a number of mechanisms, but in simple terms requires the constant comparing of the actual spend against the project budget and calculating variances.

4.3 Project cost control

Many of the cost control measures applied across business operations also relate to projects. Therefore most of the mechanisms, such as target costing, for keeping a project on budget are covered in AAT's Level 4 Financial Performance and Budgeting units and do not need detailed explanation here. This said, in some project teams, the onus will be on the accountant to create strategies to keep budgets on track and therefore the importance of this should not be underestimated.

The careful management and forecasting of project expenditure is perhaps the most important part of the financial input into the project team. The most common form for monitoring and reviewing actual against budget is with the use of spreadsheet software. This will identify favourable and adverse variances which can then be analysed to to show any interdependencies and so that the reasons for variances can be identified and remedial action taken where necessary.

Typical reasons for variances would include

- unexpected price increases in materials
- inaccurate time scales
- staffing issues
- random, unexpected events, both internal and external

Base costs must be categorised as fixed or variable at the budget outset. Management of base costs falls into three main areas:

- Short-term e.g. 'quick wins', including checking expense claims for accurancy and overspending
- Medium-term e.g. renegotiating supplier contracts

- Long-term e.g. centralisation of common functions such as reducing regional property costs and staffing

4.4 Cash flow forecasts

The project lifecycle needs to be established to forecast when funds need to be released at each phase of the project, resulting in a cash flow forecast. Cash flow forecasts are essential to ensure sufficient availability of funds throughout the project and plans for any significant outflows of cash e.g. capital expenditure items.

They can be used to explain when funds are available and how this may have an impact on the budget plan. This may be where a lease or buy decision will need to be made and the cost of financing considered.

This expenditure normally follows an 'S curve' with relatively low expenditure at the start and finish of the project and higher expenditure in the middle part. Therefore staging payments and planning the freeing of funds is critical. It is important therefore that payments to suppliers are made at a time when the project can afford to do so, and therefore that inflows and outflows are spread across the project's life cycle.

If the customer has nothing to pay until the project's completion, this represents a severe risk and likewise more than likely means the project is 'out of pocket' as suppliers will have billed for their services by this time. Up-front payments avoid this negative project cash flow, although they are difficult to negotiate. For this reason, it is essential that payments are managed in such a way as to share the risk with the other stakeholders and as such have periods of both positive and negative cash flow.

Example – Cash flow

The following data and estimates are available for ABC Ltd for June, July and August:

	June	*July*	*August*
Sales	£45,000	£50,000	£60,000
Wages	£12,000	£13,000	£14,500
Overheads	£8,500	£9,500	£9,000

The following information is available regarding direct materials:

	June	*July*	*August*	*September*
Opening inventory	£5,000	£3,500	£6,000	£4,000
Material usage	£8,000	£9,000	£10,000	
Closing inventory	£3,500	£6,000	£4,000	

Notes:

(1) 10% of sales are for cash, the balance is received the following month.

The amount to be received in June for May's sales is £29,500.

(2) Wages are paid in the month they are incurred.

(3) Overheads include £1,500 per month for depreciation. Overheads are settled the month following. £6,500 is to be paid in June for May's overheads.

(4) Purchases of direct materials are paid for in the month purchased.

(5) The opening cash balance in June is £11,750.

(6) A tax bill of £25,000 is to be paid in July.

Required:

(a) Calculate the amount of direct material purchases in EACH of the months of June, July and August.

(b) Prepare cash budgets for June, July and August.

Solution:

Note: Stock is used up by material usage, and by closing inventory. This usage Is made up partly from opening inventory. The balance must be made up from purchases.

	June	*July*	*August*
	£	£	£
Material usage	8,000	9,000	10,000
Closing inventory	3,500	6,000	4,000
	11,500	15,000	14,000
Less: Opening inventory	5,000	3,500	6,000
Purchases	6,500	11,500	8,000

Note: The main points to watch out for are sales receipts and overheads. Tackle sales receipts by calculating separate figures for cash sales (10% of total sales, received in the month of sale) and credit sales (90% of last month's sales). For overheads, remember that depreciation is not a cash expense and must therefore be stripped out of the overheads cash cost.

Cash budgets, June – August

	June	*July*	*August*
	£	£	£
Receipts of cash			
Cash sales	4,500	5,000	6,000
Credit sales	29,500	40,500	45,000
	34,000	45,500	51,000
Cash payments			
Wages	12,000	13,000	14,500
Overheads	6,500	7,000	8,000
Direct materials	6,500	11,500	8,000
Taxation	–	25,000	–
	25,000	56,500	30,500
Surplus/(deficit) for month	9,000	(11,000)	20,500
Opening balance	11,750	20,750	9,750
Closing balance	**20,750**	**9,750**	**30,250**

4.5 Reconciling budgeted and actual performance

During the project, actual costs are compared with standard costs. Any variances are isolated for investigation as to their cause, enabling corrective action to be taken as soon as possible.

Management will wish to see a clear and succinct summary of the results for the period and in particular will want any unusual or unexpected items to be brought to their attention (exception reporting).

Therefore it is crucial to anticipate and address issues of expenditure exceeding tolerances and if necessary to reduce or redeploy resources.

There are a number of forecasting methods which can be used, including:

- Linear regression
- Seasonal variation
- Moving averages
- Indexing
- Extrapolation

- Sensitivity analysis
- Sampling

All of these methods are covered in depth in the Financial Performance unit of AAT Level 4, however the following two examples show two of these methods.

Example - Indexing

The materials costs for a business for the last six months were:

	£
March	427,000
April	442,000
May	460,000
June	433,000
July	447,000
August	470,000

If the index for March is 100, what are the index numbers of the costs for each of the subsequent months and what do these index numbers tell us?

Solution

Month		*Index*
March	Base year	100.0
April	$\frac{442,000}{427,000} \times 100$	103.5
May	$\frac{460,000}{427,000} \times 100$	107.7
June	$\frac{433,000}{427,000} \times 100$	101.4
July	$\frac{447,000}{427,000} \times 100$	104.7
August	$\frac{470,000}{427,000} \times 100$	110.1

The index shows that the materials costs are generally rising although there is a fall back in June which has been made up for by the highest level yet in August.

Example – Seasonal Variation

The Sales Manager for Yankee Limited is reviewing the company's quarterly sales (shown below) for the last financial year. External information for the label printing market indicates average annual growth of 16%. The Sales Manager's analysis suggests Yankee's sales have increased by 18% over the last year. As this is better than the market average the Manager will be awarded a performance related bonus.

	Q1	*Q2*	*Q3*	*Q4*
Actual sales volume	224,000	196,000	215,000	265,000

Before the Sales Manager's bonus is calculated and paid you have been asked to verify his findings. Having carried out some research you have established the following seasonal variations.

	Q1	*Q2*	*Q3*	*Q4*
Seasonal variations	14,000	–24,000	–15,000	25,000

Required:

Calculate the seasonally adjusted sales volume for EACH of the FOUR quarters for Yankee Ltd.

Calculate the seasonally adjusted growth in sales volume from Quarter 1 to Quarter 4 for Yankee Ltd. Express your answer as a percentage, to the nearest whole %.

Should the Sales Manager be paid his bonus? YES/NO

Solution:

The seasonally adjusted sales volume for EACH of the FOUR quarters for Yankee Ltd are:

	Q1	*Q2*	*Q3*	*Q4*
Actual sales	224,000	196,000	215,000	265,000
Seasonal variations	14,000	–24,000	–15,000	25,000
Trend	**210,000**	**220,000**	**230,000**	**240,000**

The seasonally adjusted growth in sales volume from Quarter 1 to Quarter 4 for Yankee Ltd is: **14%** (£240,000 – £210,000)/£210,000 × 100 = 14.28%

Should the Sales Manager be paid his bonus? **NO**

4.6 Variance reporting

As the project progresses, the key consideration for the finance team is whether the planned budget is being adhered to. Therefore to enable cost control, it is crucial that a variance report is regularly provided to assess how closely the actual expenditure (and income) is aligned to the budgeted finances. It will depend on the project manager how in-depth or frequent this report will be presented, but most likely it will be weekly or fortnightly and will include assessment across a number of project objectives or operational areas.

Constant monitoring of the project needs to be evidenced over the lifecycle of the project. Presentation of recommendations or adjustments should be illustrated with the use of graphs, charts or trend analysis.

4.7 Lifecycle costing

Lifecycle costing is the forecasting of costs for assets over their entire life, so that decisions concerning the acquisition, use or disposal of the assets can be made in a way that achieves the optimum asset usage at the lowest possible cost to the entity. (It is simply a net present cost (NPC).)

For example, when buying a machine, a business might be offered either a poor quality machine for £20,000 or a high quality machine for £50,000. If the poor quality machine is expected to continually break down and need to be repaired all the time, while the high quality machine is expected never to break down, then life cycle costing might argue that the high quality machine should be bought, despite it being more expensive, since its total cost of ownership over its entire life will be less than the poor quality alternative.

Activity 9

A company is going to renew a machine and is undecided between two options.

Machine A costs £50,000 immediately while machine B costs £80,000. Both machines will last 4 years. They will generate net savings after maintenance costs of:

	Machine A	*Machine B*
Year 1	£20,000	£30,000
Year 2	£20,000	£20,000
Year 3	£20,000	£20,000
Year 4	£10,000	£20,000

At the end of their lives they will be disposed of, generating an inflow of £10,000 for machine A and £30,000 for machine B.

Task

Calculate the Life Cycle Cost (LCC) of the two proposals when the interest rate is 10%.

The relevant present value factors are:

	Year 1	*Year 2*	*Year 3*	*Year 4*
10%	0.909	0.826	0.751	0.683

	Cashflow	*DF*	*PV*	*Cashflow*	*DF*	*PV*
Y0						
Y1						
Y2						
Y3						
Y4						
		LCC	£		LCC	£

Therefore machine ____________ is the better option.

4.8 Earned Value Management (EVM)

Earned Value Management (EVM) helps the financial managers of projects to measure the project's performance. It is used to calculate variances based on a comparison of work performed and work planned. It can therefore be used to determine whether a project is meeting scope, time and cost goals by using contemporary data from the project and comparing it back to the original plans.

This includes three primary measurements for the each activity from a project's work breakdown structure:

- Budgeted cost of work scheduled (BCWS)
- Actual cost of work performed (ACWP)
- Budgeted cost of work performed (BCWP)

From these, variances and indices can be calculated to reflect project progress:

- Schedule variance = BCWP – BCWS (if the difference is small, the project is on course, a negative difference implies the project is behind schedule)
- Cost variance = BCWP – ACWP (if this is negative, costs have overrun)
- Schedule index = BCWP/BCWS (if this results in 1, the project is on schedule. If smaller than 1, the project has overrun)

- Cost index = BCWP/ACWP (if this results in 1, the project is on budget. If smaller than 1, the project is overspent).

4.9 Budgetary Control Scenario

Activity 10

Visiguard Ltd is a division of Alton Products plc. It makes a single product, the Raider. Just over a year ago, the chief executive of Alton Products, Mike Green, was concerned to find that Visiguard was budgeting to make only £20,000 profit in the year to 31 May 20X0. As a result, he imposed his own budget on the division. His revised budget assumed:

- increased sales volume of the Raider
- increased selling prices and
- that suppliers would agree to reduce the cost of the material used in the Raider by 10%.

The only other changes to the original budget arose solely as a result of the increased volume in the revised budget.

The original budget and the revised budget imposed by Mike Green are reproduced below, together with the actual results for the year to 31 May 2000.

Visiguard Limited
Budgeted and actual operating statements for one year ended 31 May 20X0

	Original budget	*Revised budget*	*Actual results*
	£	£	£
Sales and production volume	10,000	11,000	11,600
	£	£	£
Revenue	1,400,000	1,760,000	1,844,400
Variable materials	400,000	396,000	440,800
Production and administrative labour	580,000	630,000	677,600
Light, heat and power	160,000	164,000	136,400
Fixed overheads	240,000	240,000	259,600
Budgeted profit	20,000	330,000	330,000

Required:

Using the information provided in the two budgets, calculate the following:

(a) The unit selling price of the Raider in the revised budget.

(b) The material cost per Raider in the revised budget.

(c) The variable cost of production and administrative labour per Raider.

(d) The fixed cost of production and administrative labour.

(e) The variable cost of light, heat and power per Raider.

(f) The fixed cost of light, heat and power.

Data

On receiving the actual results for the year, Mike Green states that they prove that his revised budget motivated managers to produce better results.

Required:

Write a memo to Mike Green. Your memo should:

(a) Use the information calculated before to prepare a flexed budget statement for Visiguard including any variances.

(b) Identify TWO situations where an imposed budget might be preferable to one prepared with the participation of managers.

(c) Briefly discuss whether or not his requirement that material costs be reduced would have motivated the managers of Visiguard.

(d) Identify TWO ways in which profit could have increased without additional effort by the managers of Visiguard.

4.10 Other project control mechanisms

It is important to remember that in addition to the above accounting processes, there are other ways in which the project's budget and performance is monitored and controlled. These include project reports and progress review meetings.

4.11 Project reports

The financial report should therefore include:

- original authorised budget
- changes to the budget, including justification and authorisation
- amended authorised budget

- expenditure to date (base estimates and risk allowances)
- commitments
- agreed variations
- potential claims awaiting resolution
- orders yet to be placed
- variations pending
- future changes anticipated
- any required changes to contingency amounts

For any project packages which are not complete, the cost to complete them should also be included as a forecast.

4.12 The forecast of cost to complete

This forecast will rely heavily on an accurate assessment of the project's output. If the project relates to manufacturing, therefore, it will be easier to assess this based on the simple scale of production. If however the results are less tangible and the tasks involved require varying levels of skill and effort to complete, this will be more complex.

Perhaps the most effective indication of project progress and the cost to complete therefore is how many more person-days it will take to finish the project.

This will allow the project manager or financial controller to forecast the cost to complete, based on:

- the actual cost of completed work
- the projected cost of work in progress
- the current budgeted cost of work not yet started

4.13 Project meetings

The importance of project meetings was shown using the Example in Chapter 7. Regular project meetings are a key means of control and allow both the members of the project team and external stakeholders to keep up to date with the progress project.

Some meetings are specific to particular stages of the project – for example, project initiation and completion meetings. Others meetings will be held less frequently and are likely to include less predictable attendees – for example, ad hoc emergency and problem-solving meetings.

In terms of control, the most important are the progress review meetings which are regular and formal, providing an update on all aspects of the project. These will typically include the project manager, the project team and the customer or steering committee.

Meetings are vital forms of communication to any project and allow for the above information to be provided to all project stakeholders.

Activity 11

The following statements refer to project control. Which of the statements are correct?

Statement	Correct or incorrect?
A project control system will ensure that the project meets its deadlines.	
Performance management is only required at the end of the project.	
Reports and meetings are important elements of control within projects.	
Project progress review meetings are regular, formal meetings involving the project manager, team members and the customer or steering committee.	
The main purposes of a control system are to prevent and correct deviations.	

Activity 12

Referring back to the project in your workplace addressed in Activities 5, 7 and 8, explain how costs were managed against the original and revised budgets.

Required:

Review expenditure on the project compared to the budgeted costs and assess how effective cost control measures were.

Explain how funds were released and cash flow was managed and suggest whether they processes could have been improved.

Describe how potential excess expenditure was identified and how forecasting techniques were used.

(AAT Assessment criteria 2.1, 2.2, 2.3, 2.4)

5 Project completion

5.1 Introduction

Formal sign off of the project is the final stage of the project life cycle and indicates that objectives have been met and deliverables are to the satisfaction of all stakeholders. It is a common misconception that this stage of the project is a mere formality and as such requires little effort.

It is important though that however much energy has been sapped by the project, all members of the project team ensure that the solution for the user is satisfactory and allow a period of reflection and analysis to help with the improvement of future projects.

5.2 Completion activities

A number of activities must occur at the conclusion of the project.

- Formal sign off and agreement that the project has been delivered
- End of project meetings with stakeholders
- Organising and filing all project documentation
- Review of project organisation and procedures
- Final project report including analysis of whether the project met deadlines and budgets
- Receiving and making final payments
- Accounting for all income
- Checking and reconciling costs
- Disbanding and potentially rewarding of the project team

The customer will also wish to offer their own views on the success of the project and therefore it is likely that both internal and external review meetings will be held. Customer acceptance ultimately means payment and for this reason, this is a crucial part of the completion process.

5.3 The final report

The final report will most likely be produced by the project manager, but will focus largely on the financial success of the project. Therefore it is likely to list the objectives and deliverables identified in the PID and assess how actual achievements and time and cost budgets relate to the plans. It is likely to look at milestones and costs and state how often these were in line with the project's brief.

In terms of the financial considerations, for each work package, it will be required to report back on whether the project was managed to budget and to assess reasons for variances.

Key questions may include:

- Did the project overrun?
- Did an unknown limiting factor occur?
- Was there too little tolerance in the project plan?

The analysis included in this report will be addressed in greater depth below when project evaluation is considered.

5.4 Post completion audit

If the project is relatively large in scale it is likely that after the completion of the project a further audit is carried out to judge the management of the project and to establish whether the project was largely effective both in terms of its administration and delivery and in terms of the lasting impact on the business. This is the part of the completion likely to offer recommendations for future projects.

6 Project Evaluation

6.1 Evaluation of project costs

On completion of the project, all financial liabilities should be accounted for and all ongoing costs should be identified and have relevant accruals organised. In addition to financial costs, there may also be social responsibility costs associated with the project.

6.2 Evaluation of financial performance

The financial performance of the project can then be analysed, using a number of methods:

- **Efficiency ratios** – the relationship between inputs and outputs, with the fewer inputs/resources required to achieve the required outcome seen as the more efficient
- **Material usage** – budgeted compared to actual materials utilised for production
- **Labour utilisation** – analysis of how labour was organised, including the use of idle time variances

- **Benchmarking** – using performance indicators to judge success and comparing outcomes with best practice
- **Balanced scorecard** – involves four different perspectives: financial; customer; internal business process prospective; innovation and learning.

6.3 The balanced scorecard

The balanced scorecard approach to performance indicators recognises that historically too much emphasis has been placed on financial ratios in assessing an entity's performance. A successful business will only succeed in the long-term if it keeps its customers happy as well as by making profits. The approach therefore combines financial measures with operational, organisational innovation and customer service measures. All of these perspectives must be managed by managers if the business is to prosper in the long-term.

The balanced scorecard becomes the manager's instrument panel for managing the complexity of the organisation within a dynamic external environment.

The table below is an example of a balanced scorecard performance management system which demonstrates the role of critical success factors (CSFs) and key performance indicators (KPIs) in this process.

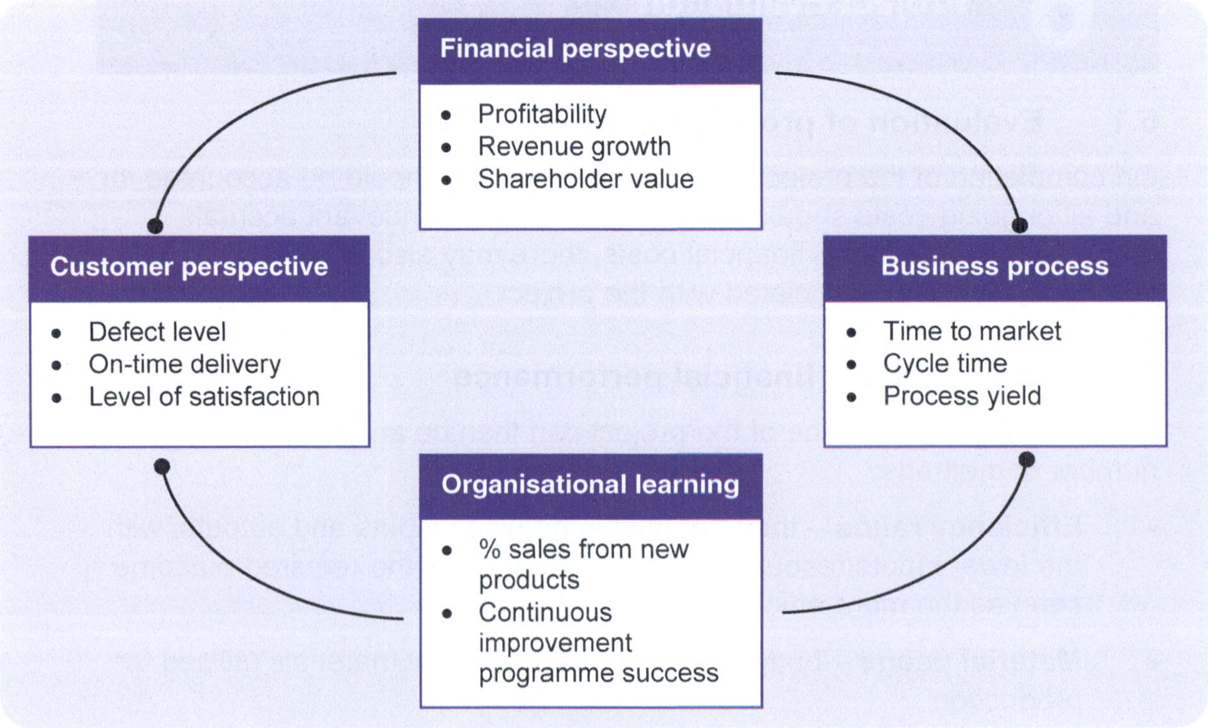

Typical key performance indicators for the balanced scorecard approach are illustrated below.

	Financial aspect	*Customer aspect*	*Business process aspect*	*Organisational learning aspect*
Strategic objective ▼	Shareholder satisfaction ▼	Customer satisfaction ▼	Manufacturing excellence ▼	New product innovation ▼
Critical success factor ▼	Grow shareholder wealth ▼	Achieve preferred supplier status ▼	State-of-the-art process plant ▼	Successful new product development ▼
Key performance indicators	ROCE	Number of new customers	Cycle times Unit cost % yield	% of sales represented by new products

6.4 Common project problems

Consider in your evaluation of the project's performance whether any of the following common hurdles were overcome and if so, how:

- Did the project overrun?
- Was the planning unrealistic?
- Did an unknown limiting factor occur?
- Was there too little tolerance in the project?

One of common obstacle, unknown limiting factors, is explored below.

Example

Meato Ltd makes and sells two dog food products, the Bassett and the Spaniel. It has a shortage of labour, which is limited to 200,000 hours per annum. This is not enough to meet the demand for both products.

	Bassett	**Spaniel**
Labour hours per unit	5	10
Selling price	£80	£100
Variable cost	£50	£50
Contribution per unit	£30	£50

Let us find the higher contribution per unit of limiting factor:

Bassett 30/5 = £6 contribution per labour hour

Spaniel 50/10 = £5 contribution per labour hour

Therefore the company should concentrate on the manufacture of the Bassett product.

Be aware though that there are other considerations:

a) In the short term, the management may be able to find a way to meet the labour demands by using overtime, agency staff or outsourcing

b) In the long run, the management must try to remove the limiting factor in this case by recruiting and training additional labour

c) It may be there is more than one limiting factor to consider

d) There may be other considerations, such as customer contracts requiring minimum order quantities.

6.5 Net Present Value

To appraise a project we need to take into consideration the time value of money. So after identifying cash flows, they should be discounted to come to a Net Present Value and determine if the project will generate more inflows of cash than outflows. If the former is the case, this is acceptable.

Activity 13

Highscore Ltd manufacture cricket bats. They are considering investing £30,000 in a new delivery vehicle which will generate savings compared with sub-contracting out the delivery service. The vehicle will have a life of six years, with zero scrap value. The accounting technician and the transport manager have prepared the following estimates relating to the savings.

The cash flows from the project are:

		£
Year	1	9,000
	2	11,000
	3	10,000
	4	10,500
	5	10,200
	6	10,100

The business discount rate is 15%.

Required:

Prepare an appraisal of the project using the discounted cash flow (NPV method) technique.

The relevant discount factors are:

	Year 1	*Year 2*	*Year 3*	*Year 4*	*Year 5*	*Year 6*
15%	0.870	0.756	0.658	0.572	0.497	0.432

Highscore Ltd

Discounted cash flow – Net Present Value method – appraisal

Year	Cash Flow	15% discount factor	PV
1			
2			
3			
4			
5			
6			
		NPV	

6.6 Reporting financial aspects of the project

To contribute effectively towards the final project report, the reporting of financial performance should

- be clear, concise and easy to understand for non-financial stakeholders
- consider all stakeholder groups (management, employees, investors, contractors)
- make recommendations and conclusions based on key performance indicators

The following activity allows you to practice some of these techniques.

Activity 14

Tempest plc is a large public company engaged in the running of cinemas throughout the UK. Some cinemas are very large with multiple screens. Typically these are based on large sites situated out of town, with on-site parking, and often with bar and snack facilities.

Other smaller cinemas with only a few screens are typically based in city centres. They have limited parking, but similar facilities for refreshments.

Currently Tempest charges the same fee per film for both types of cinema. However the number of customers per month, and spend per customer on food and drink varies greatly at each type of cinema. A project team has been set up to create Tempest's Plan for the Future. They need to judge which type of cinema is more profitable per customer and therefore the company's commercial priorities.

A typical forecast income statement and statement of financial position for both type of cinemas is shown below:

Forecast Income statement	***Out of Town***	***City Centre***
	£000	£000
Turnover	1,512	501
Cost of production		
Direct costs (90% films, 10% food)	320	108
Fixed costs	450	180
Total cost of sales	770	288
Gross profit	742	213
Administration costs (fixed)	50	50
Operating profit	692	163
Revenue from films	1,209	451
Revenue from food and drink	303	50
Gross profit margin	49%	42%
Operating profit margin	46%	32%
Number of customers per month (thousand)	150	56
Average spend per customer – Films	£8.06	£8.05
Average spend per customer – Food	£2.02	£0.89
Direct cost per customer	£2.13	£2.16
Fixed cost per customer	£3.00	£3.24

Draft a report for your Project Manager covering the following:

- Explain why the gross profit margins are not significantly different using sales price, direct costs and fixed costs to illustrate your answer.
- Explain why the operating profit margins are different.
- Which is the most profitable type of cinema and why?
- Apart from reducing fixed costs what could Tempest do to improve the profitability of the City Centre Cinemas? Use numbers to demonstrate your answer if necessary.
- Tempest suspect City Centre customers are smuggling in their own sweets and snacks – give ONE way that Tempest could investigate the extent of this smuggling? What could be done to combat it?

Use the template provided on the next page to complete your report.

To:	**Subject:**
From:	**Date:**

Why are the gross profit margins not significantly different?

Sales Price

Direct costs

Fixed costs

Why are the operating profit margins different?

Which is the most profitable type of cinema and why?

Apart from reducing fixed costs what could Tempest do to improve the profitability of the City Centre Cinemas?

Tempest suspect City Centre customers are smuggling in their own sweets and snacks – what could Tempest do to combat this smuggling?

Activity 15

Referring back to the project in your workplace covered in earlier activities, draft a final project report, to be sent to all stakeholders, including a full analysis of the financial performance of the project at completion. This should include at least two performance indicators and a cost reconciliation report, as well as recommendations for the future.

(AAT Assessment criteria 2.5, 3.1, 3.2, 3.3)

7 Compliance

7.1 Regulatory framework

There are a number of legal and regulatory requirements and standards which any project should satisfy.

In earlier chapters of this Text, the legal and ethical considerations of companies working with individuals and with other organisations were addressed.

A sound understanding of the financial regulatory framework and accounting standards is established through the other units of the AAT Level 4 qualification.

Examples include

- IAS 7, regarding cash flow
- IAS17, when considering lease or buy options

7.2 Legal requirements

There are a number of legal requirements to consider during the project:

- **The Companies Act 2006** contains guidance and rules on the formats for the financial statements, fundamental accounting principles and valuation rules and has been amended to take account of the companies who have adopted International Financial Reporting Standards (IFRSs).

  It embodies four accounting principles:

  - going concern
  - consistency
  - prudence
  - accruals.

- **The Data Protection Act 1998** states that all personal data should be kept and utilised for designated purposes. It states that accuracy and integrity must be maintained and the data must be open to inspection. Information must be secured against alteration, accidental loss or deliberate damage.

7.3 Project management methodologies

A project management methodology is a set of guidelines which defines the methods and processes to be followed to help successful delivery of the project. By providing a standard set of processes and templates, these methodologies can support any organisation's projects.

PRojects IN Controlled Environments (PRINCE2) is perhaps the most widely utilised methodology and contains a large number of control elements to ensure that projects are delivered on time and on budget. It provides a clear structure of authority and responsibility, gives an understanding of the tasks to be completed and the risks involved and includes a number of tools and products such as plans, reports and PIDs.

As part of the organisational structure defined by PRINCE2, a project assurance team are created independently of the board/committee and project team. Their purpose is to monitor quality and provide an independent view on the project's progress, split into three concerns: business assurance, user assurance and specialist assurance.

7.4 Axelos

Axelos is a joint venture set up in 2014 by the UK government and Capita, to manage and provide training in best practice in these methodologies.

For example, Axelos manages:

- Managing Successful Programmes (MSP)
- PRojects IN Controlled Environments (PRINCE2)
- Portfolio, Programme and Project Offices (P3O)

7.5 Copyright and licencing considerations

The copyright and trademark of PRINCE2 will need to be considered within all planning.

Activity 16

List the financial, legal and professional standards which must be considered throughout any project.

(AAT Assessment criteria 4.1, 4.2)

Activity 17

Insert the correct word from the Picklist below to complete these sentences:

The project stage where customer feedback would be obtained is known as (A).

At the (B) stage, the project objectives and targets for time, costs and quality are agreed and communicated (for example, Work Breakdown Structures, Gantt Charts and PQPs).

The phase when the actual performance of the project is undertaken is known as (C).

A Project (D) Document completes the first stage of the project and defines the purpose and scope of the project.

The (E) stage establishes whether the project helped the business to deliver the benefits defined in the original business case.

Picklist

Quality	Implementation	Post completion
Initiation	Planning	Completion

End of chapter answers

Activity 1

The correct answer is **C. a unique objective and stakeholders.**

Activity 2

There are a number of people involved in a project. Match the people below to the correct description.

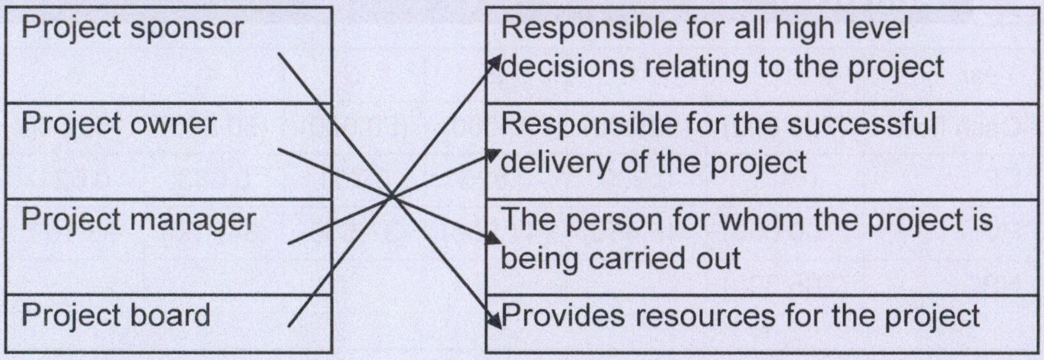

Activity 3

The correct answer is **D.**

This appears to be an issue for the manager of the employee not performing effectively and making payments in a tardy fashion. This would most likely be an issue of training and/or disciplinary action depending on the circumstances. Either way, it is clearly an example of an individual's behaviour having an impact on the business rather than being an issue requiring a new policy or serious investigation or development as the other three options are.

Activity 4

The Project Initiation Document is in fact an essential document both in the initiation and later stages of the project. Therefore the sentence should include reference to the fact that it seeks the authorisation and funding for the project in its first form and then provides a structure to the project in action, as it defines objectives, assumptions, deliverables, constraints, roles and responsibilities and the overall approach to communication and reporting.

Activity 5

This answer will depend on the individual's experience and the specific requirements of the project. They should however identify the nature of the costs (eg. capital, labour, materials, overheads, etc) and show that different project options were considered.

Activity 6

Year	*0*	*1*	*2*	*3*	*4*	*5*
Cash flow	(700,000)	(50,000)	(50,000)	(50,000)	(50,000)	150,000
DF	1	0.909	0.826	0.751	0.683	0.621
PV	(700,000)	(45,450)	(41,300)	(37,550)	(34,150)	93,150
NPC	(765,300)					

Year	*0*	*1*	*2*	*3*	*4*
Lease costs	(200,000)	(200,000)	(200,000)	(200,000)	(200,000)
DF	1	0.909	0.826	0.751	0.683
PV	(200,000)	(181,800)	(165,200)	(150,200)	(136,600)
NPC	(833,800)				

Based on the calculations it is best to **BUY** the machine, in order to save **£68,500.**

Activity 7

This answer will depend on the individual's experience and the specific requirements of the project. The budget should however identify all relevant costs and address further considerations including make or buy decisions or limiting factors. The written report to accompany the budget should explain how these decisions were reached and confirm why the chosen approach to the budget (eg. Top-down/bottom-up, ZBB) was taken with reference to other types of budget in comparison. It is important that a section is included on contingency and management reserve and in doing so to raise any obvious issues or reasons why this may prove relevant.

Activity 8

The answer will depend on the specifics of the project, however typical tools used for planning time would be the use of Gantt Charts and Work Breakdown Structures. Critical Path Analysis could be referenced, with the use of network diagrams, although the student need not provide detail. In terms of quality, a Project Quality Plan is most likely.

These two factors can have a huge impact on financial budgets and planning as if the project runs late, it may be necessary to pay extra labour costs and purchase raw materials at a premium. All overheads are likely to increase the longer the project runs and the analysis of make or buy decisions, for example, may be affected. The cost considerations of quality are key, especially within a manufacturing project, as financial adjustments may be required if production outcomes are not as planned.

Activity 9

	Cashflow	*DF*	*PV*	*Cashflow*	*DF*	*PV*
0	(£50,000)	1.000	(50,000)	(£80,000)	1.000	(80,000)
1	£20,000	0.909	18,180	£30,000	0.909	27,270
2	£20,000	0.826	16,520	£20,000□	0.826	16,520
3	£20,000	0.751	15,020	£20,000	0.751	15,020
4	£20,000	0.683	13,660	£50,000	0.683	34,150
		LCC	£13,380		LCC	£12,960

Therefore, **machine A** is the better option.

Activity 10

(a) Revised budgeted selling price:
(£1,760,000/11,000) £160

(b) Material cost per unit in revised budget:
(£396,000/11,000) £36

(c) Variable cost of production and administrative labour – high/low method:

Increase in budgeted labour cost (£630,000 – £580,000)	£50,000
Increase in budgeted volume (11,000 – 10,000)	1,000
Variable cost of labour per unit (£50,000/1,000)	£50

(d) Fixed cost of production and administrative labour:

Total budgeted cost of labour for 11,000 units	£630,000
Variable cost of labour (11,000 × £50)	£550,000
Budgeted fixed cost of labour	£80,000

(e) Variable cost of light, heat and power – high/low method:

Increase in budgeted light, heat and power (£164,000 – £160,000)	£4,000
Increase in budgeted volume	1,000
Budgeted variable cost of light, heat and power per unit (£4,000/1,000)	£4

(f) Fixed cost of light, heat and power:

Total budgeted cost of light, heat and power for 11,000 units	£164,000
Variable cost of light, heat and power (11,000 × £4)	£44,000
Budgeted fixed cost of light, heat and power	£120,000

MEMO

To: Mike Green

From: Management Accountant

Date: 22 June 20X0

Subject: Motivation and performance

I attach a budgetary control statement for Visiguard based on the flexible budget technique and wish to make the following observations.

(a) **Visiguard Ltd – Flexible budgetary control statement for the year ended 31 May 20X0**

	Flexed budget	*Actual results*	*Variances*
Sales and production volume (units)	11,600	11,600	Nil
	£	£	£
Revenue (£160 × 11,600)	1,856,000	1,844,400	11,600 (A)

Variable materials (£36 × 11,600)	417,600	440,800	23,200 (A)
Production and administrative labour (£80,000 + [£50 × 11,600])	660,000	677,600	17,600 (A)
Light, heat and power 120,000 + [4 × 11,600]	166,400	136,400	30,000 (F)
Fixed overheads	240,000	259,600	19,600 (A)
Profit	372,000	330,000	42,000 (A)

(b) There is an assumption that a participative approach to budgets and budgetary control will improve management motivation and results. However, there are a number of situations where imposed budgets may be more effective than participative budgets. These include:

- Managers' objectives may not be those of the organisation as a whole.
- Managers do not have the training, skill or technical knowledge to set budgets.
- Managers would prefer not to set their own targets.
- Time constraint whereby full participation is not practicable.

(c) Setting of budgetary targets that are not achievable can be demotivating. If managers recognise this they are likely not even to attempt to achieve the target. Impossible targets can also bring into disrepute the whole planning process; and managers may question the validity and usefulness of the budgetary process.

This might have been the case in terms of the request to reduce material costs. If Visiguard do not have an alternative supplier, the managers may have little control over material prices.

(d) It does not always follow that improved performance compared to the original budget is because managers were motivated by the budget revision.

- Actual activity was greater than the agreed revision. This may have been due to the increased energy and motivation of managers. However, there may have been, outside the control of managers, a general increase in demand for the product.
- The only cost less than planned in the budget is light, heat and power. This may have been an inaccurate forecast or because weather conditions have been milder, thus reducing heating costs. It is unlikely that the power supplier has reduced costs.

Activity 11

A project control system will ensure that the project meets its deadlines.	Incorrect
Performance management is only required at the end of the project.	Incorrect
Reports and meetings are important elements of control within projects.	Correct
Project progress review meetings are regular, formal meetings involving the project manager, team members and the customer or steering committee.	Correct
The main purposes of a control system are to prevent and correct deviations.	Correct

Activity 12

This answer will depend on the individual's experience and the specific requirements of the project. They should however present the original planned expenditure and use variance analysis to show how costs were managed and give an example of short-term, medium-term and long-term management of base costs. They should provide evidence of a minimum of two different forecasting techniques used to show how control was maintained where expenditure exceeded tolerances.

Activity 13

Discounted cash flow – Net Present Value method – appraisal

Year	*Cash flow*	*15% discount factor*	*PV*
0	(30,000)	1.000	(30,000)
1	9,000	0.870	7,830
2	11,000	0.756	8,316
3	10,000	0.658	6,580
4	10,500	0.572	6,006
5	10,200	0.497	5,069
6	10,100	0.432	4,363
		NPV =	**£8,164**

Activity 14

To:	Project Manager	**Subject:**	Profitability
From:	Accountant	**Date:**	Today

Why are the gross profit margins not significantly different?

Sales Price

The Sales price in each cinema is the same and therefore the revenue earned per customer does not have any effect on the gross profit margin.

Direct costs

The direct cost per customer is slightly higher at the City centre cinemas (£2.16 versus £2.13 at the out of town sites). This only has a small effect on the gross profit margin.

Fixed costs

The fixed costs per customer are higher per customer at the City Centre cinemas (£3.24 per customer versus £3.00 per customer). This explains the majority of the difference in the gross profit margin.

Why are the operating profit margins different?

Both cinemas have the same administrative costs despite having a different number of customers – this works out at £0.33 per customer at the out of town cinemas and £0.89 at the city centre cinemas. This cost is fixed, and accounts for the difference in operating profit margins.

Which is the most profitable type of cinema and why? (Many different answers could be given.)

The Out of Town sites earn £4.61 per customer and the City Centre sites earn £2.90 per customer. This can mostly be explained by the increased admin costs at the city centre cinemas.

Apart from reducing fixed costs what could Tempest do to improve the profitability of the City Centre Cinemas?

The average spend on food per customer is much lower at the City Centre cinemas – only £0.89. If customers could be persuaded to spend an extra £1.00 when the variable cost of food is only 10% then this would result in an extra £0.90 per customer per visit.

We could try to increase the numbers attending the City Centre cinemas – this would spread the fixed admin cost over more customers increasing profit per customer.

Tempest suspect City Centre customers are smuggling in their own sweets and snacks – give ONE way that Tempest could combat it?

Market research – ask the customers – are food prices at the cinema too high?

Look for evidence of food wrappers that aren't sold in cinemas

Tactic to combat smuggling – Offer promotions e.g. 2 for 1.

Activity 15

This answer will depend on the individual's experience and the specific requirements of the project. The report however should meet all of the criteria of the final project report, including a full analysis of the financial performance of the project including at least two performance indicators, for which the balanced scorecard, ratios or benchmarking would be suitable. In terms of effectiveness, in addition to a consideration of the financial aspects and control of costs and variances, the processes and people involved should also be considered. Recommendations could be either for the project's management or for the legacy of the project.

Activity 16

There are many standards which any project needs to comply with. Project management methodologies provide a framework within which to operate and therefore PRINCE2 and similar are important for any project team. Copyright issues in using this or other software must however be considered. It is also important to bear in mind all of the legal and ethical implications discussed in Chapter 3 – in particular the Data Protection Act – given the nature of projects and the level of research often involved. Financial procedures and professional standards include a consideration of international accounting standards and regulatory codes of conduct.

Activity 17

A is Completion

B is Planning

C is Implementation

D is Initiation

E is Post completion.

9 Spreadsheet Software and the use of Information Technology

Introduction

The use of Information Technology has already been seen throughout this Text. The use of such technology and recent innovations have totally changed the face of how modern business works.

On a commercial level, technology has opened up new opportunities and has become a core market in itself. In terms of the processes involved in organisations, it is difficult to see how many would operate without the use of automation and innovation.

This chapter offers a brief overview of the use of IT and spreadsheets in particular, making reference to earlier chapters and showing that although some regard IT as being an excuse not to use other more human or practical skills, its effective use is a skillset in own right.

ASSESSMENT CRITERIA

Spreadsheet Software

1 Use a spreadsheet to enter, edit and organise data.

2 Select and use appropriate formulas and data analysis tools and techniques.

3 Use tools and techniques to present, format and publish spreadsheet information.

This chapter also makes reference to all of the other business skills units.

CONTENTS

1 The use of IT in business
2 Spreadsheet software
3 IT within the organisation
4 IT and teams
5 IT and projects

1 The use of Information Technology in business

1.1 The impact of information technology

Developments in Information Technology (IT) and Information Systems (IS) have, and continue to have, a major impact on how businesses are run. Many of these advantageous developments have already been mentioned in this Text.

- The use of websites, e-mails and social media for marketing and communication
- The development of e-commerce as a means of selling and buying products and services
- The use of internal and external storage facilities, such as the cloud, for managing data and sensitive information
- The role of software to maintain customer records (e.g. CRM programs)
- The use of presentation software to enhance presentations
- The ability to outsource operations based on shared information
- The use of remote conferencing and homeworking facilities
- Office automation to arrange for information to be sent in high volumes
- The increased security for data storage

This chapter focuses on some of the above in greater depth and also how another form of software, spreadsheets can help the accounting function to manage finances effectively and aid the way that information can be translated to stakeholders through a variety of forms of communication.

1.2 Information Systems

Information systems (IS) refer to the provision and management of information to support the running of an organisation. Information technology (IT) is the supporting equipment that makes this possible.

In the modern world, with the advent of electronic data interchanges (EDI), information can be easily and accurately distributed to all stakeholders. This has a positive impact on the way that information can be communicated and utilised, but can also have a vital impact on decision-making.

Every company will have a variety of systems in place to aid with decision-making and to ensure the company operates efficiently. These can be categorised as follows:

- Management information systems (MIS) – provide information to monitor and control the organisation's business activities
- Transaction processing systems (TPS) – carry out essential, routine processing of day-to-day transactional date
- Decision support systems (DSS) – provide managers with information to support one-off or complex decisions, for example 'What If' analysis.

Although we will not cover this subject in any more detail at this stage, students should therefore be aware of the role that IT can play in their business, especially with regards to providing strategic data.

Activity 1

A computerised payroll package is an example of:

A a data processing system

B a management information system

C a decision support system

D a web dependent application

2 Spreadsheet Software

2.1 Introduction

This chapter will concentrate on the way that spreadsheets can be used to inform and complement the other skills and business functions referred to in this book.

For details on the mechanics and basic workings of spreadsheet software, it is advised to purchase Kaplan Publishing's AAT Level 3 Spreadsheet Software Combined Text/Workbook. This will cover much of the data entry, organisation and analysis tools required for assessment criteria 1.1 to 1.4 and 2.1 to 2.4, including inputting, sorting and filtering data, page and print setup, data validation and formulas.

This chapter will however show how spreadsheets can be used to format and enhance information and provide it in a suitable condition for decision-making. For further explanation and examples, the above Level 3 material may be of use.

2.2 Analysing information – Simple Budgets

The easiest way to manage budgets is by using a simple spreadsheets, including formulas. By using the data in the spreadsheet, the possibility of human error is removed and it is easier to perform multiple calculations and some of the analytical tools below.

Here is a sample budget plan created using Excel:

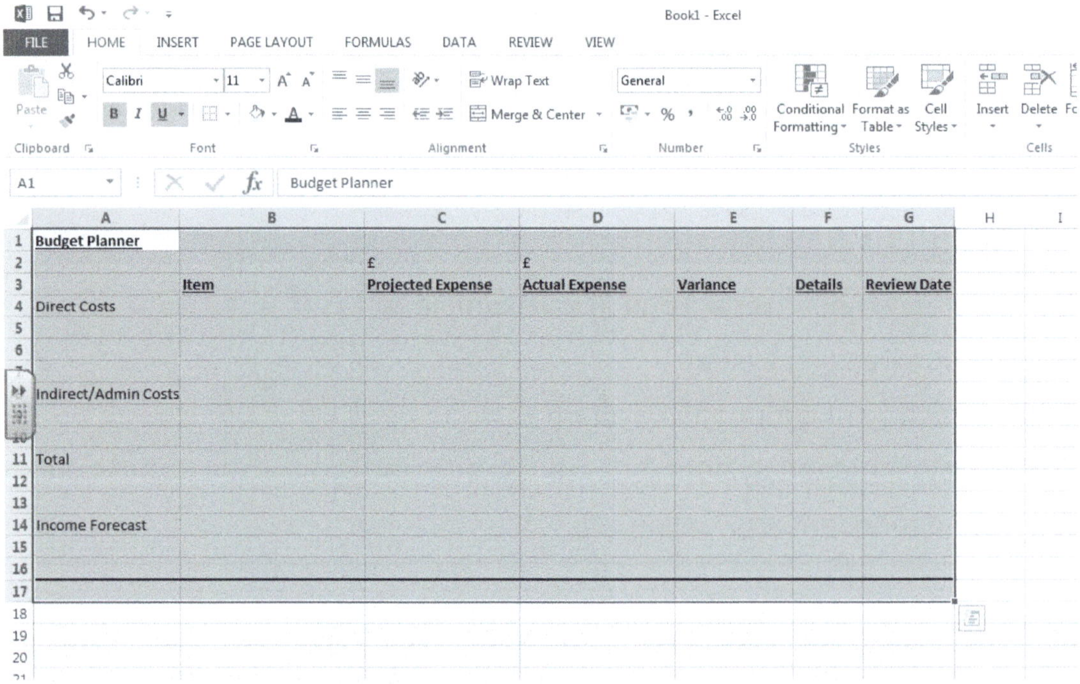

2.3 Analysing information – Pivot Tables

A Pivot Table is a tool used for turning tables of data into meaningful reports. The tool can be used to create reports from external sources, multiple-workbooks (another consolidation tool) and workbooks.

In essence a Pivot Table is a means of taking raw data and presenting it so that the user can understand what they are looking at. It is often best to think in terms of 'what would I want a report on this data to look like?' You can then set your pivot table to look like this.

Below is an example of a pivot table showing sales data, which is one common use for this form of report.

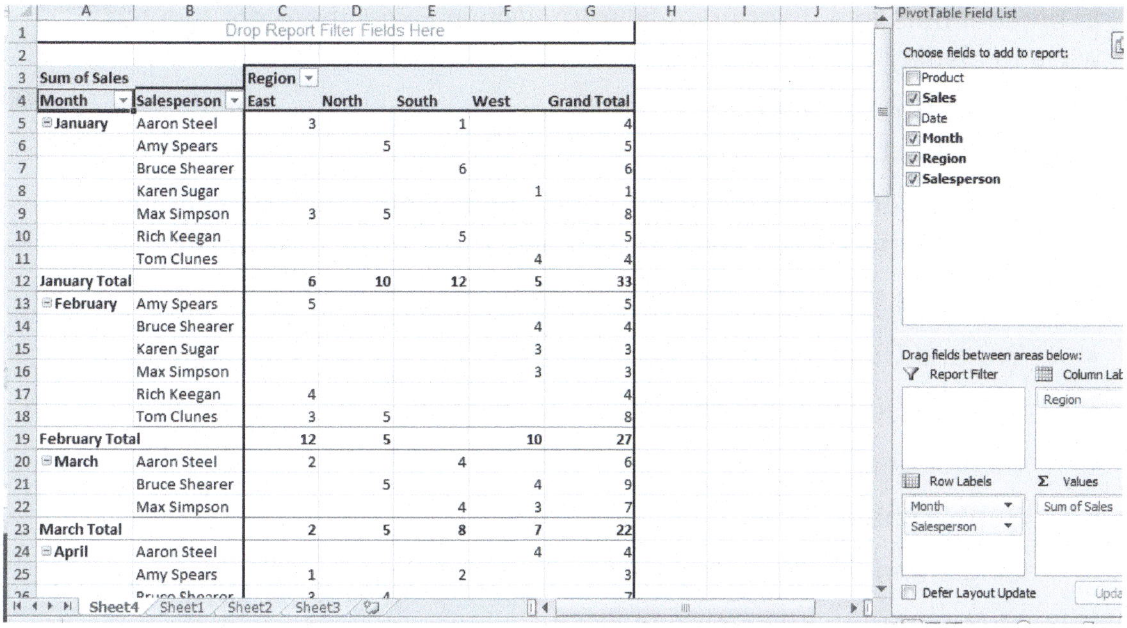

Sum of Sales		Region				
Month	Salesperson	East	North	South	West	Grand Total
January	Aaron Steel	3		1		4
	Amy Spears		5			5
	Bruce Shearer			6		6
	Karen Sugar				1	1
	Max Simpson	3	5			8
	Rich Keegan			5		5
	Tom Clunes				4	4
January Total		6	10	12	5	33
February	Amy Spears	5				5
	Bruce Shearer				4	4
	Karen Sugar				3	3
	Max Simpson				3	3
	Rich Keegan	4				4
	Tom Clunes	3	5			8
February Total		12	5		10	27
March	Aaron Steel	2		4		6
	Bruce Shearer		5		4	9
	Max Simpson			4	3	7
March Total		2	5	8	7	22
April	Aaron Steel				4	4
	Amy Spears	1		2		3
	Bruce Shearer	3	4			7

2.4 Analysing information – What If analysis and scenarios

As briefly mentioned in the previous chapter, spreadsheets can also help with forecasting and showing how different factors can have an impact on performance. Using Scenario Manager, variables can be changed to see the impact on the final outcome.

It is also possible to goal seek – in other words, 'what if' in reverse. This enables you to start with your desired outcome and will then change the variables accordingly to meet it.

2.5 Analysing information – Analysis Tools

Within Excel, additional Analysis Tools can be activated. Many of these will prove valuable when managing project finances or for any of the forecasting methods we discussed in the previous chapter. For example, the Analysis Tools include Moving Average, Random Numbers, Rank and Percentile and Sampling.

2.6 Displaying information – Charts and graphs

As addressed when covering effective communication and presentations, it is vital to present this information in a way that is accessible to the audience and will both capture their interest and make complex statistics more easily understood.

One way spreadsheets can help with this is the use of charts and graphs to present data in a diagrammatic form. Within Excel there are two basic ways to display charts and graphs:

1 **Chart Sheet** – here the chart or graph becomes the entire worksheet.

2 **Embedded** – here the chart or graph is located on the sheet that contains the data. The chart can be moved around to suit the user.

You can utilise the following types of graph:

- Bar and Column charts
- Pie and Doughnut charts
- Scatter graph
- Bubble chart
- Single and Double line graphs
- Multiple graph types on one chart

For further details on each, the Level 3 Spreadsheet Software Combined Text/Workbook provides examples.

When it comes to choosing the correct type of chart to use there are no hard and fast rules. It is generally up to the report writer to choose, and, as you are trying to show graphically what a series of numbers represent it is sometimes best to play around until the best option is found. Within each type of graph or chart you will find sub-types of the same graph with a mini-explanation of each, plus you get a preview of what your graph will look like.

A Pivot Chart is just a chart based on a pivot table. They work in exactly the same way as a normal chart. The beauty of Pivot Charts is that they change according to the filters applied to your PivotTable.

Activity 2

Detail five ways spreadsheet software can be used to improve business performance.

3 IT within the organisation

3.1 IT specialisation

Before looking at the ways in which IT can work to bring colleagues within the organisation closer together, it is also worth noting that in many cases the IT department operate entirely independently of other areas of the business, seeing other departments more as customers than colleagues. To take this to its extreme, for many smaller companies, IT services are often outsourced to external suppliers. This is not only as a cost-saving measure, it is also a necessary measure to keep up-to-date with the latest software developments and system requirements.

The outsourcing of the IT function is likely to be subject to a tendering process and a series of contractual obligations and service level agreements.

Activity 3

The outsourcing of an IT service by an organisation can lead to which one of the following:

A Increased reliance on the IT department

B Increased reliance on central departments generally

C Certain staff having responsibility for monitoring contracts

D Recruitment of additional programmers

3.2 Communication and data sharing

Due to technological developments, it is easier for colleagues to share information and communicate more easily. The use of e-mails, wireless and mobile technologies have radically changed business life and social media is an effective and easy way of communicating with large groups of business contacts in a more informal manner.

Most organisations have an intranet network, with access limited to their employees. This internet-based information-sharing portal allows for both confidential and large data to be stored more easily and accessed more widely. Corporate policies, training documents and organisational tools are often housed on the intranet, for example. An extranet is an extension of this concept, with suppliers and customers also granted access.

Groupware is the software used primarily for sharing diary functions both internally and externally. This enables meetings to be set up more efficiently and for collective calendar, address book and schedule use by those involved.

Activity 4

Many large organisations have established an intranet for the purpose of:

A providing quick, effective and improved communication amongst staff using chat rooms

B providing quick, effective and improved communication to staff

C providing quick, effective and improved communication to customers

D providing quick, effective and improved ordering procedures in real time

3.3 Customer Relationship Management Systems

One area in which the sharing of data and scheduling information can be particularly useful is Customer Relationship Management (CRM). The importance of CRM, the monitoring and management of existing and potential customer relationships, was established in Chapter 3.

CRM software enables greater co-ordination between the business departments at every level of customer relationships and enables efficient marketing communication by holding mail and e-mail addresses for mass distribution of information and promotional activities. It also keeps records of lost business and areas of concern, allowing for improved control of sales operations.

4 IT and teams

4.1 Virtual Teams

IT developments, such as e-mail and the internet, have enabled employees to work away from the office much more than was previously possible.

Remote working is therefore an example of IT allowing previously impossible business activities to occur. For example, the virtual meetings via video or telephone conference we looked at previously in this book are an example of teleworking or homeworking.

There are both positive and negative elements to remote working. On the whole, such conditions tend to lead to increased motivation and productivity, but organisational culture can be diluted and it can be difficult to control or co-ordinate across larger departments.

A virtual team is a group of people who interact through independent tasks guided by the usual common purpose of any team. Their primary link to each other is via IT resources, which enable them to communicate, send and share information and hold meetings.

Due to their nature, virtual teams can struggle to form the strong team ethic and have the defined roles described previously. The leader of the team's role is often one of co-ordination rather than hands-on management in a virtual team. Virtual teams can however prove effective – they enable people who are geographically spread to be part of the same team and therefore the quality of team members can be improved. They rely on continual communication and clearly defined roles and responsibilities to be effective.

5 IT and projects

5.1 Project Management Software

The planning and control of projects can also be supported by the use of software tools designed specifically for this purpose.

For example, software can

- Create CPA (Critical Path Analysis) network diagrams, Gantt charts to help with planning
- Provide templates for Project Initiation Documents (PID), Project Quality Plans (PQP) and Work Breakdown Structures
- Compare plans with actual results and store all results and documentation in the control period
- Create technical documents, analysis and end of project reports

Although included within the above project management software, less specialised software, for example spreadsheets can also be useful alongside this for

- Creating budgets and monitoring costs
- Allocating time across many tasks
- What If analysis – seeing the impact of the different scenarios during the project

- Managing diaries and linking project stakeholders

Unquestionably there are therefore many advantages to using software in projects, as planning, control and communication should all be more accurate and less time-consuming. Also for more complex projects, this software can manage large volumes of data and diverse activities more efficiently.

However, as with the use of IT to solve many business issues, the lack of human involvement can also reduce personal responsibility and lead to an emphasis on maintaining and managing these tools rather than the project itself.

Activity 5

Which of the following statements regarding project management software are true?

A Software can only be used to help at the planning stage of the project.

B Software improves the accuracy of drawing CPA network diagrams

C Using project management software will ensure the project's success

D Software can be used to undertake What If analysis

E Using software can improve communication during a project

Answers to chapter activities

Activity 1

The answer is **A.** It is an example of a data processing system or transaction processing system.

Activity 2

Examples of the ways spreadsheets could be used to improve performance include:

- Providing more accessible information to staff and customers using charts, graphs etc
- Analysing sales and marketing through pivot tables to analyse customer purchasing
- Keeping projects to budget as a cost control mechanism
- Forecasting and preparing for different scenarios
- Managing non-financial aspects of the business more efficiently e.g. staff rotas

Activity 3

The answer is **C.** All of the other three are the result of in-house IT service provision.

Activity 4

The answer is **B**. The intranet improves communication between staff, however it does not use chat rooms to do so.

Activity 5

The following statements are true: **B, D and E.**

Note: for D and E the software referred to can be non-project specific, although project management software does help in these areas.

Performance Evaluation

10

Introduction

The accountancy profession is often demanding – requiring individuals to perform a large volume of technical work both accurately and before key deadlines, as well as to exhibit the many other career skills covered in this Text.

For this reason, personal reflection, performance evaluation and career development are important for any accountant. These mechanisms enable them to analyse their performance and judge where it can be improved and where further training or learning is required.

ASSESSMENT CRITERIA

1 Understand how to evaluate own performance at work.

2 Be able to evaluate and improve performance using feedback from others.

3 Be able to use evaluation and feedback to develop and use a learning plan.

CONTENTS

1 Core competencies revisited
2 Performance evaluation
3 Learning and training
4 Personal development and learning plans

1 Core competencies revisited

1.1 Core competencies

To develop professionally, it is vital for professionals in any career to evaluate their own performance and encourage others to do likewise.

In order to evaluate performance in the workplace, it is firstly necessary to look at the possible criteria on which the employee will assess themselves and be judged by others.

As was briefly mentioned in Chapter 1, these benchmarks can be characterised as core skills and many have been addressed in this Text.

Therefore, as performance evaluation is discussed and you reflect on your own capabilities, bear the following skills in mind:

- Organisational and administrative
- Communication
- Presentation
- IT skills
- Team work
- Problem-solving
- Conflict resolution
- Managing information and data
- Developing and training others

Naturally, as an accountant, you will also need to assess your performance in line with your duties within the finance team.

1.2 Personal skills

There are also skills which come more naturally to some people because of their personal characteristics and social influences. These attributes may be seen as personality traits rather than skills as such, but they help individuals to apply their skills in the workplace. Examples include commitment, perseverance, using initiative, flexibility, embracing change and motivation.

Example

The above personal skills relate to the mentality of the employee and as such it can sometimes be difficult to explain or illustrate to others. Therefore it is worthwhile to think of examples where each is in action, both in a professional and personal context.

Commitment	• Being punctual and prepared for each day's work • Finishing every task to the highest standard possible • Contributing fully in meetings and encouraging others to develop their ideas
Perseverance	• Rearranging a meeting after the first one was cancelled due to a train strike • Finding an alternative way of sending statements after the IT system went down • Retaking your driving test having failed initially
Initiative	• Suggesting improvements to a process or sporting tacts • Leading the team and guiding others in the manager's absence • Looking for extra work when you have finished the report you were working on early
Flexibility	• Working on two projects at the same time and adjusting priorities accordingly • Reorganising a working day as a visiting customer is late for a meeting • Helping the marketing team to design a brochure as it will assist your team
Courtesy	• Greeting colleagues and customers in a friendly fashion • Considering the viewpoints of others when designing a presentation • Writing a Thank You note to those who sponsored you on a charity walk
Motivation	• Maintaining a CPD folder to list all of your achievements and goals for the future • Setting yourself weekly challenges to complete tasks • Upselling in a weekend retail job to be rewarded with a gift voucher

2 Performance evaluation

2.1 What is performance evaluation?

Definitions

Performance evaluation is the regular and systematic review of performance and the assessment of potential with the aim of producing action programmes to develop both work and individuals.

Performance evaluation aims to improve the efficiency of the organisation by ensuring that the individual employees are performing to the best of their abilities and by developing their potential for improvement.

It is therefore of benefit to the individual as they will develop relevant new skills and have a good grasp of their perceived performance and to the company who will stand a better chance of achieving their objectives if staff are performing effectively.

Typically, assessing employee performance involves measuring both

- quantitative measures (i.e. how many units of work the employee has completed or how many new clients they have won)
- qualitative measures (i.e. how impressive their behaviour has been in terms of their attitude towards their work and other members of staff).

Activity 1

Simone has recently undergone an appraisal interview, where she was told that her attitude at work was excellent and that she was pleasant to work with.

What type of employee performance measurement is Simone's appraisal focused on?

A. Qualitative

B. Quantitative

2.2 The process of performance evaluation

Organisations follow four main steps when assessing performance of employees:

Target-setting

(the manager and employee should agree on which goals and targets the employee is going to work towards)

↓

Monitoring

(during the period, the manager should monitor employee performance and provide regular feedback and support)

↓

Review

(usually a formal appraisal to discuss the employee's performance in relation to the pre-agreed targets)

↓

Action plan

(new targets are then agreed for the forthcoming period)

2.3 Target and objective setting

Targets are typically

- areas that the employee needs to improve (perhaps where the employee is currently making mistakes)
- linked to the overall business goals (such as increasing activity by five percent)
- development goals that will benefit the employee (and the company) and therefore increase motivation.

As with all objectives in a business, personal targets should also be SMART. It is also important that employees understand and agree to these targets. If they do not 'buy into' them, they will not put any effort in to accomplishing the goals set – especially if they do not feel that the targets are achievable. This can lead to demotivation.

2.4 Performance evaluation criteria

It is crucial that valid criteria are used when assessing employee performance. This is made more complex because job descriptions tend to have multiple dimensions, meaning that the assessment must look at a number of different criteria in order to accurately reflect the employee's performance.

Assessment criteria may include the following:

Volume of work

- within time period
- evidence of work planning
- personal time management
- effectiveness of work under pressure

Quality of work

- level of analytical ability
- level of technical knowledge
- accuracy
- judgement exercised
- cost effectiveness

Knowledge of work

- gained through experience
- gained through training courses
- gained prior to employment

Personal skills

- decision-making
- capabilities
- flexibility
- adaptability
- assertiveness
- team involvement
- motivation

Management skills

- communication skills
- motivation skills
- training and development skills
- delegation skills

Activity 2

Give an example of how you have exhibited at least three of the personal or management skills above in the workplace.

Having defined the core competencies to be evaluated, there are a number of ways for individuals to assess their own performance and be assessed by others. Scorecards are a popular way to start this process, where the employee and/or their manager will rate achievement using performance scores or grids.

A personal SWOT analysis chart may also prove worthwhile. This would typically be performed by both the manager and employee and evaluates which aspects of a job an individual likes and dislikes on the one hand, and those aspects that an individual does well and not so well in on the other.

This process can prove particularly useful as an indication of how the employee is performing in line with the requirements of the job description and can also assess their current position for the start of a learning and training plan, as will be covered later in this chapter.

	Strengths	**Weaknesses**
Opportunities	Tasks the person likes and does well	Tasks the person likes but does not do well
Threats	Tasks the person dislikes but does well	Tasks the person dislikes and does not do well

Example

Jason works as a customer services representative at Windsor Electricals. As part of his defined targets, he is responsible for responding to key client enquiries within 24 hours and is judged on the number of customers who say they were satisfied with his performance.

He has been asked to self-evaluate his performance in preparation for a review with his manager using scores of 1 to 10, with 1 representing poor achievement and 10 being exceptional. For this role, the criteria are as follows:

	1	2	3	4	5	6	7	8	9	10
Responding to phone queries promptly										
Responding to e-mail queries promptly										

Verbal communication skills										
Providing detailed information										
Product knowledge										
Customer satisfaction										
Team working										
Use of IT systems										
Accuracy of work										
Time management										
Organisation										
Promotion of brand and business development										

When doing so, Jason can refer back to the SMART objectives he was originally set. For example, responding to the telephone queries in a given time and a defined percentage of satisfied customers.

Example

Jason is also asked to perform a SWOT Analysis on his work based on his current job description. In order to do so, he identifies the areas on the scorecard marked as 3 or below as weaknesses and 8 or above as strengths. He also includes specifics. For example, his use of the computerised ordering system is exemplary and therefore worthy of mention when referring to his IT expertise. Likewise, he feels his key client newsletters are particularly illustrative of his high score for providing detailed written communications.

When looking at opportunities and threats, Jason identifies opportunities for further development and training. He has given himself a score of 5 for business development as he does not currently have many chances to incorporate this into his daily work, but it is something he would like more exposure to. Again some of the lower scores he has given can be used to identify the threats in the SWOT analysis and he therefore suggests further training and new strategies in these areas.

Example

Jason's SWOT Analysis:

Strengths

- Telephone skills (prompt and productive)
- Written communication skills (key client newsletters)
- IT skills (ordering system)
- Attention to detail and product knowledge

Weaknesses

- Does not always use own initiative
- Struggles to work in a team
- Prioritisation of workload
- Business development/ sales and presentation skills

Opportunities

- Departmental restructure
- Large new client with specific needs
- Continuing admin qualification

Threats

- Restructure may mean new staff / priorities
- No current opportunity to develop a business development career

Activity 3

To identify your own strengths and weaknesses for a SWOT analysis, complete the following grid, with reference to your current role/skills:

	1	2	3	4	5	6	7	8	9	10
Personal organisation										
Accuracy of work										
Efficiency of work										
Providing detailed, useful information										
Knowledge of systems and product										
Written communication										
Verbal communication										
Listening skills										

Presentation skills										
Use of IT and data systems										
Customer relationships										
Negotiating and persuading others										
Team working										
Problem solving and conflict resolution										
Managing and adapting to change										
Sense of ownership and responsibility										
Creative thinking and innovative ideas										
Commercial awareness										
Legal and ethical awareness										
Flexibility and adaptability										
Contribution to decisions										
Self-reliance and motivation										
Adherence to job specification										

Using your scores and related analysis, create and start to complete your SWOT analysis chart (this may be added to when learning and training are discussed later in the chapter).

2.5 Performance appraisal meetings

Definitions

Appraisal is the normally formal process by which the employee is assessed by their manager. Most appraisals will address the progress, performance and attitude of the member of staff.

Appraisals have many benefits, as shown in the following table:

Benefits for the employer	Benefits for the employee
It provides a formal system for assessing the performance and potential of employees, with a view to identifying candidates for promotion.	The employee gets feedback about performance at work, and an assessment of competence.
It provides a system for identifying ways of improving the competence and addressing the skills gaps of employees, in order to raise their level of efficiency and effectiveness.	A formal appraisal system offers the employee an opportunity to discuss future prospects and ambitions, such as promotions or moving to a different department.
It is a valuable system for human resource planning, and ensuring that employees are ready for promotion, to fill management job vacancies that arise.	An appraisal interview may be used as a basis for considering remuneration and rewards.
If it is well managed, communications can be improved between managers and staff and so improve working relationships.	It can be used to identify and agree measures for further training and development and to establish expectations for the coming period.
It monitors human resource selection processes against results – has the organisation been hiring the right people?	It is an opportunity to ensure that work of particular merit is recognised.
It allows for assessment of the job specification in action.	It provides a forum for the employee to voice concerns about work area that the employee is unhappy with.

The performance appraisal must follow a defined process. This can be summarised as follows:

- **Step One:** The manager will identify the criteria for assessment based on the business and employee objectives, job analysis and requirements and the individual concerned.
- **Step Two:** Both the manager and the employee will then assess their performance based on the criteria.
- **Step Three:** There will be a meeting or interview to discuss the manager and employee's views and see where they reach agreement.
- **Step Four:** Conclusions are reached and an action plan is created.

Example

Returning to the example of Jason, who works as a customer services representative at Windsor Electricals, having completed his initial self-evaluation described above, his manager Ali arranges an annual appraisal meeting to discuss Jason's progress.

Prior to the meeting, Ali reiterates the targets stated above and confirms his intention to compare Jason's actual performance against these targets. Any areas where he deviates from the targets (in either a positive or negative way) can be discussed and are likely to form the basis of Jason's annual bonus and pay rise for next year.

Any areas that Jason is struggling with, or would like to gain additional skills and knowledge in, can be used to identify training and development opportunities for the coming year.

Finally, the appraisal can then be used to agree what Jason's targets will be for next year.

Activity 4

Explain the benefits of continually assessing and reflecting on your work. Give examples of how this performance evaluation has been and could be achieved, by both yourself and others.

(AAT Assessment criteria 1.1, 1.2, 1.3)

2.6 Barriers to effective performance appraisal

This seems like a relatively straightforward process. However, there can be conflict should the employee and their manager disagree on certain points raised. It is at this time that both the two participants need to decide whether they are going to solve the issues jointly or whether one or the other will take a more assertive tone. Managers can therefore adopt a 'tell and sell' approach (where they persuade the employee that their views of them are correct), a 'tell and listen' approach (where both sides have their say separately) or a 'joint problem-solving approach (where the manager acts as a counsellor to encourage the employee to identify their own problems).

If not handled carefully, appraisals can therefore cause demotivation for employees. Likely reasons for this include:

- the appraisal is seen as a one-sided process
- the conversation is unproductive and pointless

- the appraisal meeting is a box-ticking exercise rather than seen to be of any worth
- goals and objectives are not discussed and no points of action are identified

As a general rule, for effective appraisals with staff managers should typically exhibit 4 F's:

- Firmness – they must address the negative as well as the positive
- Fairness – they should treat all employees the same
- Factually correct – they should not rely on opinions alone.
- Frequency of use – they should appraise performance regularly and purposefully.

Lockett argued that in addition to the prescribed fairness of the management, the following other aspects of the appraisal process should be monitored to ensure it is effective for both the company and the employee:

- Relevance – does the system have a useful purpose and is it relevant to the needs of both the organisation and the individual? Do the appraisal criteria link to the needs of both parties?
- Serious intent – is the management committed to the system or has it simply been thrust on them by the HR department? Do the appraisers have training in interviewing and assessment techniques? Is there a demonstrable link between performance and reward?
- Co-operation – is the appraisal a participative, problemsolving activity, with the appraisee being given time and encouragement to prepare for it? Is a jointly agreed conclusion arrived at by the end of the appraisal?
- Efficiency – is it costly and difficult to administer and does it seem too time-consuming compared with the value of its outcome?

Activity 5

Which of the following is an objective of the appraisal process to an employer?

A. It enables them to identify underperforming employees for punishment

B. It helps the business to recruit the best possible employees

C. It helps to identify skills gaps in employees

D. It reinforces management authority over employees

Activity 6

Mainwaring and Sons is currently undertaking an appraisal of the performance of its employees. Many employees have complained that the outcome of their appraisal had no link to the pay rise or rewards that they received.

According to Lockett, what aspect of a successful appraisal process appears to be missing?

A. Relevance

B. Serious intent

C. Co-operation

D. Efficiency

2.7 Goal setting

As part of the appraisal process, the tasks the person does not do well are examined and reasons are established for this perceived under-performance.

Particular weaknesses will be identified as causing the failure to carry out certain tasks satisfactorily. This should then inform a personal set of objectives in order to overcome these weaknesses. These goals can be achieved through a number of methods, ranging from simply more concentration on the problem area by the employee to formal, long-term training.

Therefore in terms of personal improvement, further actions can be categorised as follows:

- Short-term measures to improve performance in the current role and address shortfalls relating to the specific job specification.
- Long-term plans to develop skills and methods in order to both enhance current performance and allow further professional development.

Whereas the former can be addressed by modifications in work patterns and personal behaviour and organisation, the latter will often require extra learning, training and coaching, as discussed in Part 3 of this chapter.

Example

Let us return to the example of Jason, who works as a customer services representative at Windsor Electricals.

After his meeting with Ali, Jason has been advised that his time management requires improvement. Although Ali acknowledged that

Jason's workload was vast and that other departments could assist him further to provide information more promptly, Jason was struggling to prioritise the many tasks he had to perform.

Rather than seeking formal training or going on a course, Ali and Jason discussed some strategies to address this problem.

Jason started by prioritising his tasks using a ranking system. He then allocated each a realistic timeframe and gave them stipulated time slots. Instead of doing the task which would take longest first, he did those which were most important.

Although his strategy changed several further times to address this issue, Jason did not require further training and Ali, who is naturally organised, was able to make further suggestions.

When setting both short-term and long-term targets, all performance and development goals should be **SMART:**

- **S**pecific – all objectives should be specific and clearly understood by all parties. It should not be vague or open to interpretation.
- **M**easurable – they should have a quantifiable yardstick of achievement so that success can be clearly monitored.
- **A**chievable – it is important to avoid discouraging people with unattainable objectives, which they could never deliver even when performing to the best of their abilities.
- **R**elevant (or realistic) – the goal needs to be within the scope of the employee's abilities and something they will be happy and able to work towards completing.
- **T**ime bounded (or timely) – there should be a deadline to complete the objective so that efforts are purposeful.

Example

Jason's SMART objectives included:

- Responding satisfactorily to all key client enquiries within 24 hours.
- A minimum of 80% of customers saying they were satisfied with his performance in the quarterly service review.
- To pass the intermediate level of his professional qualification within the next 12 months.
- To review IT ordering processes and create a training folder for all staff within 3 months.
- To keep a weekly log of new strategies to improve time management skills and watch at least three videos on the topic.

In all of the above, the goal can clearly be understood, has a point of reference for measuring success, seems both relevant and achievable given Jason's role and experience and has a time constraint. Therefore these could be termed SMART.

Activity 7

Using your SWOT analysis, take one of the areas you have defined as a weakness. Along with a manager or mentor, create a strategy to improve your performance in this area by taking a new approach or using a new system.

After a fortnight, assess if the new strategy has improved your performance and the next steps forward as a result.

(AAT Assessment criteria 1.4)

3 Learning and training

3.1 Learning, training and development

Often performance evaluation leads to the identification of development, learning or training needs to either rectify issues with the individual's performance or to enable them to embrace new skills or responsibilities. Most organisations view training and development of staff as an essential investment. Due to the obvious importance of training and development, a systematic approach should be taken in order to maximise its effectiveness.

Definitions

Education is defined as the activities which aim at developing the knowledge skills, moral values and understanding required in all aspects of life rather than a knowledge skill related to only a limited field of activity.

Training is the planned and systematic modification of behaviour through learning events, programmes and instruction which enable individuals to achieve the level of knowledge, skills and competence to carry out their work effectively.

Training therefore usually implies a planned process to modify attitudes, skills or behaviour that will help the individual to improve their performance in their job. It is therefore job-oriented rather than personal.

Definition

Development is the growth or realisation of a person's ability and potential through conscious or unconscious learning and educational experiences.

Development takes a broader view of the acquisition of skills and knowledge than training, concerned more with changes in attitude, behaviour and potential than with immediate skills. It relates more to helping the growth of the individual for future roles.

It is often argued that development is therefore more general, more future-oriented and more individually-oriented than training.

The benefits of learning and training include:

For the individual	For the organisation
Improved skills and (dependent on the type of training) qualifications.	Increased motivation of employees, leading to higher productivity
Increased confidence and job satisfaction.	Increased competence and confidence, meaning higher quality and fewer mistakes.
Better ability to current job.	Low staff turnover, saving the organisation time and money
More scope for promotion to a new job or to be able to perform other roles.	Skilled workforce, leading to more innovation and a better customer experience.

3.2 The training and development process

Stage 1: Identification of training needs

How does a company know that it needs to train its workers? There are a number of possible methods. These include:

- **Performance appraisal** – As already explained, most line managers appraise their staff or carry out a performance review at least annually. During this, the manager can review past performance, discuss the employee's aspirations and use this to identify possible training and development opportunities in the future.
- **Formal training needs analysis (TNA) -** This involves identification of the skills, knowledge and experience needed for a particular job and comparing this to the skills, knowledge and experience of the current jobholder. If the jobholder is lacking any of these required skills, this is referred to as a learning gap, which can be filled using

training. TNA may also be triggered by external changes to the organisation, such as new government legislation.

- **Observation** - There may be signs that staff require additional training, such as poor productivity or high numbers of mistakes. There is evidence that inadequate training leads to workers failing to meet production targets, leading to frustration. This means that, in addition, managers should monitor labour turnover, absenteeism rates or the level of grievances within the organisation.
- **Organisational strategy -** Training and development must be linked to the overall business strategy. There should be senior support for the training programme and it must be seen to support the needs of the organisation itself.

Training merely for the sake of training is likely to be a waste of time and money.

Stage 2: Setting objectives for training

This stage examines what the proposed training programme is supposed to accomplish. Objectives need to be clearly stated, measurable and specific, outlining the effect that training should have on the performance and abilities of the employee being trained.

When an organisation considers sending a junior member of its accounts department on a professional accountancy course, they will have several learning objectives, including:

- the employee will be able to achieve a pass mark in all of his accountancy exams.
- the employee will be able to produce an error-free analysis of the organisation's management accounts each month without supervision.

Stage 3: Programme design and delivery

Training and development of individuals can include:

- formal training courses – both in-house and external
- mentoring
- coaching
- computer-based learning
- self-managed learning

Groups may have slightly different training and development methods, including:

- lectures
- discussions
- case studies and role play
- business games

Stage 4: Evaluation and validation of the training programme

Once complete, evaluation of the training programme aims to assess whether it was successful and whether the training achieved its objectives. It will also enable the organisation to ensure that it is using the right tools for training. Further analysis will be required to see whether the individual is able to utilise what they have learnt and is applying it within their role.

3.3 The importance of learning in the workplace

Definition

Learning can be defined as 'the process of acquiring knowledge through experience, which leads to changes in behaviour'. It includes acquiring new skills, knowledge or attitudes, or a combination of all three.

There are three types of learning.

- Formal – this is undertaken deliberately and occurs when individuals 'learn' and 'study'. It is often classroom-based and highly structured.
- Informal – this is also usually deliberate, but is not highly structured. Examples include networking, coaching and mentoring.
- Incidental – this is a by-product of another activity. For example, attending a formal classroom course may also help a student to learn how to keep their attention focused for a long period.

Some employers (often smaller businesses) see investment in learning in the workplace as a drain on their resources – using up valuable time and money. However, there are many advantages to employees undertaking work-related or work-based learning.

- It can lead to increased competence, understanding, self-esteem and morale within the workforce and therefore improved productivity and better route for developing staff for promotion.
- It may improve the level of creativity and innovation of workers in the organisation, giving an advantage over competitors.
- People who enjoy learning are more likely to be flexible in times of constant change.
- If workers are not given learning opportunities, there is a risk that they will feel undervalued, lose motivation and look for work elsewhere.

Organisations where learning is promoted tend to gain significant advantage over competitors, especially in fast-changing markets. These 'Learning Organisations'

- generate and transfer knowledge throughout the organisation
- learn from others and from past experience
- tolerate risk and failure as learning opportunities
- have a systematic, ongoing, collective and scientific approach to problem-solving.

Therefore, learning in the workplace can be of great advantage to both the individual and the company. As suggested earlier, it is from their learning that employees can deal with conflict and change more effectively and contribute to the business with new ideas and systems to improve efficiency and the commercial offering.

As a result, the learning organisation became a source of competitive advantage for many companies and knowledge across hierarchies and departments was embraced and encouraged.

3.4 Workplace learning

Although workplace learning is still often through more traditional methods – face-to-face tuition geared towards qualifications or formal acknowledgement – much workplace learning is more practical and responsive. It is also more collaborative, as experiences and ideas are shared and problems are solved through mutual learning.

Formal training will be covered later in this chapter, but it is worth noting here that instead of attending organised courses, there are other more active and collaborative means of learning. In many ways, learning occurring within the workplace and therefore in a meaningful, relevant and supportive environment, can be more beneficial.

Participative strategies seen in the workplace include

- Mentoring
- Workshops
- Networking
- Project work
- Case studies and scenario-based exercises
- Work shadowing

3.5 The learning process

It is important to understand how people learn, as this will allow an organisation to create suitable training programmes for its employees.

Two theories that help with this are those proposed by Kolb and Honey & Mumford.

3.6 Kolb: experiential learning cycle

Kolb suggested that learning is a series of steps based on everyday experience. He argued that classroom learning is false and that actual learning comes from actually undertaking tasks and learning from them.

Kolb identified four learning stages that must be addressed:

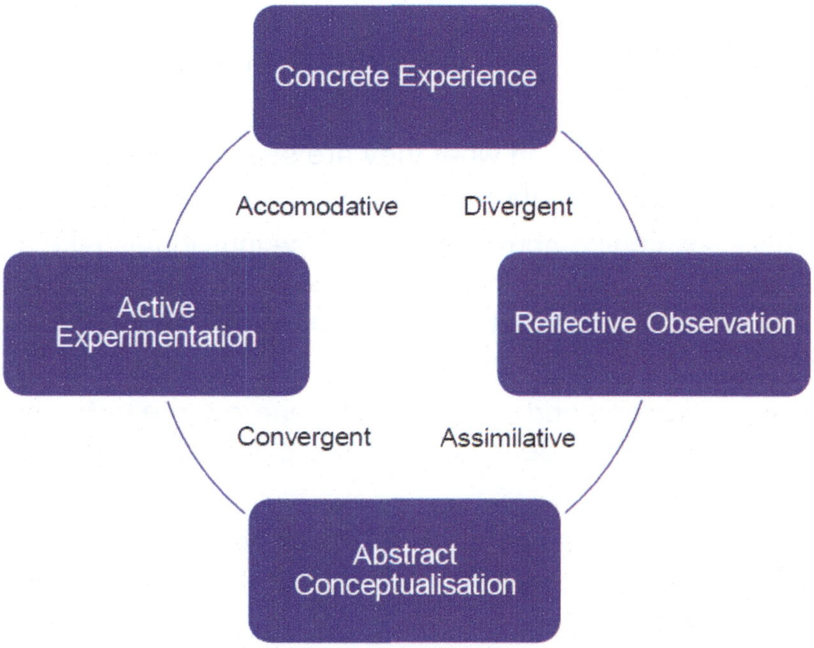

According to Kolb, successful learning is a cycle that progresses through all four stages of the stages identified above.

Example

For instance, if you want to learn how to use a new computer system:

Concrete experience – you may decide to start using the new computer system, without any training or guidance.

Reflective observation – having failed to accomplish everything you wanted, you spend some time identifying the problems you had and which tasks you were unable to perform successfully on the new system.

Abstract conceptualisation – having identified the problem areas, you go to the instruction manual and look up how to undertake these tasks.

Active experimentation – once you have read the instructions relating to the areas you were uncertain about, you then go back to the computer system and try them again to see if you are now able to perform all the tasks you needed to accomplish.

Kolb argued this is an ongoing loop, as using the system again may well trigger new problems or issues (new concrete experiences) which trigger the cycle again. It also does not matter at which stage you begin, for example you could start at the reflective observation stage by watching others using the system.

Kolb also identified four different learning styles adopted by individual learners (as shown on the diagram above), based on where they start on the learning cycle.

Each style is a combination of two elements from the cycle.

- Divergent – feeling and watching – these people prefer to watch rather than do, reflecting on what they are seeing from various angles before trying it for themselves.
- Assimilative – watching and thinking – these individuals take a concise, logical approach. They prefer good, clear explanations rather than undertaking practical examples. They then need time to think through what they have seen.
- Convergent – thinking and doing – these learners prefer to apply ideas and enjoy testing ideas out in practice to see if they really work.
- Accommodative – doing and feeling – these people have a strong preference for concrete experiences and active experimentation (hands-on approach).

Activity 8

Mandeep works for a sales department. The processes for raising a sales invoice have recently changed. He has asked to watch another member of staff, who has been trained in the new process, raise a sales invoice before he attempts to do it himself.

According to Kolb, where is Mandeep starting on the learning cycle?

A. Concrete experience

B. Active experimentation

C. Reflective observation

D. Abstract conceptualisation

3.7 Honey and Mumford: learning styles

Honey and Mumford built on Kolb's earlier work and came up with four alternative classifications of learning styles. They argued people learn more effectively if they are aware of their learning style preferences.

- **Activists** – are primarily interested in self-discovery; they ask 'What if?' questions. In terms of learning they need a variety of new, challenging and interactive activities where they have opportunities to shine. They like to touch and experiment and as a result business games, competitive tasks, role-playing exercises and group discussions work well for them. They are dynamic, open-minded and enthusiastic so are not shy of problem-solving or peer feedback.
- **Reflectors** – are primarily interested in personal meaning; they question, 'Why?' They tend to take a step back and need time to think over, assimilate and prepare for activities, or to review what has happened and reach decisions without pressures and tight deadlines and therefore lectures or considered discussions are helpful to them. They look for an instructor who is both a taskmaster and a guide, offering them insight and interpretation, as they can be seen as indecisive.
- **Theorists** – are primarily interested in facts as they lead to conceptual understanding. They question, 'What?' These learners need opportunities to question, probe and explore methodically assumptions and logic. They are uncomfortable with subjective judgements and lateral thinking, instead looking to maximise certainty and identify interrelationships between ideas and events. They are likely to use case studies, theoretical readings and reflective thinking exercises.
- **Pragmatists** – are primarily interested in how things work. They need to try out ideas and techniques to see how well they work in practice. They like making practical decisions and tend to be frustrated with open-ended discussions. They thrive on constructive group work.

It is generally agreed that a combination of different types of learners will make an effective team in an organisation. In discussing an issue, the most likely question the Reflector will pursue is why it is important; the Theorist, in contrast, will be interested in what it is all about; the Pragmatist will be concerned with how it can be applied in the real world; and the Activist will be keen to know what would happen if they were to apply it here and now.

Most individuals exhibit a clear preference for one style of learning and may struggle to switch between them. People with such a clear style preference will therefore tend to learn more effectively if learning is geared to their personal preferences.

A feature of Honey and Mumford's model is that it provides suggestions about the best ways for individuals to learn. The most effective learning methods are different for each learning style.

- Activists – have a practical approach to training, are flexible and optimistic. They prefer practical problems, enjoy participation and challenge, are easily bored and have a dislike of theory. They must have hands-on training.
- Reflectors – need an observational approach to training. They need to work at their own pace – slow, cautious and non-participative – where conclusions are carefully thought out. They do not find learning easy especially if rushed. They are best when carrying out an investigation or work shadowing, allowing them to draw their own conclusions.
- Theorists – require their learning to be programmed and structured and therefore prefer classroom based courses. They like time for analysis and for their training to be provided by people who share the same preference for ideas and analysis.
- Pragmatists – need to see a direct value and link between training and real problems and aim to do things better.

Activity 9

With reference to the theories above, what sort of learner are you and how does this influence your development?

(AAT Assessment criteria 3.1, 3.2)

3.8 Mentoring and Coaching

Sometimes individuals other than your manager may become involved in your personal development. For example, mentors (usually experienced members of staff) are widely employed to offer advice to newcomers. They tend to offer practical support, impartial advice and help with the personal development plan of the employee in a less formal manner than the appraisal. They tend to serve as a role model and as such can be a valuable source of wisdom and inside knowledge on how the company works.

Coaching tends to focus on specific objectives, with an expert providing tips on how to excel in a focused area.

Activity 10

Assess how learning and development can benefit you as an employee and the organisation as a whole. Provide at least three examples for both.

(AAT Assessment criteria 1.4, 1.5)

4 Personal development and learning plans

4.1 Personal development and learning plans

A personal development plan is a clear developmental action plan for an individual that incorporates a wide set of developmental opportunities including formal training.

During their career, employees are increasingly encouraged to manage their own development. In consultation with management, they might be asked to set up personal development plans whereby they set targets and propose actions/activities to achieve them.

Development is more general than training, is more forward-looking and orientated towards the individual, and is concerned with enabling the individual to fulfil his or her potential.

Training	Development
Immediately practical	No immediate practical application
Connected to job performance	Over time it enables a person to deal with wider problems

4.2 Foundations for the learning plan

Prior to the creation of a personal development or learning plan, it is essential to perform two steps which have already been covered in this chapter.

Firstly, an analysis of the employee's current position and performance is required. This will probably be in the form of the SWOT analysis referred to earlier, however it is crucial to also include developmental progression as well as on the job, reactive training when referring to the weaknesses, opportunities and threats in the analysis.

Secondly, following the above analysis, personal goals should be set for the individual. Having drawn conclusions from the SWOT analysis, SMART objectives should be identified and all further training, learning and development activities should be intrinsically linked back to these objectives.

Activity 11

Using your previous SWOT analysis (adding to it if necessary), identify at least three opportunities to personally progress through further learning, training or developmental activities.

Using these, state a minimum of three goals which would enable you to develop/progress in these areas.

(AAT Assessment criteria 1.6, 1.7, 2.2, 3.1)

Learning and development plans provide both structure and motivation to the development process. They enable both the individual and the company to easily and clearly ascertain exactly where development opportunities are being sought and how well they are progressing.

In addition to seeking career development or CPD (Continuing Professional Development) opportunities focusing on those areas where the individual believes they may excel in the future, learning or training plans may also be designed to rectify perceived areas for improvement. Therefore, it is common for identified weaknesses to be included, along with relevant training to solve the problem.

Example

Mary is a Store Manager for MC Fashion, a leading retail company. She has met with her Regional Manager, Betty, to discuss her Personal Development Plan for the year ahead.

Mary is an experienced manager, who has been asked to include three different development elements in her plan:

- An area for learning
- An area where improvement is required
- An area where she feels she is strong and could benefit the company and her career progression through greater focus

Betty provided Mary with information about various business and management courses and identified her lack of IT skills as being one area where Mary could improve her own performance. Betty also felt that Mary is particularly good at developing and training her staff and felt others could benefit from her ideas.

Here is the Personal Development Plan created for Mary:

Skill / development	Target	Purpose/ outcome	Action to be taken	Success criteria	Review date
Management	Start to study for accredited qualification	To obtain new knowledge, to prepare for future roles.	Source best qualification and register for tuition. Attend and study, sharing best practice.	Pass termly assessment. Present new ideas to managers meeting.	1/1/15
Use of IT in running the store	Continue to develop awareness.	To improve sales performance and commun-ications with staff and customers, in current role.	Attend training and workshop sessions. Work with business mentor. Try three new strategies.	Produce a report detailing progress to the board. Successfully complete courses.	1/6/15
Developing people, HR	Improve training in store by creating a new policy.	To improve in current role and develop others.	Full review of training procedures. Consultation and networking for ideas. Draft and test policy.	Completion of research report and presentation to line manager with proposal.	1/1/15

Activity 12

Using the three areas for improvement identified in Activity 11, draw up a development plan covering each. Send this as a memo to your manager, giving reasons why this plan is valuable for your development.

(AAT Assessment criteria 1.8, 2.2, 3.2)

4.3 Monitoring and measuring

Once an individual's goals and personal ambitions have been defined and a development plan constructed, it is crucial to monitor progress.

When drawing up and implementing the plan, some degree of control is necessary to monitor the extent to which the programme is achieving the goals and stated objectives. Control processes give people structure, define methods and indicate how their performance will be measured. For the individual, it is reassuring to know what is required and how the outcome will be measured.

As part of this process, regular and relevant feedback can be provided to enable the individual to know how well they are progressing in terms of the specified goals and to reassure them that they are on the right track and are achieving satisfactorily. Likewise, managers need to know the plans and objectives are realistic and well understood.

- Feedback should be clear and frequent and this can only be achieved if there is continuous monitoring of the task.
- Feedback can also have a motivating effect by providing recognition of work done which in turn provides the incentive to sustain and improve performance levels.
- Recognition, praise and encouragement create feelings of confidence, competence, development and progress that enhance the motivation to learn.

There are many different types of feedback which can be sought, either by the employee or the manager. Here are examples of both formal and informal feedback:

Formal feedback

- Monthly progress meetings with the line manager to check everything is on track
- Questionnaires sent to colleagues and customers to assess the individual's performance
- Written reports, activity logs or the updated PDP sent to the manager by the employee
- Group or individual training sessions focusing on an area of development and measuring progress accordingly

Informal feedback

- Discussing progress and solutions with colleagues
- Regular, unscheduled chats in the office or via e-mail with the manager
- Asking for less structured feedback from other managers, customers and peers
- Observations in the office
- Comments made in all communications which relate to one of the goals (eg. being thanked for organising an event so efficiently)

Example

Ali asked Jason to send her a regular report logging the new strategies he has tried (formal) and suggests a meeting in three months to discuss progress on this matter (formal).

Jason in the meantime speaks with his colleagues to get their insight (informal) and picks up on a couple of compliments from customers in terms of his speed of response (informal).

After a month, Ali asks for progress on the training course across the office (informal) and as soon as Jason has attended she asks him to feed back to the rest of the team in a workshop (formal).

4.4 Evaluation of learning

It has been suggested that there are five levels at which evaluation can take place.

Reactions – of the trainees to the training, their feelings about how enjoyable and useful it has been.	End-of-course questionnaires – obtain immediate feedback on the perceived value of the training but may not be the best way of evaluating the effectiveness of the programme.
Learning – what new skills and knowledge have been acquired or what changes in attitude have taken place as a result of the training.	Attainment tests – limited to the immediate knowledge and skills improvement and may not indicate whether the learning will be transferred to the workplace or job. Interviews – appraisal or performance reviews provide an opportunity to discuss the individual's progress during and after a training and development programme.
Job behaviour – at this level evaluation tries to measure the extent to which trainees have applied their training on the job.	Observation – the end results of the learning and development can be assessed by observation of improvements in job performance levels. Career development – the speed of promotion of an individual may be used as an indication of the effectiveness of the training and development and also the level of support given to the development plan by the organisation.

Organisation – training may be assessed in terms of the ways in which changes in job behaviour affect the functioning of the organisation	At the departmental level the effective training and development of staff can mean the achievement of targets, goals and objectives measured in terms of output, productivity, quality, etc.
Ultimate value – this is a measure of the training in terms of how the organisation as a whole has benefited.	Measured in terms of greater profitability, survival or growth.

Whatever evaluation method is used it should be done before, during and after the event.

- Before the event will clarify the existing skills, knowledge and attitudes to help the trainer plan the event and provide a yardstick by which to measure them.
- During the event will identify the rate of learning, allowing the trainer to pace the learning to suit the trainee and offer remedial help where needed.
- After the event can be immediately after the training or over a long time. It should link back to the objectives of the training (discussed in an earlier stage) and check that they have been accomplished.

Ultimately, the learners themselves have a responsibility to seek out learning and development opportunities and take full advantage of them. However, the Human Resources department, mentors and line managers will necessary be involved during every part of the process.

Activity 13

Returning to the development action plan in Activity 12, evaluate your learning/training to date and evaluate your work for improvements.

(AAT Assessment criteria 2.4, 2.5, 3.3, 3.4)

Activity 14

Using your most recent appraisal, detail the following:

a) The feedback of your personal performance provided

b) Your own self-appraisal and how this differed

c) The actions and objectives set as a result of the appraisal

Now consider in preparation for your next appraisal:

a) How your work has improved and why

b) Your options for career progression and further development in your current role

c) The development of a personal learning plan

(AAT Assessment criteria 1.6, 1.7, 2.1, 2.2, 2.3, 2.4, 2.5, 3.1, 3.2)

Activity 15

Your department has not been performing well and as a result you have been asked to perform a training needs analysis for yourself and your colleagues. Which of the following would be effective ways to gather information for this purpose (it may be more than one option)?

Method	Effective?
Analysing questionnaires and attitude surveys issued to staff	
Interviewing managers elsewhere in the organisation about their views on development needs	
Observing individuals working	
Holding group discussions with the department to identify common issues	

Activity 16

Felipe joined the finance department of Butterworths a year ago. He is surprised that in that time he has never been given any clear targets or objectives and he has had no opportunity to discuss his performance with his line manager, Christian.

Other members of the department feel the same and discussed the matter with Christian. Christian was surprised at their feedback as he suggested to them that if there were problems with their performance, he would have raised them to the individuals concerned. His lack of involvement should therefore, he argued, be seen as a good thing.

When meeting with another manager Christian explained that he had never undertaken performance appraisals for his staff as he felt they were a pointless waste of time.

Suggest ten reasons, both in favour of the employee and the company, the other manager could provide to support the use of formal appraisals to convince Christian.

Answers to chapter activities

Activity 1

The correct answer is **A Qualitative.** This is a less tangible aspect of the employee's performance and therefore difficult to measure quantitatively.

Activities 2-3

These answers will depend on the individual's relevant experience and skills.

Activity 4

There are many benefits to self-evaluation and reflecting on your own work, including the identification of strengths and weaknesses to identify areas for both improvement and recognition. Self-evaluation can help to identify training needs and career development opportunities and desires. It can also allow the individual to reflect on their relationships with others in the work place and views towards certain aspects of their role in order to make them more productive in their role.

In terms of evaluating performance, this can be achieved through formal appraisals with managers or informal discussions with others, seeking the feedback of both colleagues and external stakeholders if desired. Frequent meetings with a manager or mentor can allow more regular evaluation. In some cases, personal evaluation can be a group activity – with peer workshops or the use of assessment centres or tests similar to those in the recruitment process.

Activity 5

The correct answer is **C appraisals help to identify skills gaps in employees.**

The appraisal process is certainly not designed to punish employees and only applies to existing staff, meaning that it will not help with recruitment. It is also designed to improve communication between managers and employees, not reinforce the differences between them.

Activity 6

The correct answer is **B Serious intent** seems to be missing as rewards are not linked to the appraisals' outcomes and therefore there is nothing to suggest they are taken seriously, even if they do comply with company objectives or have some benefits.

Activity 7

The answer will depend on the individual's strengths and weaknesses and whether or not the strategy for improvement is appropriate. The student should show they have been able to reflect on their attempts to improve and make informed recommendations for further action.

Activity 8

The correct answer is **G reflective observation** as Mandeep is watching others first and reflecting on their experience before attempting anything personally.

Activity 9

The answer will depend on the individual's learning preference and personal attributes. Activists will tend to prefer hands-on, practical training, reflectors prefer to draw their own conclusions from slower, more reflective exercises, theorists will typically prefer classroom courses or more analytical training and pragmatists will usually appreciate learning that relates directly to their daily work and involves constructive, practical work.

Activity 10

Benefits of learning and development for the employee include:

- Developing new skills or utilising identified expertise
- Learning from the expertise of others to improve performance
- Formal qualifications to assist with future employment opportunities
- Career development, including promotions
- Opportunities for increased remuneration

Benefits of learning and development for the employer include:

- Greater skills, understanding and competence within the workforce
- Increased morale and self-esteem amongst employees
- Innovation, creativity and the sharing of ideas can lead to increased productivity
- Embracing learning can help to recruit better candidates
- A workforce more open to change and new concepts
- More natural and obvious succession planning

Activities 11-14

This answer will depend on the individual's SWOT analysis and the areas they feel require development. All plans should include SMART objectives. Reasons in favour of learning plans include increased structure, accountability, motivation and transparency for the individual. Criticisms of these plans include the perceived lack of flexibility.

Activity 15

All of the methods listed would be effective ways to gather information.

Activity 16

Benefits for the company include:

- It could provide a fairer and more frequent means of assessing employees' work and areas for improvement.
- It could inform reward decisions.
- It could aid with succession planning.
- It could help to set personal and company targets.
- It could improve efficiency and effectiveness across the staff.

Benefits for the employee include:

- It could provide a fair and understandable basis for remuneration.
- It could offer detailed feedback about performance.
- It could offer an opportunity to discuss concerns.
- It could help to identify training needs.
- It could recognise high quality work.

If managed correctly, the process should also enable more productive upward and downward communication.

Skills-based scenario - a project in practice

11

Introduction

This chapter features an example of a project of a fictitious company, Wonderstuff Ltd.

Through the scenarios addressed in the chapter, the understanding developed earlier in this Text can be put into context and shown in action. This chapter therefore combines all aspects of the previous ten chapters and as such serves as a good basis for how work-based evidence can be obtained.

1 Review at Wonderstuff Ltd

You have recently started working for Wonderstuff Ltd, a provider of nutritional supplements and health products. The company has approximately fifty employees, mostly located at a Head Office in Northern England. They also have a retail outlet in a central London location.

The organisation is divided into the following departments:

- Product Development
- Production and Purchasing
- Warehouse, Distribution and Logistics
- Sales and Marketing
- Customer Service and Administration
- Legal, Contracts and Human Resources

Each of these six departments has a divisional head, who reports into the Managing Director. The accounting function has typically been outsourced, so it is only recently that Wonderstuff Ltd has had its own dedicated accounts team, including yourself. As such, all three members of the team report directly into the Managing Director.

Wonderstuff Ltd have been showing healthy growth for some time and are now looking to establish new products and diversify. However, before this is possible, the Managing Director wants to perform a full review of departmental spending and budgeting and control procedures.

Given the expertise of the new accounting team, he has asked you to lead this review. When performing your research, the Managing Director has made it clear he is looking for input from all areas of the business and would welcome a fresh approach to thinking.

Task One

Given the brief above, create a plan of action for how you will perform the above review. Include the following points:

1. **Who should be involved and how will you communicate with them?**
2. **The nature and content of your initial communications with colleagues**
3. **The meetings and workshops you would organise – their purpose, participants and desired outcomes**
4. **How you will report your findings back to the Managing Director**

5. **How and where you will use the following skills in this exercise and any barriers you will need to overcome:**
   a. **Verbal communication/presentation skills**
   b. **Written communication skills**
   c. **Problem-solving skills**
   d. **IT and software skills**
   e. **Time management and organisational skills**

2 The Super Shakes Project Team

As part of a their commercial development strategy, Wonderstuff Ltd are looking to develop a new product range, known as Super Shakes – healthy, fruity milkshakes to be sold primarily in a Central London location.

To research, develop and market the new range, a project team has been set up.

As a key member of the accounts department, you have been asked to organise the project team. Your first task is to recruit a team of individuals to work together on the project and to explain the structure of the team. You have access to all departments, skillsets and ranks of employee, but should ensure a mix of levels, departments and competencies where possible.

Task Two

With reference to at least two theories of team work, write a memo to your Managing Director to describe the sort of people you require in the team.

As well as defining team roles, you should also include the responsibilities each team member is likely to have within the project and some of the general skills needed for effective team work.

In addition to this, highlight the roles and responsibilities of the team leader and indicate if you feel you would be suitable, giving reasons.

3 External analysis

Having formed the project team successfully, you have discovered from some of the others in the team that Wonderstuff Ltd do not appear to spend any time on either competitor or external market analysis.

Task Three

Write an e-mail to the Marketing Director to ask whether this is the case and to stress both the importance of competitor analysis, the mechanisms and methods which could be used, sources of information and the likely benefits to Wonderstuff Ltd. Also indicate as part of your e-mail some of the ways different organisations can be compared with reference to organisational structure and culture.

4 Improving performance

Henry is part of the project team. His main role within the company is as the Customer Services Manager, a department which was producing satisfactory results before he took over. However, recently, several of his staff have asked whether jobs in the sales and marketing departments are available. There have been a number of unexpected mistakes and information is not being communicated properly.

Henry comes in early every day, stays late, takes large amounts of work home and is showing definite signs of stress and strain. In the meantime, his staff members appear bored and disinterested. Some have also been heard complaining that they lack direction, objectives and opportunities to progress. They have however not been given a chance to express this to Henry, who remains separated from them.

Task Four

Henry has asked for your views on the issues in an ad hoc meeting. Write briefing notes for the meeting, to cover the following:

- **Reasons why this situation may have occurred**
- **How the problems could be solved**
- **How Henry could utilise performance appraisal and why it is so important**

5 Managing Project Finances – Cost Analysis

As a result of favourable initial project research, the new strawberry milkshake has gone into production and uses natural strawberries instead of the usual artificial flavour and colouring. It was introduced in June. You now need to produce an analysis of initial costs and present to the project team.

You have been provided with the following operating statement for June:

Variances	*Favourable*	*Adverse*
Direct materials (milk) price	£800	
Direct materials (milk) usage		£400
Direct materials (strawberries) price		£1,600
Direct materials (strawberries) usage		£1,875

The company's Shake Expert has given you the following information about the strawberry milkshake production in June:

June is the month in which strawberries normally start to ripen in England. However, this year, the month of June has been unusually cold and rainy, and therefore we had to purchase imported strawberries for the first two weeks of the month. Towards the end of the month, English strawberries were used.

The imported strawberries came from the Netherlands, where June was also unusually rainy. This led to the strawberries being smaller in size and having a less concentrated aroma.

The rainy weather had an opposite effect on the production of milk in the UK, which was considerably higher than during the same period last year. This led to Wonderstuff being able to secure a deal to purchase 1,000 litres of milk at a reduced price from their regular suppliers, as their storage capacity was fully utilised.

The expected mix of milk to strawberries was 1 litre of milk for 300 g of strawberries. However, due to the Dutch strawberries' lack of aroma, this had to be changed to 400 g of strawberries for every litre of milk.

In June, we hired a new Shake Mixer to replace an experienced Mixer who was recruited by the competition.

Towards the end of the month, it was noted that the usage of milk was higher than expected. When this was questioned, the new Shake Mixer explained that some of the milk had gone off on one of the few hot days of the month as he had left the refrigerator door open by mistake. The Shake Expert had doubts about this explanation, and recalled that the new Shake Mixer had mentioned during his recruitment interview that all his friends and himself had always been fans of milkshakes.

Task Five

Using this information, prepare a presentation for the Project Team to summarise progress to date, providing possible reasons for the variances noted, by considering the following:

- **The availability of milk and strawberries on the market**
- **The ratio of strawberries to milk**
- **The recruitment of the new Shake Mixer**

Discuss whether any action could have been taken in respect of the quality of the strawberries, and the reliability of the new Shake Mixer.

6 Marketing and Communication

Following the success of the new natural strawberry milkshake, Super Shakes is examining the possibility of changing its business model towards an approach based on promoting all-natural products and advertising an ethical stance. The new strategy will involve higher levels of promotional activities and the return to more traditional manual production processes.

The project team are responsible for recommending marketing strategies for the new Shakes and therefore you are required to formulate a brief proposal on how the new product could be marketed and a suggestion for a pricing strategy to suit market conditions.

You have asked the Marketing team for their input and the Marketing Director has e-mailed you with the following five bullet-points:

- The major global soft drinks brands still dominate this market
- They are able to use more sophisticated tactics to appeal to youngsters in particular
- Although we have a loyal customer base, awareness of Wonderstuff's brand identity is poor
- This product is very similar to many others and to cheaper, cost-effective alternatives
- There is not much money left in the marketing budget

Task Six

Provide a brief marketing proposal, to be sent as a memo to the Marketing Director for feedback, suggesting five possible types of promotional activity to support the new product launch.

7 Future Recommendations

The forecast income statement under the new strategy and the actual figures for the previous year are shown below:

Last year's actual figures are based on an average selling price of £3 per milkshake and sales of 255,000 milkshakes.

The forecast scenario uses an average selling price of £5 and sales of 180,000 milkshakes.

Income statement	***Last Year Actual***	***Forecast Scenario***
	£	£
Turnover	765,000	900,000
Cost of production:		
Direct (raw) materials	204,000	216,000
Direct labour	280,500	288,000
Fixed production overheads	153,000	90,000
Total cost of sales	637,500	594,000
Gross profit	127,500	306,000
Selling and distribution costs	35,000	178,000
Administration costs	50,000	50,000
Operating profit	42,500	78,000
Gross profit margin	16.67%	34.00%
Operating profit margin	5.56%	8.67%
Direct materials as a percentage of turnover	26.67%	24.00%
Direct materials cost per unit	£0.80	£1.20
Direct labour cost per unit	£1.10	£1.60
Fixed production cost per unit	£0.60	£0.50

Task Seven

Prepare a final presentation with accompanying slides and a one page written report for a meeting with the Managing Director of Wonderstuff Ltd to discuss developments with the Super Shakes range given the data above.

He will expect an explanation of why the gross profit margins and operating profit margins are different. Suggest which course of action to take and recommendations for the future, with clearly explained reasons.

8 Stakeholder Communication

The Super Shakes range has been a great success and as the product manager, you have been praised by people at all levels of the organisation for your input.

Given the success of the new ethical premise behind the product, as a post-project activity, you have been asked to communicate the rationale behind Super Shakes, the outcomes of product's launch and potential for the future to three stakeholders, including one external group.

Task Eight

Identify three stakeholders (at least one external).

Make notes on how the stakeholders can be classified, including reference to organisational structure and culture and Mendelow.

For each stakeholder:

a) **Determine the purpose behind and best method of communication**

b) **Draft the relevant communication (e.g. presentation notes/ slides; promotional literatures; e-mail; meeting agenda, etc.**

c) **Explain the differences between the audiences and the communication.**

d) **Design a means of feedback from the stakeholder group that you can present to your board.**

Solutions to Tasks

Task One

Much of the answer to this task will depend on the strategy the individual chooses to adopt. Given that the review is looking at budgetary control, it is most likely that the budget-holders will be the most appropriate staff to involve in the process.

As a relative newcomer, an informal but focused e-mail or face-to-face conversation may be the best way to approach these individuals, especially if they are the divisional heads with considerable status. It would probably be wise to stress the Managing Director has requested the review. It would also be worth considering if there are individuals of a lower position who are fundamental to cost control – for example, those in departments responsible for procurement and purchasing.

As a starting point, questionnaires or a workshop may work best to seek initial views, as well as acquiring the relevant financial data. After this, a meeting of all divisional heads and other staff mentioned above could be organised.

The outcome of initial meetings or workshops would be to find out information and seek suggestions and feedback. Later meetings would be more formal, with the purpose of formulating a new policy and then introducing it.

It should be noted, especially if looking to control costs, that videoconferencing or virtual meetings may be more cost-effective, although as the Head Office is substantial, most key personnel are likely to be there. An off-site meeting could be an option if this is both cost-effective and if the purpose is to either allow an informal atmosphere to enable the free flow of ideas or if the team dynamic seems to require it.

Verbal communication and presentation skills are likely to be seen both in running the meetings and also when feeding back to the Managing Director where a presentation to summarise key points, with an accompanying, detailed report is probably the best way to put points forward.

Written skills will be evident in the report as well as when e-mailing participants of the meetings and providing follow-up notes and action plans.

Problem-solving skills could be required should the divisional heads prove awkward to deal with or where there are conflicts between them. Also some types of meeting may be subject to unexpected difficulties to overcome.

IT and software will be used to present ideas and analyse both financial data and personal feedback from those involved.

Scheduling meetings and keeping this process on track and to time will require considerable organisational skills.

Common barriers would be difficulties in communicating with those of a different status within the business, diary clashes when trying to schedule meetings and antagonistic participants in meetings and presentations. As the floor has been opened up for change, many people are likely to wish to express their views and therefore it could be difficult to stop certain characters from dominating.

Task Two

MEMO

Accountant > Managing Director

The project team needs around ten people from a variety of different departments and of varying levels in the company's organisational hierarchy. For this reason, the matrix structure would prove a good way to organise the project team.

In terms of departments therefore, as a minimum we would need someone from Product Development, a representative from Production, a member of the Logistics team, people from both Sales and Marketing, one of the Customer Services department and a person with legal or HR expertise, in addition to myself. This should cover all key business functions and enable us to have all perspectives for input into the project.

I would recommend that the people are not all senior managers, as operational and day-to-day knowledge will be crucial in terms of implementation and ensuring overall buy-in.

We can use Belbin's team roles to help get the right the people. Belbin suggested all good teams should have the following:

- Leader – a co-ordinator, a balanced and disciplined individual
- Shaper – someone highly task-driven and extrovert to promote activity in support of the Leader

- Plant – an ideas person, often quite introverted, but thoughtful
- Monitor-evaluator – someone to keep the team's ideas realistic by looking for potential issues
- Resource-investigator – a networker able to source solutions and look for alternatives
- Company worker - an administrator we can trust to have an eye for detail
- Team worker – someone to promote good relationships within the team
- Finisher – a progress chaser, keen to see us through to the end of the project satisfactorily
- Expert – we perhaps need someone with specific knowledge of Shakes to analyse and consult

One person could have multiple roles and likewise, more than one person can play many of the support roles.

Bearing Tuckman's theory in mind, it is crucial we get to know these roles quickly, to go from Norming to Performing. Having said this, if it is a long-term project, we must be aware of complacency (Dorming).

For this project, our Product Development representatives would work well as Plants and Monitor-evaluators and some of the more forceful personalities in the Sales and Marketing team would be excellent as Shaper or Finisher given their extroverted nature. Our HR/legal people have the eye for detail and knowledge of company procedures to be excellent as the Company worker.

I would allocate specific responsibilities and targets throughout the project. For example, the production team will have their own output targets and our marketing representative will have monthly promotional projects.

General skills needed for effective team work were defined by Cloke and Goldsmith. These ten skills should be apparent to keep the project team productive and happy:

- Self-management
- Responsibility
- Leadership
- Strategic planning
- Feedback and evaluation

- Communication
- Successful meetings
- Resolving conflicts
- Supportive diversity
- Enjoyment

Of these skills, leadership is vital and it is crucial that the team leader is able to organise, co-ordinate and mentor the team members to fulfilling many of the other skills. Conflict resolution is a key part of this.

A leader needs to motivate their team, whether through a rewards system, or other managerial methods. The style of leadership can be determined by using a number of theories, including Mintzberg and Drucker's theories of leadership skills.

Drucker claimed effective managers perform five key functions: setting objectives, organising, motivating, establishing yardsticks and developing people. Mintzberg split ten skills into the Interpersonal, Informational and Decisional. For anyone to lead the team successfully they need to exhibit as many of these as possible.

A team leader can exhibit a number of styles – as more of a people-oriented person, I would be categorised as having a 'Country Club' style according to Blake and Mouton and as I like to involve others, this would be deemed participative (consults) by Ashridge Management College. Others may be more task-oriented or lean more towards Tell/autocratic approaches.

Handling conflict is one crucial part of being a team leader – leaders have to make the crucial decision of whether to intervene or not. There are four alternative approaches – avoidance, suppression, negotiation and resolution, but which is correct depends on the circumstances.

Given my experience of leading the budgetary control initiative and my knowledge of project finances and team work, I feel I have the knowledge to be a good leader. I also feel the style above would work well on this project.

The Accountant

Task Three

E-mail to: The Marketing Director

From: The Accountant

Date: Today

Subject: Use of Competitor and External Analysis

Dear Marketing Manager,

As part of my work with the project team, there have been a few concerns regarding the level of external market and competitor analysis is being effectively conducted and/or used here at Wonderstuff Ltd. I hope you do not mind if I seek clarification regarding this, as the project team has been briefed with looking at new product development and therefore market research is essential to our activities.

For any company it is important to understand the markets they operate in and how they are going to compete against their rivals for business. This analysis will not only allow us to understand our competitors' strengths and weaknesses, but also our own and therefore to assess our relative competitive advantage and how we can use it to drive the business forward. Competitor analysis is therefore crucial to strategy formulation.

We need to be aware of changes in our marketplace and how external factors can have an impact on us moving forward. One way to look at these factors is through a PEST analysis, looking at political, economic, social and technological issues that influence the way we operate. Without a good understanding of the government's latest policies and recent legislation (Political factors), for example, we may either miss opportunities or respond to restrictions too late. Likewise, social factors include the way the public respond to trends – this is crucial for us at Wonderstuff, as we need to respond to lifestyle and dietary views.

I would also suggest we use Porter's Five Forces model when looking at particular opportunities. This enables an analysis of barriers to entry and considers the attractiveness of a market. It considers the relative power of buyers and sellers, rivalry, new entrants and how available substitutes are.

If we do not pick up on these issues quickly enough, our competitors will. We need to be aware of new entrants to the market, new products and the promotions they are offering, as all could reduce our customer base and have a serious impact on our business.

Competitor analysis should avoid such a decrease in sales, keeping the company profitable and reactive to any shifts in consumer behaviour.

Competitors can also suggest different paths, which we may choose to follow or oppose.

I would suggest looking at our competitors' websites, annual reports, newspaper and online news articles and trade media presence initially. We could also conduct market research and reviews, and perhaps even try to purchase from one or more of them ourselves. We could look at their organisational structure, including the decision-making processes, and their culture, using McKinsey's 7-S model as a framework.

Hopefully this provides some ideas and I am happy to discuss in more detail if you have some spare time.

Kind regards,

Accountant

Task Four

Henry's problems seem to stem from three main problems – a lack of delegation, a lack of communication and a lack of performance appraisal.

He seems unable or unwilling to delegate and as a result is completing a number of operational day-to-day activities which his staff could manage. Whether he is unsure of how to delegate or does not trust others is unclear, but the situation is likely to get worse as staff leave and more inexperienced people join the team.

His personal circumstances could be affecting his performance, but it is causing the department to lack strategic planning or direction and therefore results are suffering.

To solve this problem, he needs to delegate responsibility to others in his team and in doing so increase their motivation. He needs to make it clear to staff which tasks he wants them to perform and to allocate resources and objectives to each. This will reduce his stress and workload, allowing him to concentrate on non-routine activities.

It will also aid the staff, as they will gain minor management experience, extra training and, in some cases, specialised roles. This should lead to greater and quicker productivity, mutual decision-making and increased job satisfaction. Having said this, there may be increased staff costs if formal promotions are required and the right people must be entrusted.

In terms of communication, Henry should try to involve staff more and praise/encourage them to keep interests levels higher and promote a better atmosphere. Although as a manger, some distance is desirable, his separation from his staff is having a detrimental impact.

Performance appraisal would be one way this could be achieved – it will enable a sense of direction and idea of career progression for the staff as Henry will set targets and monitor them accordingly. This in turn could mean Henry is more happy to delegate.

Performance appraisal will also aid with succession planning if turnover of staff remains high in the department, although with the recognition performance appraisal brings and the opportunity for the team's issues to be heard, it is likely to be a more healthy department anyway.

Task Five

The structure of the Slides is up to the individual but they should be relatively brief in content and include images and charts/graphs to show some of the statistics provided.

Extra research on the ingredients may be included to add colour.

As with all presentations, the audience should be considered (on this occasion the rest of the project team).

Where explanation is required, the following should be included (in brief):

Possible reasons for the variances

- **Direct materials (milk) price variance** – The price variance for milk is £800 favourable. This appears to be due to the company seizing an opportunity to purchase 1000 litres of milk at a reduced price, as a result of market saturation due to increased production of milk.
- **Direct materials (milk) usage variance** – The usage variance for milk is £400 adverse. According to the Shake Mixer's explanation, this is due to the fact that some milk was lost as a result of the refrigerator door being left open on a hot day. However, the Shake expert seems to suggest that he believes this increased usage may have been caused by the Shake Mixer using the milk to make milkshakes for himself and his friends. This seems to be corroborated by the strawberry usage variance, which is also adverse.
- **Direct materials (strawberries) price variance** – The price variance for strawberries is £1600 adverse. This is probably due to the purchase of imported strawberries from the Netherlands as a result of the scarcity of strawberries on the UK market. These may have been more expensive per kilogram than budgeted, or the

additional transport costs incurred could have caused the adverse variance.

- **Direct materials (strawberries) usage variance** – The usage variance is £1,875 adverse. This appears to be due to the need to increase the ratio of strawberries to milk as a result of the Dutch strawberries lack of aroma. Part of this variance could also be explained by the use of strawberries by the new Shake Mixer for his own benefit.

Action which could have been taken

- **Quality of strawberries** – the company could have tried to import strawberries from warmer countries such as Spain. However, the better quality of such strawberries may not have offset the higher transport costs. Alternatively, the company could have delayed the launch of the new strawberry milkshake until the time when English strawberries became available.
- **Reliability of the Shake Mixer** – the company could have tried to retain the previous experienced Shake Mixer by giving him additional incentives. Alternatively, the company could have been more careful in recruiting the new Shake Mixer, who appears to be at best negligent with the ingredients, if not plainly dishonest about the reasons why some of the milk has gone missing.

Task Six

MEMO

Accountant > Marketing Director

It seems that our primary objective needs to be to create awareness within the target market, using as little money as possible. Therefore I would suggest both conventional advertising and some PR and promotional activities. Due to the cost restrictions, I have ruled out TV and the mass print media.

Suggestions:

- Lifestyle/health magazines – place an advert and/or offer a promotion/sample (this is a targeted market so less risky or costly than mass media)
- Sales promotions – giveaways to both key trade (e.g. supermarkets) and consumers (e.g. at gyms)
- Trade promotions and exhibitions – focused on the core market to start with (e.g. health shows)

- Customer promotions – price reductions for first month to penetrate the market (penetration pricing)
- Coupon offers – rewards for purchasing, including vouchers to get a free Shake
- Public relations – seek endorsement from relevant celebrities or get exposure at large events, write press releases

Please let me know your thoughts.

Task Seven

Content:

The explanations should include the following content:

Why are the gross profit margins different?

Sales Price / Sales Volume

The sales price is 66% higher under the forecast scenario, which will result in an increase in the G.P. margin, however the forecast sales volume is 29% lower (75,000/255,000) than last year, which would contribute to a reduction of the gross profit margin.

Materials

The materials cost per unit is 50% higher under the new scenario, which would contribute towards a lower gross profit margin. This may be the result of the use of more expensive natural ingredients.

Labour

Labour cost per unit is £1.60 for the forecast scenario, up from £1.10 last year. Again, this should reduce the margin for the forecast scenario. This could be explained by the more labour intensive production techniques the new scenario involves.

Fixed costs

Fixed costs reduce by 17% in the new scenario, which should help improve the G.P. margin. As a result of the use of more manual techniques, Super Shakes may be able to reduce the use of equipment and dispose of some, which would lead to a lower depreciation charge.

Which is the dominant factor and why?

Even though the sales volume is lower and variable costs per unit are higher, the gross profit margin under the forecast scenario is substantially higher than last year. This appears to be due primarily to the significant increase in selling price.

Why are the operating profit margins different?

The higher operating profit margin in the new scenario appears to be primarily influenced by the increase in gross profit. However, this favourable influence is largely offset by the significant increase in sales and distribution costs.

Recommendation, with reasons, as to which course of action to take

Based purely on the forecast information, it would appear that the new forecast scenario would be a favourable solution, as it would generate a larger return. However, the sales volume is lower than last year and therefore the market share is lower. It may be worth setting the price slightly lower to avoid the loss of market share.

Presentation:

The final presentation should be a brief overview of the above and should also include:

- Charts and graphs to show important statistics
- Images and appropriate animation
- A strong start and finish
- Three key points with bullet-points or crucial words for you to speak around in the presentation
- Aspects which grab the Managing Director's attention

Note: This presentation is for a high level decision-making at the top of your company and therefore should be business-like and professional, as well as thought-provoking and analytical

One Page Written Report

This should include the same core analytical statements as the presentation and shown above but more detail should be provided – therefore longer lists of bullet-points or full paragraphs of more detailed explanation are more appropriate. Some more complex charts or statistical data can be incorporated.

Task Eight

Examples of the stakeholders could be:

- The company's employees
- Shareholders
- Suppliers (connected)
- Customers (connected)
- The local community (external)
- The local council (external)
- The government (external)
- A pressure group (external)

The above could either be general stakeholders or those relating specifically to the project. If the latter, they should be referred to as Project Sponsors/Users/Team etc.

Using Mendelow's Matrix, the stakeholders can be classified and the level of effort the communication is worth can be ascertained. The stakeholders who both have a lot of influence and require more work are defined as Key Players so will require more information and to be made to feel important. Those requiring Minimum Effort should have a less complicated and efficient means of communication.

Communication to the stakeholders will depend on the audience. Whereas the purpose for the company employee's and shareholders and a Project Sponsor will usually be to inform, the public and potential customers will usually be marketed to with sales messages.

Key clients may appreciate a glossy corporate brochure, whereas the local council are likely to appreciate a meeting or presentation supported by a factual document.

The student should provide reasons for providing the different forms of information to the three stakeholders and show how the message will change accordingly, including use of statistical information, language and multimedia. All should have different needs which need to be specifically addressed.

In terms of feedback, a form could be devised to be handed out at the end of a meeting with local residents or following the receipt of either e-mailed or printed information.

Typical criteria would include factors such as the clarity of information provided, quality of written/oral communication, appropriateness to the audience, professionalism, levels of interest and enthusiasm and how well the brand was represented.

It should also be noted that the feedback could be utilised to inform future communications as part of a performance evaluation process.

Practice Assessment

The following questions are designed to test understanding using AAT QCF-style questions. As the Business Skills units are largely evidence-based, this does not serve as a simulation of the actual assessment.

Task One

Each company has its own organisational structure and culture.

a. Which of the following is NOT a key feature of an organisation?

A Controlled performance	
B Collective goals	
C Social arrangements	
D Creation of a product or service	

b. Which of the following statements regarding the entrepreneurial structure is usually correct?

A It allows for defined career paths for employees	
B It enjoys strong goal congruence throughout the organisation	
C It can cope with significant diversification and growth	
D Control within the organisation tends to be weak	

c. Which of the following structures is best placed to address the need for co-ordination between different functions in complex situations?

A Functional	
B Divisional	
C Matrix	
D Geographical	

d. Which is the correct definition of the term 'span of control'?

A The number of employees reporting to one manager	
B The number of managers to whom one employee reports	
C The number of levels in the hierarchy	
D The number of employees at each level of the organisation	

e. Which of the following is a benefit of centralisation of decision-making and processes?

A Reduced training costs within the organisation	
B Better local decisions due to local expertise	
C Better motivation of staff	
D Increased flexibility	

f. The **(A)** is the network of relationships that exist within an organisation and arises through the common interests and friendships between members of staff.

When people of the same status but from different departments come together to share views this is known as **(B) .**

The **(C)** is a communication network which connects people with common interests and usually circulates rumours and gossip.

Choose from the picklist below the correct words to fill gaps A, B and C.

Picklist

Negotiation	Grapevine	Scalar chain	Body language
Upwards communication	Lateral communication	Informal organisation	Organisational culture

g. Which of the following statements referring to organisational structure are true and which are false?

Statement	**True/False**
A virtual organisation exists where all non-core activities are outsourced to third parties.	
Entrepreneurial structures typically suffer from slow decision-making.	
An organisation's span of control is unaffected by the nature of the work the organisation undertakes.	
A matrix structure may increase conflict between managers.	
Tall organisations typically have a narrow span of control.	

Task Two

RPA Ltd manufactures a wide range of products, ranging from domestic tools to bicycles and sporting equipment.

a. RPA Ltd wishes to use a structure that will allow for each of its product ranges to be managed separately, but also wishes to minimise its overall administrative costs.

Which of the following organisational structures would be most appropriate for RPA Ltd to adopt?

A Divisional	
B Entrepreneurial	
C Functional	
D Matrix	

b. RPA Ltd plans to open a series of new manufacturing plants in France and Germany to broaden its European business.

Which level of strategy planning would this decision relate to?

A Functional	
B Strategic	
C Tactical	
D Operational	

c. To establish areas for potential business development, RPA Ltd need to perform an analysis of customer views. Which of the following business departments is most likely to be concerned with the identification and satisfaction of customer needs?

A Production	
B Research and development	
C Marketing	
D Purchasing	

d. When planning their expansion into new territories, RPA Ltd must be aware of a number of external factors which may have an impact on their business. The management have identified four key issues:

i. Plans to build new roads
ii. Anti-pollution legislation
iii. Fuel taxes
iv. Minimum wage and local employment laws

Which of the following categories within a PEST analysis would all of the above relate to?

A Political	
B Economic	
C Social	
D Technological	

e. The management of RPA Ltd need to bear in mind the needs of their stakeholders when making crucial decisions. The following stakeholders have been identified as being important:

i) Company employees

ii) Customers

iii) Pressure groups

Choose one word from the Picklist 1 and one from Picklist 2 below the best words to describe the three groups above:

Picklist 1

Primary
Secondary

Picklist 2

Internal	Connected
External	Minimal effort

f. According to Mendelow, which of the following is the correct approach for RPA Ltd to take towards stakeholders who have low levels of power and low levels of interest?

A Minimal effort	
B Keep informed	
C Keep satisfied	
D Key players	

Task Three

The ability to communicate effectively with customers and other stakeholders is essential to the survival of any company. Marketing is a vital part of this communications strategy.

a. A company with a marketing orientation believes which of the following is key to corporate success:

A selling products actively and aggressively	
B meeting customer needs better than competitors	
C the level of sales, advertising and sales promotion	
D producing goods and services of optimum quality	

b. Which ONE of the following is part of the marketing mix?

A Purchasing	
B Profit	
C People	
D Public relations	

c. Which ONE of the following is an example of direct marketing?

A Writing an article for a trade journal	
B Targeting individual customers with promotional material	
C Posting blogs to draw attention to the organisation	
D Public relations activities	

d. When considering which form of communication will be most effective, which of the following is the most important consideration?

A How to use as much technology as possible	
B How to address the needs of the recipients	
C How to make the sender look impressive	
D How to provide as much information as possible	

e. Match the definition with the relevant type of communication:

Communication between people at the same level within an organisation.	Downwards communication
A lack of this means that managers get little feedback from more junior employees.	Upwards communication
This refers to communication between different levels and departments.	Diagonal communication
A lack of this means that junior employees will be unaware of their manager's plans and goals.	Lateral communication

f. E is a team leader. The team tends to communicate via e-mail, where all of the messages are sent to E and E then forwards on the messages to relevant team members if he feels that they need to be made aware of the contents.

Which communication pattern is Y using?

A The Y	
B The wheel	
C All channel	
D The circle	

g. E writes a briefing document for his department on new working from home measures, including deadlines for a risk self-assessment to be completed by all team members. This document is placed on the company's intranet.

On the date of the deadline, E has had few completed forms and is told that many of the staff had not seen the document, as they access the intranet infrequently.

Which aspect of the communication process has caused this problem for E?

A He has chosen the wrong channel	
B He has encoded the message poorly	
C His communication has suffered from too much noise	
D His communication has not been accurately decoded	

Task Four

Tasty Treats Ltd is a manufacturer of pet food.

a. Tasty Treats is currently reviewing the quality, packaging and design of the tinned food it supplies for dogs. What element of the marketing mix is the company considering?

A Product	
B Place	
C Price	
D Promotion	

b. Tasty Treats analyse their potential market into sub-groups, identifying customers with common needs and behaviours in order to target them through their marketing. Which of the following describes this technique?

A market research	
B market development	
C segmentation	
D product adaptation	

c. Tasty Treats need to decide their pricing strategy. They are considering charging a very low price when their new products are first introduced to gain rapid growth in market share. Which of the following best describes this strategy?

A loss leader pricing	
B market penetration	
C skim pricing'	
D product penetration	

d. When selling the pet food products, Tasty Treats needs to bear in mind a number of legal obligations to its customers.

Which of the following is NOT a typical requirement of sale of goods legislation?

A The seller must have legal title to the goods being sold	
B Goods sold must be fit for purpose	
C Item descriptions must be accurate	
D Goods must be reasonably priced	

e. Which of the following would raise ethical issues for Tasty Treats given the nature of the business?

(i) The materials used in the production of the pet food

(ii) How the pet food is advertised

(iii) The working practices and conditions of Tasty Treats' suppliers

(iv) How much Tasty Treats pays its own staff

A (i) and (ii) only	
B (i), (iii) and (iv) only	
C (ii), (iii) and (iv) only	
D (i), (ii), (iii) and (iv) only	

f. Tasty Treats is considering implementing a corporate social responsibility (CSR) policy. However it is concerned that there may be potential problems with this policy. Which ONE of the following is a legitimate drawback of a CSR policy?

A Loss of business focus causing a downturn in sales	
B Failure to attract high quality employees	
C Increased materials costs	
D Reduced emphasis on training and retention causing a loss of key business skills	

g. A meeting of senior managers at Tasty Treats has been called in order to discuss the CSR policy. Mark each statement below regarding the organisation of meetings as either true or false.

Statement	**True/False**
Meetings are more productive where there is no agenda and proceedings can take their natural course.	
When organising a meeting to discuss key business issues, it is best to invite as many people as possible.	
Everyone in the meeting should take their own minutes so there is no need for a co-ordinated follow up.	
Virtual meetings can be as effective as face-to-face meetings.	
Off-site meetings are always a better option than those held in the office.	

Task Five

For teams to operate effectively, members of the team must adopt particular roles and exhibit certain skills and attributes.

a. Belbin suggested nine team roles which a group requires in order to prove effective.

Which of the following includes two of the roles defined by Belbin?

A Negotiator, Initiator	
B Diplomat, Spokesperson	
C Shaper, Plant	
D Secretary, Co-ordinator	

b. Match the following team roles with the appropriate personality:

A is a quiet person, who often reserves their opinion until directly asked for it. A offers creative ideas when the team faces problems.	Finisher
B is respected by all team members for his analytical skills, but tends not to be invited to social occasions as he is often tactless.	Monitor-evaluator
C is always keen to ensure any potential conflicts and issues within the team dynamic are identified and resolved and that everyone works well together.	Plant
D has a keen eye for detail and identifies minor aspects and errors other people miss. He works well to deadlines but is often reluctant to involve others.	Team-worker

c. Which is the stage of team development during which the effectiveness of work will be at its lowest according to Tuckman?

A Performing	
B Storming	
C Forming	
D Norming	

d. Which of the following statements is correct with regards to the differences between individuals and teams?

A Teams tend to enjoy synergies which cannot be achieved by individual workers	
B Teams tend to make decisions more rapidly than individuals	
C Individuals are less likely to make definite decisions and rely on compromises	
D There are fewer controls in place when groups make decisions	

e. Group working can bring many advantages but it can also have some negative effects. Match the effect with the description below.

Groups can end up taking decisions which are riskier than the individual members would take.	Conformity
Group members reach consensus without critically testing, analysing and evaluating ideas.	Risky shift
Individuals within the group can be persuaded to accept decisions which they know to be wrong.	Groupthink

f. Which of the following skills are listed by Cloke and Goldsmith as being key for successful team work:

i) Encouraging competition

ii) Shaping successful meetings

iii) Strategic planning

iv) Resolving conflicts

A (i) and (ii) only	
B (i), (iii) and (iv) only	
C (ii), (iii) and (iv) only	
D (i), (ii), (iii) and (iv) only	

g. Mintzberg identified ten skills effective team managers require. These skills included those of:

Figurehead

Leader

Liaison

Which of Mintzberg's three main categories do the above skills of a manager belong to?

A Interpersonal	
B Decisional	
C Informational	

Task Six

A new IT system is being implemented at RPA Ltd to improve efficiency.

a. The board of RPA Ltd are considering outsourcing the IT operations to a consultancy company in a foreign company. The existing IT department at RPA Ltd is considered excellent, which is important in the industry in which they operate.

Which of the following statements regarding this possible outsourcing is correct?

A It is a good idea as outsourcing will reduce the risk of security breaches internally	
B It is a good idea as it is likely to increase skills and understanding at RPA Ltd	
C It is a bad idea as it could cause a loss of competitive advantage	
D It will be easy to bring the IT function back in-house if problems arise with the contractor	

b. The IT Manager asks junior staff within the department for their opinions on a new system, but retains the final say on which system will be purchased.

According to the Ashridge Management College, what management style is being adopted here?

A Joins	
B Tells	
C Consults	
D Sells	

c. Shelby is part of the project team set up to manage the implementation of the new system. She is described as being 'committed to the task, can be aggressive and challenging, but will always promote activity'. Which of Belbin's roles does this describe?

A Shaper	
B Team Worker	
C Finisher	
D Plant	

d. There is some resistance to the new system in the accounting department. The departmental manager offers staff bonuses to encourage them to use the new system, as well as relying on her own personal charisma. Which TWO of the following sources of power is the manager planning to use?

A Reward	
B Legitimate	
C Referent	
D Coercive	
E Expert	

e. To encourage buy-in to the new system, managers have been asked to assess staff motivation. Link the needs of Maslow's hierarchy below to the relevant statement to aid with this process.

A has been offered a large pay rise in recognition of his hard work on several recent projects.	Basic
B has been offered a permanent contract with her company, giving her access to a good pension scheme.	Security
C has been offered her first ever job. The pay she receives is due to cover her essential living costs.	Ego

f. Enlargement, enrichment and rotation are terms associated with which ONE of the following?

A Adjustments to an individual's content and role	
B Improvements brought about by competitive benchmarking	
C Market and product development strategies	
D Customer approval ratings	

Task Seven

A project is a unique undertaking to achieve a specific objective. Consequently, projects have defined and specialised schedules and their own allocation of resources.

a. Which ONE of the following is NOT one of the purposes of a project budget?

A responsibility for expenditure	
B motivation of employees	
C co-ordination of staff	
D costing of units	

b. At what stage in the project life cycle is the scope of the project determined?

A Planning	
B Initiation	
C Growth	
D Control	

c. The Project **(A)** provides the resources for the project.

In the PRINCE2 structure, the team that provides an independent view of how the project is progressing, reflecting business, user and specialist interests is called the project **(B)** team.

The Project **(C)** is responsible for overall project output.

Fill gaps A, B and C using words from the Picklist below:

Picklist

Steering	Assurance	Support	User
Owner	Manager	Sponsor	Team

d. Which of these is NOT a control element within projects?

A Project reports	
B EVM	
C Project meetings	
D Feasibility study	

e. Which of these meetings would take place regularly with the objective of providing an update on the status of the project?

A Team meetings	
B Progress review meetings	
C Problem solving meetings	
D Business review meetings	

f. Which of these techniques would be used at the completion stage of the project?

A Progress reports	
B Gantt chart	
C External review	
D Scenario planning	

g. A final report is produced at the end of the project. Which of the following would NOT be included in the final report?

A Actual achievement in relation to costs and schedules	
B Customer's requirements and original project deliverables	
C The extent to which the benefits defined in the business case have been achieved	
D List of deliverables which the customer received	

h. The following statements all refer to the role and attributes of a project manager. Select which are True and which are False.

Statement	**True/False**
They are responsible for selecting, building and motivating the project team	
They make all high level decisions relating to the project	
They provide the resources for the project	
They are the main point of contact with the management hierarchy	
They must have all of the technical skills required in the project	
They must be effective communicators	
They must adopt a democratic style of leadership	
They may have to negotiate on a variety of issues	

Task Eight

The role of accounting and accountants is essential in any project, especially with relation to the managing of finances and ethical considerations.

a. Which of the following is an advantage of a top-down/imposed budget?

A Decision-makers are experienced	
B Staff at lower levels are likely to feel greater ownership and motivation	
C The budget is flexible and continually updated.	
D Overall corporate strategy is likely to be irrelevant.	

b. Which ONE of the following would NOT be a suitable way of addressing expenditure exceeding tolerances in a project?

A Indexing	
B Moving averages	
C Seasonal variation	
D Critical Path Analysis	

c. For which aspect of the balanced scorecard would successful new product development be a performance indicator?

A Organisational learning	
B Business process	
C Financial perspective	
D Customer perspective	

d. Which of the following is considered one of the five Fundamental Principles in the Code of Ethics?

A Courtesy	
B Reliability	
C Social responsibility	
D Objectivity	

e. Which of the following is a value that organisations try to encourage within their corporate culture in order to encourage staff to act ethically?

A Empowerment	
B Integrity	
C Satisfaction	
D Objectivity	

Task Nine

Training, learning and development can have considerable benefits for both the individual and the organisation.

a. Which TWO of the following are features of a 'learning organisation'?

A Learning from others and past experience	
B Avoidance of the risk of failure where possible	
C A detailed system of controls over employee activities	
D Generation and transfer of knowledge throughout the organisation	

b. Link the definition with the correct term

The activities which aim at developing skills, values and understanding required in all aspects of life.	Education
The growth or realisation of a person's ability and potential through conscious or unconscious learning.	Training
The planned and systematic modification of behaviour through learning events, programmes and instruction.	Development

c. Kolb has suggested that there are four stages in the learning process. Which of the following is not one of the four stages?

A Experience	
B Active experimentation	
C Observation and reflection	
D Divergent	

d. Using Honey and Mumford's learning styles, match the employees with the correct learning style:

V prefers a hands-on approach to learning and dislikes reading text.	Activist
W learns by watching others attempt something first and then trying to imitate them.	Pragmatist
X prefers to understand the principles behind something.	Reflector
Y prefers to see practical, applicable examples.	Theorist

e. Which of the following is NOT a usual purpose of performance appraisal?

A To identify training and development needs	
B To ensure that work of a particular standard is recognised	
C To terminate an employee	
D To help with a company's succession planning	

f. Which of the following is most likely to be a goal of a personal development plan?

A Meeting weekly sales targets	
B Increasing market share	
C Getting a pay rise	
D Developing skills and expertise	

Task Ten

Lewis has recently been appointed as a manager at RPA Ltd. He is responsible for a finance and administration team with ten members of staff.

a. Lewis is concerned that a member of his staff is not performing effectively at work. Which of the following could be a consequence of the staff member's ineffectiveness?

A Loss of reputation and customers	
B Reduced need for employee training	
C Increased staff motivation	
D A rise in productivity	

b. Two members of Lewis's team have been arguing over who is responsible for sending out the monthly overseas statements. Lewis feels that although the conflict is obvious, it is not serious and will sort itself out over time. Which conflict management strategy is Lewis adopting?

A Denial	
B Suppression	
C Reduction	
D Resolution	

c. Lewis is required to complete his staff's annual appraisals. Which of the following is NOT a normal stage in the performance appraisal process?

A Review	
B Delegate	
C Set targets	
D Action plan	

d. When setting objectives for his staff, Lewis is aware that these should be SMART. What does SMART stand for?

A Specific, Manageable, Accountable, Relevant, Timely	
B Specific, Measureable, Achievable, Relevant, Timely	
C Scientific, Measureable, Achievable, Realistic, Timely	
D Scientific, Measureable, Authoritative, Responsible, Timely	

e. Lewis has completed the performance appraisal for Moses. Moses was informed that his work was unacceptable, with Lewis giving examples to back up this view. He told Moses that if there was no sign of significant improvement, Lewis would be forced to take further action.

Which approach was Lewis employing?

A Tell and sell	
B Tell and listen	
C Joint problem solving	
D Job enlargement	

f. According to Blake and Mouton's managerial grid, managers can be classified by their level of concern for people and concern for production.

Lewis has been told that he has a high concern for his staff but is not as concerned by output. Which of the following would best describe Lewis?

A Impoverished manager	
B Team manager	
C Country club manager	
D Task manager	

Practice Assessment Answers

Task One

a. **D** Organisations do not need a product or service to sell in order to exist, for example a club or orchestra are organisations.

b. **B** As the entrepreneurial structure is run by one person this will lead to strong control, a clear strategic direction and better goal congruence.

c. **C** A matrix structure combines the benefits of decentralisation with those of co-ordination so has a degree of flexibility to make quicker decisions.

d. **A** It is the number of employees reporting to one manager, whereas C is the scalar chain.

e. **A** As the training can be co-ordinated more efficiently especially for junior staff. B, C and D are typically advantages of **de**centralisation.

f. **(A)** is Informal organisation.

(B) is lateral communication.

(C) is grapevine.

g.

A virtual organisation exists where all non-core activities are outsourced to third parties.	False
Entrepreneurial structures typically suffer from slow decision-making.	False
An organisation's span of control is unaffected by the nature of the work the organisation undertakes.	False
A matrix structure may increase conflict between managers.	True
Tall organisations typically have a narrow span of control.	True

Task Two

a. **A** The divisional approach enables RPA Ltd to manage the products separately. The matrix structure would also enable this, but due to the number of managers and complexity involved, would prove to be more expensive and therefore not keep costs low as is required.

b. **B** As strategic planning involves making plans for the whole business, such as which markets to enter and exit.

c. **C** Marketing departments are most concerned with customer needs. Research and Development focus on product and service innovation.

d. **A** These are all political issues, as they result from governmental policy and resulting legislation.

e. The choices from the picklists would be as follows:

i) Company employees – Primary, Internal

ii) Customers – Primary, Connected

iii) Pressure groups – Secondary, External

f. **A** If stakeholders have little interest in the company and no real power of its progress, minimal effort would be all that is required.

Task Three

a. **B** A marketing orientation puts the customer's needs above all other factors. A could be termed sales-orientation. D could describe product-orientation.

b. **C** People is one of the 7 P's. The others are Product, Price, Promotion, Process, Physical evidence and Place.

c. **B** Direct marketing involves direct communications with a target audience, such as direct mailing).

d. **B** The audience and their needs are crucial whether communicating in verbal or written form. Quality and relevance of information are more important than the amount of information conveyed.

e.

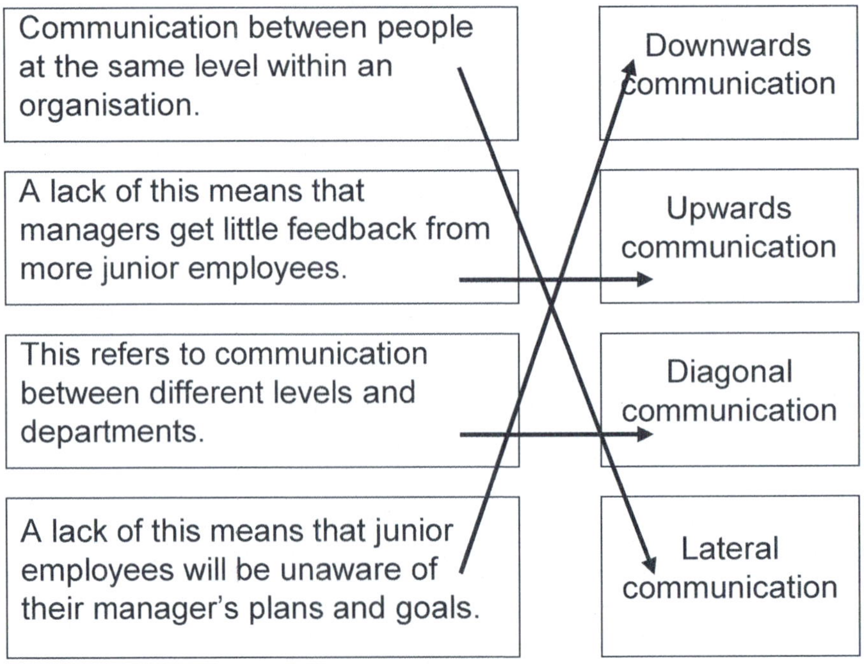

f. **B** In the wheel, communication goes through one central person. In the Y, the message works up a chain before reaching the person who can contact others. In the all channel, everyone communicates freely, whereas the circle involves a message being passed from one person to another).

g. **A** As the team members rarely access the intranet, these seems like the wrong channel for E to use to communicate with them. There is no obvious reason to suggest it has been poorly written or misunderstood as would be the case for the other options, it simply has not been seen).

Task Four

a. **A** Quality, packaging and design would all fall under the Product category in the marketing mix.

b. **C** Segmentation is the name given to dividing potential customers in this way).

c. **B** Market penetration involves setting a low price when introducing a product to gain market share.

d. **D** Goods would not normally need to be reasonably priced. When selling the pet food products, Tasty Treats needs to bear in mind a number of legal obligations to its customers.

e. **D** All of the factors would raise ethical issues.

f. **C** Due to the desire to find ethical sources, materials costs may rise. On the contrary, CSR policies are likely to result in better quality employees and should have no impact on business skills. If managed and marketed correctly they can lead to an increase in sales.

g.

Meetings are more productive where there is no agenda and proceedings can take their natural course.	False
When organising a meeting to discuss key business issues, it is best to invite as many people as possible.	False
Everyone in the meeting should take their own minutes so there is no need for a co-ordinated follow up.	False
Virtual meetings can be as effective as face-to-face meetings.	True
Off-site meetings are always a better option than those held in the office.	False

Task Five

a. **C**

b. A is the Plant

B is the Monitor-Evaluator

C is the Team-worker

D is the Finisher.

c. **B Storming** is the conflict stage where co-operation is at a minimum and jobs are not completed to an acceptable standard accordingly.

d. **A** Teams tend to be slower at making decisions than individuals and rely more on compromises. The involvement of more people in the decision-making process means that teams have better control as there are a number of people to review the decisions being made.

e.

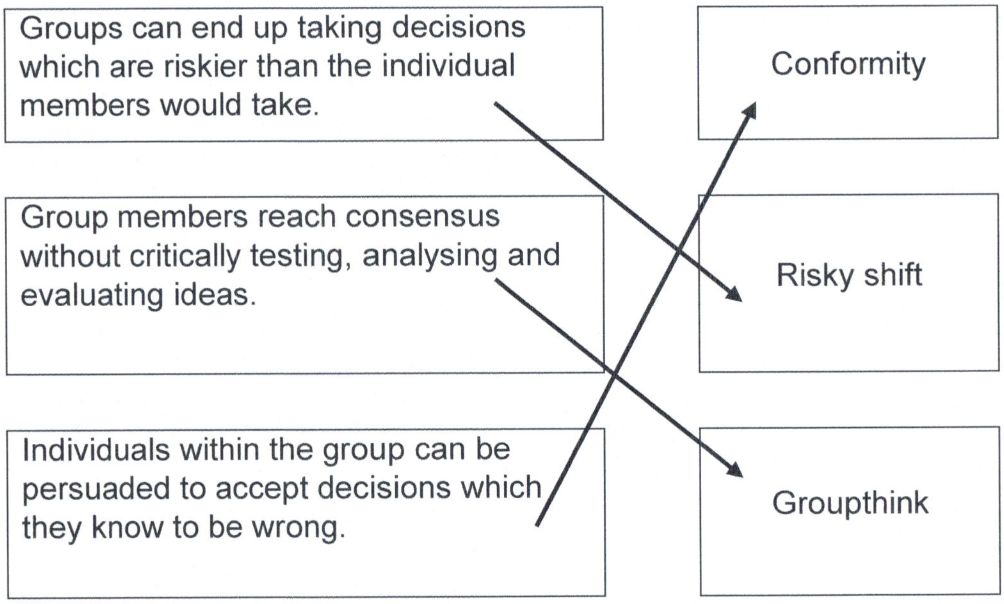

f. **C** Cloke and Goldsmith promote the idea of collective responsibility and supportive diversity rather than competitive behaviour within a team.

g. **A Interpersonal** is the category which the skills of Figurehead, Leader and Liaison fall under in Mintzberg's classification of management skills.

Task Six

a. **C** is the correct statement – as the existing IT department is highly skilled and enabling the company to have a competitive edge, outsourcing may not be the best option. Were services to be outsourced and staff laid off, it would be difficult to bring the IT function back in-house at a later time. Outsourcing brings its own, different security risks as a third party will be involved.

b. **C** As the IT manager is encouraging the views of junior staff and participative decision-making, this would be an example of Consults.

c. **A The Shaper** is always committed to the task and will promote activity. The Plant is more thoughtful, the Team Worker is concerned with relationships within the group and the finisher is the progress chaser who ensures that deadlines are met.

d. **A and C** (A refers to the a use of reward and C suggests using her relationship with her employees).

e.

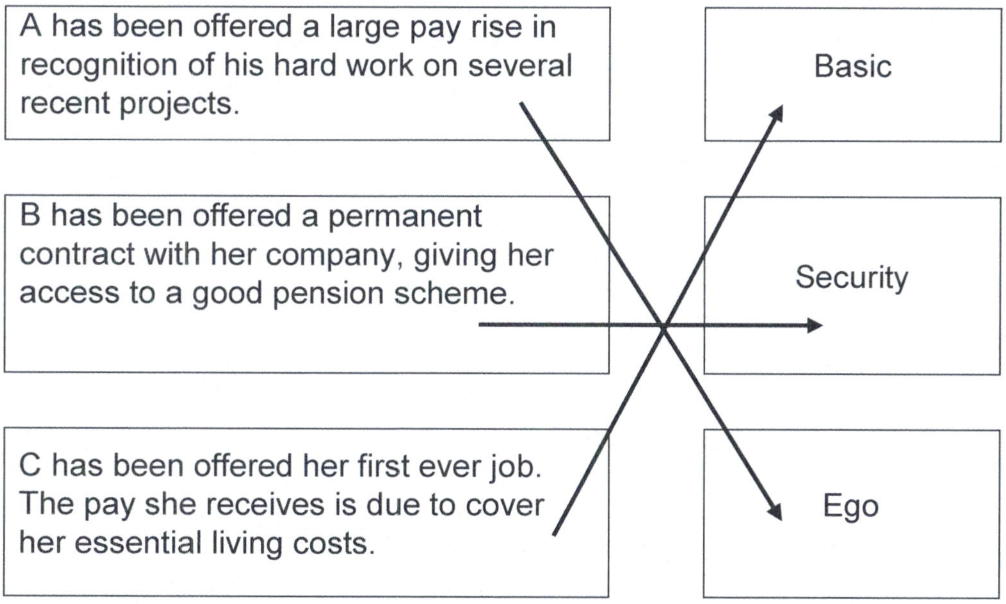

f. **A** Job enlargement, enrichment and rotation were suggested by Herzberg as ways of changing an individual's content and role.

Task Seven

a. **D** Costing of units would be the purpose of a cost schedule or standard cost card. A, B and C are purposes of the project's budget.

b. **B** The scope of the project explains what should be included in the project deliverables. This has to be decided before planning can occur.

c. (A) is Sponsor.

(B) is Assurance.

(C) is Manager.

d. **D** The feasibility study is used at the initiation stage to determine whether a project is worthwhile. A, B and C are all used for control.

e. **B** The progress meetings should be regular and provide an update on all aspects of the project. Team meetings may also be fairly regular but often not as formal or performance-focused. Problem-solving meetings will be ad hoc. The business review meetings tend to come at the end of the project to reflect on its impact.

f. **C** The external review allows the customer to confirm if their requirements have been met. Gantt charts and scenario planning are utilised more in the project planning phase. Progress reports are used as a source of control.

g. **C** Whereas A, B and D would be commonplace in the report, analysis of the benefits in terms of the business case would normally not be fully ascertained until some time after the completion of the project.

h.

They are responsible for selecting, building and motivating the project team	True
They make all high level decisions relating to the project	False
They provide the resources for the project	False
They are the main point of contact with the management hierarchy	True
They must have all of the technical skills required in the project	False
They must be effective communicators	True
They must adopt a democratic style of leadership	False
They may have to negotiate on a variety of issues	True

Task Eight

a. **A** As the budget is decided by the senior management, they are likely to be more experienced. B is a benefit of bottom-up budgets. C refers more to rolling or attainable approaches to budgeting and involves a flexibility unlikely in top-down budget.

b. **D** Critical Path Analysis is used to plan and prioritise project activities.

c. **C** This would relate to organisational learning as an outcome of new product innovation.

d. **D** Objectivity is one of the five Fundamental Principles in the Code of Ethics, along with Integrity, Professional Competence and Due Care, Confidentiality and Professional Behaviour.

e. **A** Empowerment is one of the values promoted to safeguard against ethical threats. These can be remembered using the acronym HOTTER

Task Nine

a. **A and C** are features of a 'learning organisation'.

b.

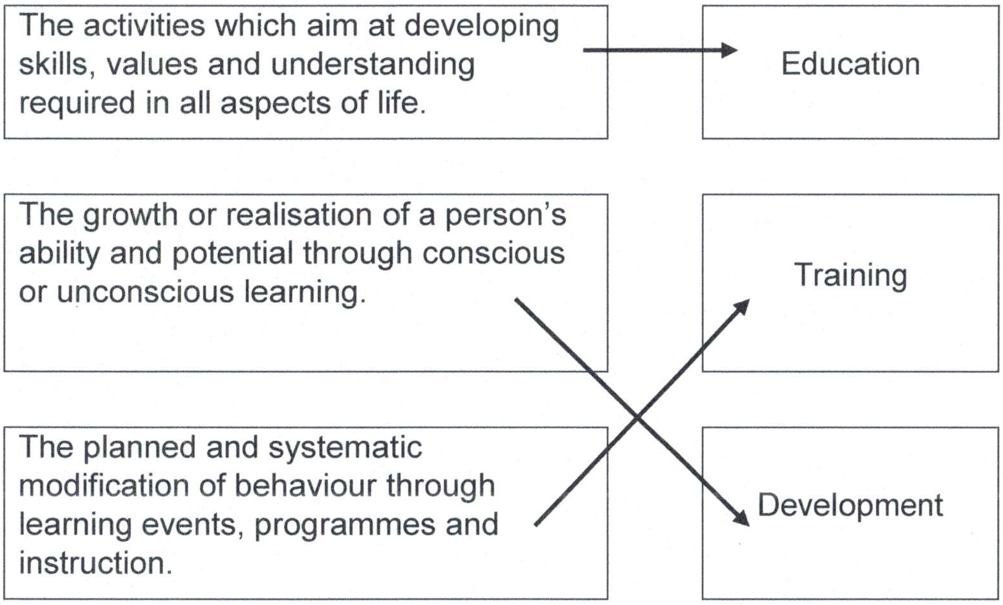

c. **D** is a style of learning, whereas the others are all stages in the learning process.

d. V is an Activist.

W is a Reflector.

X is a Theorist.

Y is a Pragmatist.

e. **C** As very rarely would an appraisal be organised to or coincide with a decision to terminate employment, for which disciplinary or other forms of meeting would be more appropriate.

f. D A personal development plan should look to future career progression rather than short-term, company-wide or remuneration issues.

Task Ten

a. **A** is a likely result of the team member's poor performance. As an individual, he/she may also be lacking in concentration, motivation or productivity.

b. **A** Due to a lack of intervention, denial is evident.

c. **B** Although delegation could be discussed, it is not part of the process. Even where self-evaluation is prominent, the responsibility for the appraisal remains with the manager.

d. **B** (SMART objectives should be Specific, Measureable, Achievable, Relevant and Timely).

e. **A** This is an example of Tell and Sell as Lewis has informed Moses of his views and given reasons for them. There does not seem to be any form of participation in the discussion for Moses.

f. **C** Lewis' focus on people make him a Country club manager. If he were more interested in output at the same time, he could potentially be a Team manager.

INDEX

A

Anthony triangle, 23

Attainable budgets, 259

Ashridge Management College, 114

Axelos, 287

B

Balanced scorecard, 280

Belbin's team roles theory, 96

Blake and Mouton's – Managerial grid, 115, 116

Bottom-up budgets, 259

Boundaryless structures, 33

Brand management, 59

Business-to-business, 58

Business-to-consumer, 58

C

Cash flow forecasts, 267

Centralisation, 34, 35

Change control, 265

Charts and graphs, 301, 302

Cloke and Goldsmith, 123

Coaching, 330

Code of conduct, 71

Commercial organisations, 13

Communication process, 135, 136, 137

Companies Act 2006, 286

Conflict, 117, 118, 119, 120, 121

Consumer protection, 70

Contingency planning, 260

Contract of employment, 72

Contractual obligations, 67, 68, 69

Core competencies, 7, 310

Corporate culture, 35

Corporate governance, 73

Corporate social responsibility (CSR), 66

Cost classification, 255

Critical path analysis, 264

Customer Relationship Management (CRM), 60, 304

D

Data Protection Act 1998, 286

Decentralisation, 34, 35

Delegation, 25

Development, 322

Divisional structure, 31

Drucker's five basic functions, 113

E

Earned Value Management (EVM), 273

Entrepreneurial structure, 30

Evaluation of learning, 337, 338

F

Feasibility, 251

Forecast of cost to complete, 276

Forecasting methods, 269

Formal communication, 132, 133

Formal groups, 92

Functional structure, 30

G

Gantt charts, 263

H

Herzberg's two factor theory, 106, 107

Honey and Mumford: learning styles, 330, 331, 332

I

Ideal budgets, 259

Indexing, 270

Informal communication, 132, 134, 135

Informal groups, 92

Informal organisation, 36

Information systems, 298

Information technology, 298, 299, 300, 301, 302, 303, 304, 305, 306

Intranet, 303

K

Key performance indicators, 281

Kolb: experiential learning cycle, 329, 330

L

Leadership, 111

Learning, 324, 325, 327

Learning organisations, 327

Lifecycle costing, 272

Limiting factors, 257

M

Management accounting, 3

Management skills, 313

Marketing, 58

Marketing mix, 145, 146

Maslow's hierarchy of needs, 104

Matrix organisation, 32

Mendelow's matrix, 56

McKinsey's 7-S framework, 62

Meetings,
- agendas, 224, 225
- group dynamics, 229, 230
- leadership, 231, 232
- minutes, 227, 228
- off site, 219

planning. 215, 216, 217, 218, 219, 220, 221, 222
project, 211, 212, 276
role & Purpose, 208, 209, 210
video conferencing, 220
Mentoring, 332
Mintzberg's ten skills, 113
Mission statements, 19
Motivation, 103, 104, 105, 106, 107, 108, 109, 110, 111

N

Net present value, 282
Non-verbal communication, 132
Not-for-profit organisations, 13

O

Objectives, 18, 19, 20, 21
Organisation charts, 29
Organisational structure, 30, 31, 32, 33
Organisations, 12
Outsourcing, 303

P

PEST analysis, 40
Performance appraisal, 318, 319, 320, 321, 325
Performance evaluation, 310, 311, 312, 313, 314, 315, 316, 317, 318, 319, 320, 321, 322
Performance related pay, 110
Personal development plans, 333, 334
Personal skills, 310, 311, 313
Peters and Waterman, 101
Pivot tables, 300
Place, 149
Porter's five forces, 44
Price, 147, 148
PRINCE2, 287
Private sector, 13
Presentations,
content, 172, 173, 174, 175, 176, 177
delivery, 179, 180, 181, 182
evaluation, 195, 196, 197, 198, 199, 200
preparation, 168, 169, 170, 171, 172, 194
rehearsal, 178
software, 183, 184, 185, 186, 187, 188, 189, 190, 191
Product, 146, 147
Professional ethics, 76, 77, 78, 79, 80, 81
Project completion, 278, 279
Project cost control, 266, 267
Project initiation document, 253
Project life cycle, 250
Project planning, 261, 262, 263, 264
Project management software, 305
Project reports, 275, 276
Project stakeholders, 249, 250

Promotion, 149

Public sector, 13

R

Regulatory framework, 286

Role theory, 91

Rolling budgets, 259

S

Sale of goods act 1979, 68

Scalar chain, 27

Seasonal variation, 271

Span of control, 27

Spreadsheet software, 299, 300, 301, 302

Stakeholders, 54, 55

Strategic marketing process, 149, 150

Supply of goods act 1982, 69

SWOT analysis, 37, 38, 39, 40, 315, 316

T

Time management, 7, 8, 9, 10, 11

Time stealers, 8

Top-down budgets, 259

Training, 324, 326

Treasury, 3

Tuckman's stages of team development, 97, 98

V

Variance reporting, 272

Virtual teams, 304, 305

Vroom's expectancy theory, 108

W

What If analysis, 301

Work breakdown structures, 262

Workplace learning, 326

Z

Zero based budgeting, 259